IDEA POWER

"*As we move from the Information Age of the 80s to the Idea Age of the 90s, ideas become a company's greatest resource. Innovative thinking is the key to short-term competitive advantage as well as long-term growth capability.*

"*Idea Power, a compact compendium of leading-edge creativity techniques and resources, can help make innovation a systematic process in any company and allow the company to realize its full innovative potential.*"

—Henry Andersen
Director, Diamond IdeaGroup
Mitsubishi Heavy Industries America, Inc.

IDEA POWER

Techniques & Resources to
Unleash the Creativity in
Your Organization

Arthur B. VanGundy

American Management Association

New York • Atlanta • Boston • Chicago • Kansas City • San Francisco • Washington, D.C.
Brussels • Toronto • Mexico City

*This book is available at a special
discount when ordered in bulk quantities.
For information, contact Special Sales Department,
AMACOM, a division of American Management Association,
135 West 50th Street, New York, NY 10020.*

Library of Congress Cataloging-in-Publication Data

VanGundy, Arthur B.
    *Idea power : techniques & resources to unleash the creativity in
your organization / Arthur B. VanGundy.*
        p.   cm.
    Includes bibliographical references (p.   ) and index.
    ISBN 0-8144-5045-8
    1. Creative ability in business.   I. Title.
HD53.V36   1992   *92-17225*
658.4'063—dc20   *CIP*

Printing number

10   9   8   7   6   5

To
Dr. Donna J. Nelson

Contents

Preface

Organizations, like people, must grow or they will die. Today's business environment is unpredictable and companies cannot rely on old ways of doing things. Increasing domestic and international competition demands that businesses develop new approaches to making and selling their products. Business as usual will work no longer. But other factors also dictate the need for new approaches: (1) Technological advances have outpaced our ability to keep up with developments in one field, let alone several; (2) knowledge is generated faster than anyone can absorb it; and (3) increasing production costs and fewer employees mean companies must do more with less.

To meet these and other competitive challenges, growing numbers of companies are turning to *creativity training*. This training equips employees with the attitudes, skills, and behaviors they need to identify important problems and generate their solutions. Our overburdened educational system does not teach creative thinking. Schools are overwhelmed just trying to teach the basics to an often undermotivated student population. So that leaves business to train its people to be creative. And growing numbers of companies are doing just that.

But how can such an intangible skill be taught? This book was written to answer that question. Creativity training requires knowledge of the creative process and the tools and techniques to achieve it. Much of this information is scattered throughout a variety of publications and training manuals. *Idea Power: Techniques & Resources to Unleash the Creativity in Your Organization* pulls together these resources to help you plan and conduct your own creativity training program. The manual is divided into four parts:

- Part I, Introduction to Business Creativity, discusses issues in organizational creativity and innovation (Chapter 1) and describes the

Creative Problem-Solving process (Chapter 2). This process has been tested scientifically and found superior to other creativity approaches.

- Part II, Creativity Training, is the core of this book: It provides four chapters on creativity training. Chapter 3 discusses the basic skills needed to facilitate problem-solving groups. Chapter 4 presents creative thinking exercises that stimulate students' thinking processes. Chapter 5 explains how to design creativity training courses, with samples of course outlines and training objectives, and descriptions of existing programs. The last chapter covers how to conduct and facilitate problem-solving retreats. Many companies use a retreat environment to generate new product ideas and resolve company problems.

- Part III, Idea-Generation Techniques, offers details on using individual (Chapter 7) and group (Chapter 8) idea-generation methods.

- Part IV, Resource Materials, outlines the tools and technology of creativity training. Chapter 9 lists movies, audiocassettes, books, idea-generation tools, and other resources. The two remaining chapters present reviews of computer software for individuals (Chapter 10) and groups (Chapter 11). Computer software is a relatively new area of creativity training, but it may be just the ticket to give your company that competitive edge.

I am indebted to many people for the material in this book. My university students have offered constructive comments over the years. My business clients have made helpful suggestions, especially in applying Creative Problem Solving to the "real world." The companies that provided review copies of their products or literature also contributed to this book. Gerald Haman, president of Creative Learning International in Chicago, was especially helpful. Finally, and most important, I thank my friend and colleague Professor Donna J. Nelson for her helpful comments and suggestions in putting the book together, as well as her assistance in editing and proofing some of the writing. Her help and encouragement were invaluable; I dedicate this book to her.

A.B.V.

Part I

Introduction to Business Creativity

1

Organizational Creativity and Innovation

"We want to become more competitive."

This statement represents the reason many companies are now focusing on creativity in solving business problems. Today's businesses face increasing pressure on a variety of fronts, such as in new-product development, marketing, distribution, and customer service. These pressures have prompted them to examine how they function, finding that traditional bureaucratic approaches are no longer effective. Instead, businesses need creative ways of responding as they move toward what many have characterized as the "idea age." This change in approach has been described in recent magazine articles in *Time, U.S. News & World Report, Success, Business Week, Newsweek,* and *Psychology Today.*

Companies such as 3M, Hershey Foods, Procter & Gamble, and Xerox are turning to creativity training. According to *Training* magazine (May 1990), this type of training has increased more than sixfold, rising from less than 4 percent of companies in 1985 to over 26 percent by 1989. Indeed, a study by the American Society for Training and Development reports that 31 percent of U.S. companies plan to offer creativity training during the next three years and 38 percent plan to offer problem-solving training.

Creativity training helps employees view problems from different perspectives and generate unique solutions. Frequently, the focus is on research and development (R&D) or new-product development. Many companies, however, now realize that creativity training is important for all their personnel. For instance, Du Pont plans to train all 140,000 of its employees worldwide. Even governments are getting into the act: Singapore, Canada, and several European countries now offer their employees creativity training.

The Bottom Line

Technological advances, shorter production cycles, global trade possibilities, federal regulations, changing consumer demographics, and a fluctuating labor force dictate the need for creative approaches to business. However, in many companies internal politics and turf battles, poor communication networks, a "head-in-the-sand" syndrome, or bureaucratic bungling prevents businesses from being creative.

Data on R&D spending and the number of patents filed provide some direct evidence of this lack in business creativity. According to the National Science Foundation, R&D spending is expected to rise very little in the next few years—in spite of increased competitive pressures. Of ninety-two companies surveyed, fully one-third said they were freezing or decreasing their R&D budgets, and the U.S. Patent and Trademark Office reports that only a little over one-half of U.S. patents have gone to U.S. residents. In the meantime, the number of patents awarded to foreigners since 1963 has risen from 18.6 percent to about 47 percent. The top three U.S. patent recipients were Japanese. Of course, patent quantity may not be a valid indicator of creativity. But the National Science Foundation also tried to measure patent quality and found that Japanese innovations may be more *significant* (based on frequency of citation), on average, than U.S. products.

These statistics alone should cause businesses to become more innovative. They don't seem to have much direct effect, however. What does seem to affect U.S. business is the dollar—after all, that's the purpose of business. And in this context, business creativity is all the more important. It has great bottom-line significance to U.S. companies because, in the long run, greater creativity will mean better products, greater sales, and larger profits at lower cost. Linking profit to creativity gets a manager's undivided attention. For example, Frito-Lay reported cumulative, documented savings attributed to its creativity training program.

The Current Business Scene

Assessments of corporate creativity appearing regularly in business publications have cited the factors responsible for stifling creativity in many organizations. The most important are:

- *"Mergermania."* Management often believes that acquiring new technologies will spur innovation. What it usually acquires instead are new headaches. Merged companies aren't always compatible, and innovation—at least in the short term—suffers as a result.

■ *Emphasis on managerial control.* If companies expect to control all phases of the innovation process, they may be disappointed. Creative efforts require employee participation, and traditional financial controls are not appropriate for long-term innovation efforts.

■ *Short-range thinking.* Pressure from stockholders causes management to focus on quick returns with tangible, financially measurable results. Only a few companies recognize the long-term potential of paced efforts to innovate.

■ *Analysis paralysis.* Because of educational background and training, most managers analyze new ideas to death. The actual or potential value of many ideas goes unrecognized as calls go out for more and more data. Creativity often takes a back seat to statistical analysis, and the predictable outcome is loss of competitive advantage. Creativity and innovation require well-timed action.

■ *Rigid hierarchical structures.* Bureaucratic structures promote efficiency when the environmental factors are known and are relatively stable. An unpredictable environment, however, requires a more responsive organizational structure. It is not surprising, then, that bureaucratic structures hinder innovation in many companies.

■ *Emphasis on "home runs" over singles.* A push for the "big idea" or prime product frequently drives new-product development efforts; managers push for the one $50 million idea rather than five $10 million ideas. Although the home-run approach can pay off, many potential single runs may be eliminated. Market research is still more of an art than a science. Some ideas initially thought of as singles often turn out to be home runs when given a chance. Moreover, many singles can add up to a few home runs.

■ *Market versus technology-driven product planning.* An age-old dilemma in product development is whether to emphasize market research or technological development. Many new product ideas come from consumers and suppliers; however, new products also can come from technological advancements. It requires vision to anticipate customer needs and reactions. After all, Alexander Graham Bell did not invent the telephone because a company's market research department determined there was a customer need.

■ *Pressure to do more with less.* Budget constraints make it difficult for companies to innovate. For example, they often punish their R&D departments for cutting costs; the more the department saves one year, the less it has to play with the next year. Zero-based budgets, personnel cutbacks, and reduced product-cycle times make it difficult to increase innovation. Paradoxically, the more companies have to cut back, the more creative they *must become*.

■ *Unclear innovation processes*. It is somewhat surprising that employees often are unclear as to their company's innovation processes. Managers often assume everyone knows how to innovate. Instead, most employees are knowledgeable about organizational politics and turf protection. Management needs to articulate a clear innovation message. It must set up structures that allow ideas to flow between appropriate departments. Contrary to what many think, organizations can manage the innovation process.

■ *Perceptions that creativity is for "creatives" only*. Many managers have the attitude that creativity is something you either have or you don't have. They view personnel in the "creative" professions (e.g., artists) as the only creative people in their organization. This stifles innovation. If managers don't believe their employees are creative, they probably won't be. Creative ideas can come from anywhere in a company; R&D, new-product development, and graphic design are not the only potential sources of new ideas.

A Climate for Innovation

Training in creative thinking can overcome innovation barriers. Before training can be effective, however, managers must consider other factors. For example, there needs to be a climate conducive to creative thinking. Organizational innovation requires a climate—within both individuals and groups—that fosters creative thinking. No training program can succeed without it.

The concept of *organizational climate* defies logical definition. It is a state of being that is determined more readily by subjective perception than quantifiable analysis. In general, an organization's *climate* refers to the overall work conditions, whether psychological, sociological, technological, political, or economic. For that climate to be hospitable to innovation, some situations must exist:

■ *Risk taking*. Any change involves risk. Organizations assume risk whenever they try to better themselves. Sometimes they fail and sometimes they succeed. If they fail occasionally, they may become reluctant to take more risks, and playing it safe becomes the norm. They then redefine success by lowering their sights. But these organizations forget that failure is not built on success. It's the other way around: Success is built on failure. Simply put, you can't succeed unless you fail. And you can't fail unless you assume some risks. This doesn't mean mortgaging the farm, of course. "Prudent" risk taking should be the norm.

▪ *Autonomy.* Generating creative ideas requires freedom of thought. An innovative climate encourages employees to think of new ways to do things. Companies such as 3M, S. C. Johnson & Son, and Hershey Foods give their R&D employees the time and money to explore "blue sky" ideas on their own. Although the press of long-term projects makes it difficult to use this time, the net effect is a climate that encourages free thinking.

▪ *Clear performance-reward contingencies.* This rather academic-sounding phrase simply means managers should link rewards with specific performance. It is easier to motivate employees who can see a direct connection between their efforts and expected rewards. If the organizational climate supports this connection, more innovative behavior is likely.

▪ *Tolerance of differences.* An innovative climate recognizes that not everyone is alike—the world would be a pretty dull place if they were. Although organizations certainly would be simpler to manage, conformity has its downside. Creativity thrives on different perspectives. The more different people are, the greater the diversity of solutions they can provide. Management must recognize that it must not only tolerate different viewpoints but also encourage them.

▪ *Top management support.* Creating and maintaining an innovative climate begins at the top. Management must support and encourage innovation for any new thinking to occur. Furthermore, top management must set the tone for the organization's creative climate. Therefore, it must make its position on innovation clear and provide the resources needed to nourish and sustain it.

▪ *Initiating and encouraging ideas.* To survive and grow, organizations require a continual flow of ideas—the lifeblood of any organization. A climate conducive to creativity must encourage all employees to initiate these ideas. Otherwise, an organization may overlook the vast reservoir of untapped creativity it needs to innovate.

▪ *Positive responses to new ideas.* Just encouraging new ideas is not enough. Companies with creative climates must also respond positively. Management philosophy must respect ideas and give them fair hearing. Managers don't have to like every new idea, but they can ensure that they consider both their positive and negative qualities. Employees who know their ideas will receive a balanced evaluation will be more likely to continue submitting ideas.

An Innovation Blueprint

Just as building a house requires a blueprint, so does building an organization's creative climate. It is important to know what obstacles will be encountered and how they should be overcome.

Perhaps the most important element of an innovation blueprint is an innovation vision. Management should develop and articulate a vision that describes the creative environment it desires, and it also should include employee representatives to develop this vision. Organizations should tie this vision to their strategic plan.

Just as important as the vision itself, however, is the way companies implement it. Management continually needs to remind employees of that vision and provide clear examples of its support. For instance, management should reward innovations promptly, giving recognition throughout the company.

It is especially important that employees affirm and commit themselves to the organization's vision for innovation. For instance, a man was walking down a street when he came upon three men working at a construction site. All the men were doing the same job. He asked the first worker what he was doing. The man replied, "Breaking up these rocks." The man then asked the second worker what he was doing. This worker said, "I'm earning a living." The man asked the third worker and he responded, "I'm building a cathedral!" Clearly the third was a man of vision: He understood the larger significance of his work.

As part of an innovation blueprint, the vision might include the following ingredients:

- Encouragement of prudent risk taking
- Encouragement of off-the-wall ideas
- Balanced evaluations of all new ideas
- Positive response to initial idea proposals
- Patience with new ideas, giving them a chance to grow
- Opportunities for interdepartmental interaction

Management can build the innovation blueprint around three components: people, process, and structure. Although overlap exists, each makes a specific contribution to the innovation vision.

People

The people component involves human resources to achieve the vision. Therefore, companies need to do the following:

- *Provide top management support.* As mentioned, employees must perceive that top management supports innovation activities.

- *Create the perception of performance gaps.* Management should create work standards that result in employee-perceived performance gaps. That is, management should provide detailed information about current and desired performance levels. Most workers appreciate such feedback. More important, performance feedback often results in perceptions of gaps. These perceptions, in turn, help motivate employees to achieve higher levels. And motivated, high-achieving employees are more likely to innovate.

- *Reward risk taking.* Management must reward prudent risk taking. One large corporation took this approach to an extreme for a while. Whenever a major project failed, the company would fire a cannon to "celebrate" a nice try. In another company, a group of R&D employees spent several months on a project that failed. Although the product represented a sound, marketable concept, it was discovered that it would have been too difficult and costly to manufacture. The project manager notified the work team members that he wanted to meet with them in his office ASAP. On the way to his office, most of the team members feared they were going to be fired. They were surprised to learn, however, that the manager wanted only to congratulate them for their original bright idea and their effort in trying to bring it to market. Of course, if you celebrate too many failures, you won't be too innovative. The point is to create a spirit that tolerates reasonable levels of failure.

- *Provide adequate financial resources.* Financial resources obviously aren't in the same category as human resources. However, employees need adequate financial support to pursue creative projects.

- *Create a spirit of teamwork.* Social units can empower employees to produce their best efforts. When work groups are cohesive, individuals don't want to let down other team members. If they believe in the goals of their team, they will be motivated to help achieve them. So, how does management create a spirit of teamwork? Provide opportunities for informal social interactions. Make sure employees understand departmental and organizational goals, and check for employee commitment to them. Finally, look for ways to create lighthearted competition among work groups.

- *Encourage use of product champions.* In new-product development, many good product ideas never get out of the system. If no formal structures exist for ensuring a fair hearing of new ideas, a product champion can push for an idea. Such individuals typically believe strongly in the product concept and are willing to promote it vigorously.

▪ *Expose employees to outside ideas.* Organizations often become stagnant dealing with the same old ideas. An infusion of new ideas can motivate and stimulate employees to think of new ways of doing things. Use outside speakers to introduce new topics; in-house newsletters and corporate libraries also stimulate the flow of ideas.

▪ *Conduct problem-solving retreats.* Many companies conduct off-site retreats to deal with strategic problems such as determining new directions for a product line or solving a tricky marketing problem. The effectiveness of such retreats depends on how task oriented they are; the agenda should be somewhat structured. Retreats also can have a beneficial team-building effect, especially across departments. Informal contacts at retreats often lead to resolution of organizational problems. Chapter 6 provides a more detailed discussion of such retreats.

Process

Companies need to spell out the innovation process. Employees often are unaware of the options available for processing new ideas, especially ideas that fall outside of traditional management channels. Here are three steps to help clarify that process:

1. *Review or revise suggestion systems.* Suggestion systems have been around for many years. Unfortunately, they are not always successful. Employees often fail to see their ideas implemented, or screening procedures are so restrictive that very few ideas receive attention. Nevertheless, suggestion systems can contribute to organizational innovation if implemented properly. Management must make clear the process for evaluating ideas and dispensing rewards.

2. *Establish an innovation council.* Many companies have such councils to structure the innovation process. Perhaps the most well-known example is Eastman Kodak, which created a separate organizational structure for collecting and reviewing new-product ideas. You must be careful, however, that the council remains responsive to changing environmental conditions and internal organizational needs. It is easy for such structures to become absorbed by the formal organization and lose their effectiveness.

3. *Provide time for "pet" projects.* A number of organizations provide time for employees to experiment with personal projects. The success rate of these projects often is high, since personal interest usually motivates the employees. They typically develop outside the traditional planning process and are funded with special budgets. In most cases, companies allow 10 to 15 percent of employee time for these projects,

but it doesn't always work out that way. Success of pet project programs depends on at least four factors: (1) Management must give employees adequate time to work on their projects, since most employees on these programs already work long hours; (2) it should view these pet projects as rewards and not punishments; (3) it should provide adequate funding, staff, and other resources, since skimping on resources is not likely to result in much innovation; (4) organizations must integrate the project results with their innovation process, giving pet project ideas the same consideration as those coming from more formal projects.

Structure

Organizations contain formal and informal communication networks, which help form a company's structure and help determine its innovation effectiveness. For instance, a marketing manager needs to receive new-product information quickly and efficiently. Moreover, this information must be of high quality. An inappropriate or dysfunctional structure thus might jeopardize product quality. The following are steps to establish a structure that supports an innovation vision:

1. *Differentiate the structure.* An organization must have specialized functions to respond to constantly changing factors in its external environment. The more factors in an environment and the more uncertain they are, the more specialized the organization must be. That is, when an environment is complex and changing, a greater number of departments must deal with the external environment. For instance, a high-tech industry such as computer manufacturing must be relatively specialized to deal with many variables shaping the computer market.

2. *Integrate the structure.* The more specialized (differentiated) an organization, the more coordination is needed among functional departments. However, this presents somewhat of a dilemma. It is difficult to achieve both high differentiation and integration—as differentiation increases, coordination requirements increase correspondingly. Several researchers, such as Lawrence and Lorsch, argue that organizations can handle this problem with a variety of "integrative" devices (e.g., liaison positions, cross-departmental task forces, and special integrating departments).

3. *Establish creativity rooms.* Many companies have creativity rooms to promote creative thinking among their employees. Because they provide different ways for employees to interact, these rooms can affect organizational structure. A typical creativity room contains books, idea-generation aids, and miscellaneous materials. They also usually include

arrangements for group brainstorming. Some creativity rooms even have computer data bases of ideas contributed by employees throughout the organization.

4. *Improve the R&D–marketing interface.* In the area of new-product idea generation, the R&D–marketing interface plays an important role in structure. In typical bureaucratic fashion, the R&D and marketing departments may not interact in productive ways. Marketing needs information from R&D about new products; if R&D doesn't provide this information accurately and on time, it could delay the launch of a new product. Frequently, such delays arise from simple misunderstandings, but an innovation blueprint should spell out how these departments should best interact.

5. *Introduce cross-training.* Train employees in different functional areas. They can spend one or two weeks with coworkers in other departments to learn about their jobs. Of course, no one expects them to learn all the skills involved, but they can develop an appreciation for general job duties, with that knowledge increasing their perspective.

Many other variables may be included in an innovation blueprint. As important as these variables are, they are not sufficient for guaranteeing an innovative organization. However, they will help create an organizational climate conducive to creative thinking, with employees skilled in Creative Problem Solving.

2

Creative Problem Solving

All organizations require new ideas to remain innovative and competi-tive. If the organization has a climate conducive to creative thinking, it can be assured of a certain number of new ideas. However, there is no guarantee. Sustained creativity requires a systematic problem-solving approach. For example, the ideas needed for competitive positioning can't be expected to arise whenever needed. Instead, organizations must be able to develop innovative solutions on demand as well as anticipate the creative responses needed for future problems. In short, organizations must become proficient problem solvers.

Creative Problem Solving (CPS) is a systematic problem-solving model that employees can use every day. CPS guides the doer through a series of divergent and convergent problem-solving activities. Each activity is designed to help with one of six problem-solving stages:

1. Objective finding
2. Fact finding
3. Problem finding
4. Idea finding
5. Solution finding
6. Acceptance finding

CPS has been used widely around the world in business, govern-ment, and education. Although several other models exist, CPS is one of the few that has been researched and shown to be effective for producing unique ideas. CPS works best when existing or conventional solutions don't work. It must be used appropriately, however.

Using CPS Appropriately

To use CPS appropriately, make sure that (1) you solve the correct problem, (2) CPS is the most efficient approach, and (3) your problem is suitable for CPS. Only certain types of problems are suitable for CPS.

1. *Solve the "correct" problem.* Appropriate use of CPS requires basic assumptions about a problem situation. Management philosopher Russell Ackoff once said that we fail more often trying to solve the incorrect problem correctly than the correct problem incorrectly. That is, it is better to work on the correct problem and have trouble resolving it than to solve an incorrect problem. A lot of good solutions won't work if you apply them to the wrong problem.

For instance, if you have a problem retaining employees, you might define your problem as, "In what ways might we recruit more personnel?" You then would generate a list of ways to do this. However, this definition might not be the most productive one. A better definition might be, "In what ways might we retain our current employees?"

2. *Use the most efficient approach.* If you know you have defined the problem correctly, next determine if CPS is the most efficient approach for reaching a solution. Don't try to reinvent the wheel. If a more efficient method exists, avoid CPS and try the traditional method. But remember that traditional methods are not always the most efficient. We use them only because we have been conditioned to do so.

Here's a simple exercise to illustrate this point: Draw a small circle about half an inch in diameter. Fill in the circle using a pen or pencil. Finished? Does your circle look more like *a* or *b* in Figure 2-1?

Figure 2-1.   Fill-in-the-circle exercise.

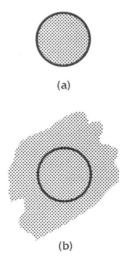

(a)

(b)

Both responses are correct. The areas within the circles are filled in, thus "solving" the problem. If your response was like *a*, you used a traditional method. Although correct, you expended effort to stay within the circle. But *b* also is correct, since the circle is filled in. The *b* method, however, was more efficient. Simply scribbling across the circle is easier than trying to stay within the confines of the line.

Most people choose *a* as their response. If you did, there are at least two reasons. You may have thought you were just following instructions. The problem asked you to "fill in" the circle, thus *implying* you had to stay within the circle. However, what the problem implied and what it told (or didn't tell) you are two different things. Most of us make assumptions about situations that are not totally correct. In this case, the instructions did not include the criterion of neatness. In fact, it contained no criteria. If you were influenced by a criterion such as neatness, it was because *you* decided to add it. The result was a less than efficient problem-solving approach.

A second reason you may have chosen *a* is due to your conditioning. From a very early age we all have been conditioned to "stay within the lines" and that neatness counts. While these guidelines help in structured situations with clear-cut criteria, they can be major obstacles when creative solutions are needed.

3. *Evaluate the problem type.* After you have tried a ready-made, efficient solution and found it lacking, you have to get more creative. You must test a variety of assumptions that might block your thinking, and you may need a variety of solutions to consider. This is where CPS can help. Before looking at how CPS can help, it is important to understand the nature of a problem and of problem solving.

A problem can be defined as a gap between a current and a desired state (Simon, 1977). Another way to state this is that a problem is a gap between "what is" and "what should be." What is a gap is relative and subjective, of course. Any two people might perceive the same situation differently. If a problem is a gap between two states, then problem solving must be the process of closing that gap—in other words, transforming the current state into the desired one. To use the earlier personnel example, the problem might involve developing ways to change the current state of employee retention to a more desired one (e.g., decreasing the loss rate from 12 to 3 percent). Problem solving includes all the actions you take to reduce this rate.

CPS works best in situations in which you have exhausted traditional problem-solving methods. These routine or ready-made solutions are known as well-structured problems. For these problems, you generally have a pretty good idea about the problem states and how to transform the current state into the desired state. For instance, frequently you can look up these transformations in a manual or ask an expert.

Other problems, however, are not solved so easily. These problems have much less information available about them and are more ill-structured. That is, there is ambiguity about the problem states or how to transform the current state into the desired state. To solve them, you need to use divergent thinking—that is, you need to think of many different potential solutions.

To test your understanding of problem types, determine which of the following situations would be appropriate for CPS:

1. Sales of a formerly successful product have become sluggish.
2. A machine on the production line breaks down repeatedly.
3. It is difficult to get new products to market.
4. Increasing expenses require cost-cutting measures.
5. A new food product has flunked consumer taste tests.

Of those listed, problems 1, 3, and 4 probably are most appropriate for CPS. All could benefit from a divergent search for many possible solutions (i.e., ways to increase sales, market a new product, and cut costs). Problem 2, however, would be solved best by looking for a specific cause, which a qualified technician should be able to locate quickly. Problem 5 could be appropriate for CPS, but only after you had tried more routine solutions. A more efficient first step is to consult with a food scientist who specializes in human taste research. You might try CPS only if he or she can't suggest a solution.

History of CPS

CPS grew out of the work of advertising executive Alex Osborn (1963), now recognized as the father of brainstorming. Osborn proposed that creative thinking involves three stages: fact finding, idea finding, and solution finding. Fact finding contains two substages: problem definition and preparation. Idea finding helps generate potential ideas, and solution finding helps evaluate and select the best ideas.

One of Osborn's other major contributions was his brainstorming rules:

1. Quantity breeds quality.
2. Defer judgment.

3. The wilder the better.
4. Seek combination and improvement.

The first two are the most important. The more ideas you generate, the greater the odds a high-quality solution will result. The defer-judgment rule separates idea generation from idea evaluation. Otherwise, you focus too much on evaluation and limit the total number of ideas. Separating these processes also helps encourage a climate more conducive to creative ideas.

CPS next was influenced by psychologist Sydney J. Parnes. Parnes conducted several major research studies on CPS and modified the process. For instance, he added new stages (problem finding and acceptance finding), which placed greater emphasis on problem definitions and solution implementation. He also noted that each stage should begin with a divergent search for data (without evaluation) and conclude with a convergent selection of the most important data. Next, Scott Isaksen and Donald Treffinger (1985) refined the model further by adding a preliminary problem-solving stage: objective finding. This stage helps identify a target area to resolve (i.e., the primary concern, challenge, or opportunity).

Overview of the CPS Process

As mentioned previously, the CPS process involves six stages, although you probably won't need all the stages for every problem. Sometimes, for instance, you may wish to begin with problem finding or idea finding, depending on how much information you have and the time available. The ground rule is to defer judgment. Always list the data before you evaluate.

Each stage contains a set of *divergent* and *convergent* activities. That is, there is an initial search for data and then a narrowing down of the data. The most important divergent activity is generating data without evaluation. During convergence, you can use hits and hotspots to select the most relevant data. *Hits* are the specific items you identify as important or relevant to a particular stage (the best objectives during objective finding, the best facts during fact finding, etc.). *Hotspots* are clusters of related hits that are optional in the sense that logical or related data groupings may not always appear. Normally you use the hits or hotspots during the next stage in the model.

The basic activities in each stage are as follows.

Objective Finding

This stage identifies a target problem area. To use objective finding, you diverge, generating a list of all problems facing you. Then you converge, selecting the most relevant problem area. You state your problem using the format "In What Ways Might I (or We)?" This is abbreviated "IWWMW?" For example: "IWWMW reduce our marketing expenses?"

Figure 2-2 shows how to use objective finding. List all problem areas that represent concerns, challenges, and opportunities in your personal or work life. Next, converge using a three-step process:

1. Identify the most relevant or important problem topics (hits).
2. Select the one hit that is most important to you.

Figure 2-2.   Objective finding.

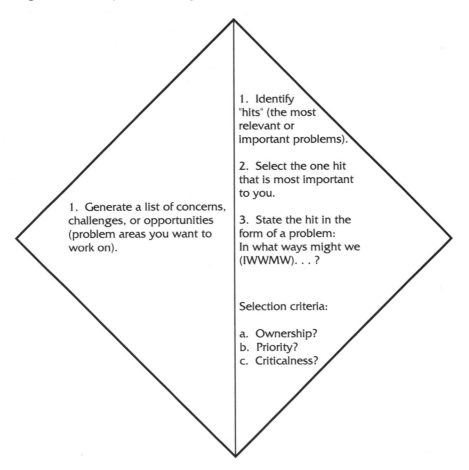

3. State the hit in the form of a problem using the format "IWWMW?"

To evaluate the hits, use the criteria of *ownership* (are you motivated to solve it?), *priority* (how important is the problem?), and *criticalness* (what is the urgency in solving this problem?). Denote hits with stars, underlines, circles, or highlighting pens. At the end of this stage, you should have identified the one problem you most need to work on next.

Fact Finding

This stage increases your overall understanding of the problem. You may need to reframe it to create a more productive perspective; this, in turn, helps you generate unique ideas. Fact finding helps you collect relevant data that can suggest different ways of restating your original definitions.

The fact-finding process is shown in Figure 2-3. First, diverge, generating a list of everything you know about the problem. Use the Five W's and think of one or two questions, each beginning with one of the words *Who? What? Where? When? Why?* Then answer each question. After generating responses to these and other questions, move to convergence, identifying hits among the responses. Then, if necessary, group your hits into common categories known as hotspots.

Problem Finding

This stage uses fact-finding hits to develop the most productive problem definition possible. As shown in Figure 2-4, the specific activities are:

1. Review all the fact-finding hits and use each hit as a stimulus to redefine your original problem statement.
2. Use these stimuli to generate a list of problem redefinitions.

For problem-finding convergence, identify the best redefinitions (hits) and select one with the greatest solution potential. To help make this decision, use three criteria: *ownership* (are you motivated to solve it?), *likelihood of stimulating many ideas*, and *freedom from criteria* (does the definition limit the range of possible definitions to a specific criterion such as cost?).

Idea Finding

The fourth stage in the CPS model helps structure your search for potential solutions. Idea-finding activities are shown in Figure 2-5.

Figure 2-3. Fact finding.

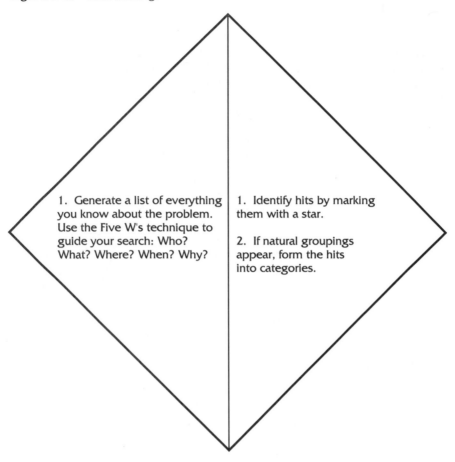

1. Generate a list of everything you know about the problem. Use the Five W's technique to guide your search: Who? What? Where? When? Why?

1. Identify hits by marking them with a star.

2. If natural groupings appear, form the hits into categories.

The primary divergent activity during idea finding is to generate many ideas using a variety of idea-generation aids:

1. Withhold judgment and generate a list of all possible ideas. This purge activity helps get rid of conventional ideas.
2. Use formal idea-generation techniques to prompt ideas. Chapters 7 and 8 describe these techniques.
3. Converge and identify idea hits. If natural categories of hits appear, group them together (e.g., finance, personnel, or marketing hits).
4. Select the best ideas or categories of ideas, using one or two broad criteria such as cost or time involved.

Figure 2-4.   Problem finding.

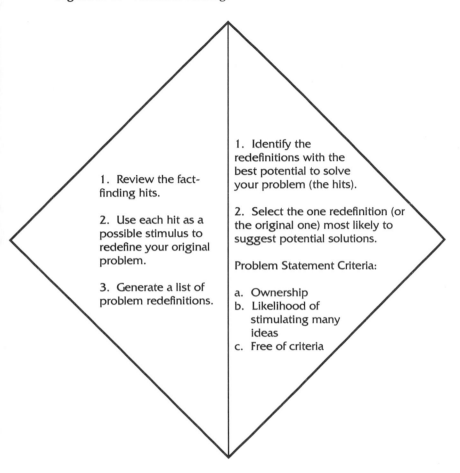

1. Review the fact-finding hits.

2. Use each hit as a possible stimulus to redefine your original problem.

3. Generate a list of problem redefinitions.

1. Identify the redefinitions with the best potential to solve your problem (the hits).

2. Select the one redefinition (or the original one) most likely to suggest potential solutions.

Problem Statement Criteria:

a. Ownership
b. Likelihood of stimulating many ideas
c. Free of criteria

Solution Finding

This stage helps you select a solution capable of solving your problem. You also can use it to transform ideas into more workable solutions.

There are two solution-finding divergent activities (see Figure 2-6). First, defer judgment and generate a list of general criteria to evaluate your solutions (e.g., time, cost, and feasibility). Other criteria may be related directly to your problem (e.g., criteria for improving a computer system might include compatibility with existing systems). Next, examine all your ideas and decide which ones you could transform into more workable solutions.

Convergence during solution finding also involves two activities.

Figure 2-5.   Idea finding.

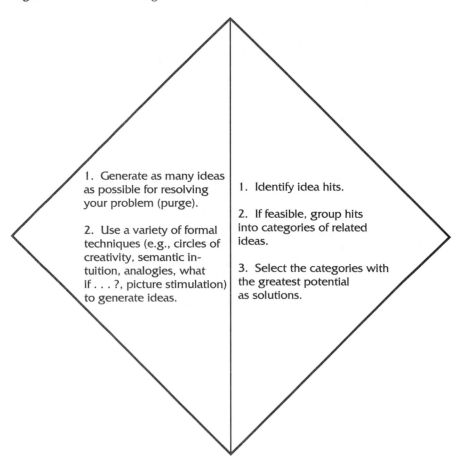

1. Generate as many ideas as possible for resolving your problem (purge).

2. Use a variety of formal techniques (e.g., circles of creativity, semantic intuition, analogies, what if . . . ?, picture stimulation) to generate ideas.

1. Identify idea hits.

2. If feasible, group hits into categories of related ideas.

3. Select the categories with the greatest potential as solutions.

Review the criteria and select the most important ones. Then use the criteria to select the best solution or combination of solutions. If you have time, use a weighted decision matrix to make your decision; follow these steps:

1. Rate the importance of each criterion on a five-point scale (1 = not very important; 5 = very important).
2. Use a similar five-point scale and rate each solution against each criterion.
3. Multiply the importance rating of each criterion by the rating for each solution.
4. Add up the products for each solution.

Figure 2-6. Solution finding.

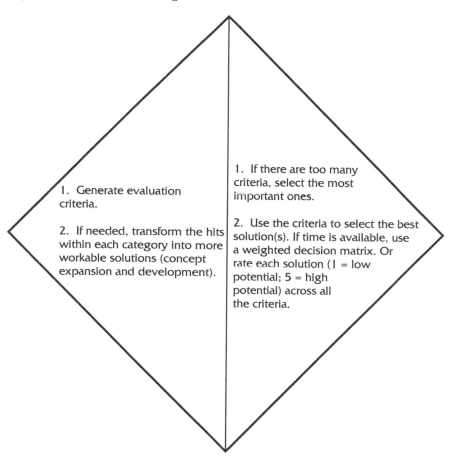

1. If there are too many criteria, select the most important ones.

2. Use the criteria to select the best solution(s). If time is available, use a weighted decision matrix. Or rate each solution (1 = low potential; 5 = high potential) across all the criteria.

1. Generate evaluation criteria.

2. If needed, transform the hits within each category into more workable solutions (concept expansion and development).

5. Select the solution with the highest score (or select a combination of solutions).

Acceptance Finding

The last stage of the CPS model helps you implement your solution successfully. As shown in Figure 2-7, major divergent activities involve: (1) listing potential implementation obstacles and ways to overcome them, (2) developing both preventive actions and contingency (backup) plans, and (3) generating an action plan to implement your solution. Include in this plan every step needed to ensure resolution of your problem. During acceptance-finding convergence, you should select the

Figure 2-7. Acceptance finding.

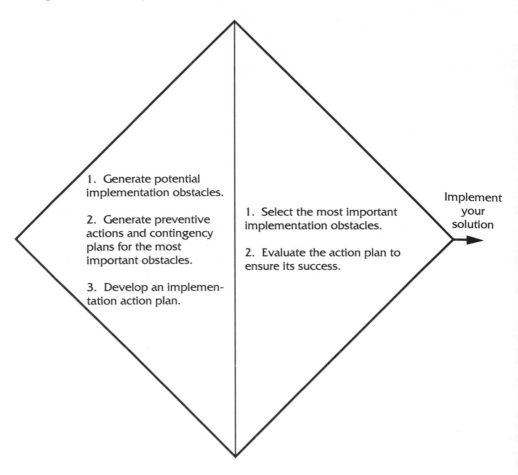

most important implementation obstacles. Finally, evaluate your action plan and make any needed improvements.

Creative Problem Solving in Action

The best way to learn how to use the CPS process is to practice it and receive feedback on how well you did. Since this is a book, you will have to settle for an example and practice on your own. After reading the illustration, take the time to practice with your own situation.

In this section we look at how to use CPS to deal with a business problem. Keep in mind that you rarely will use all six stages for every problem. And you frequently may want to return to previous stages. CPS is designed for flexibility. However, let's look at all six stages using an example of a major airline.

Objective Finding

Assume that the vice-president of marketing for FlySafe Airlines sends you the following memo:

To: John Smith, Human Resources Director

From: Mel Jones, Marketing Vice-President

Subject: Creative Problem-Solving Facilitation

As you know, our earnings for the first two quarters were down significantly over last year. And our stock has fallen dramatically over the last three years. Moreover, our major competitor, Air Turbulence, has gained considerable market share in recent years.

President Bump has asked me to generate ways to reverse our financial position. I told him that your personnel are equipped to facilitate Creative Problem-Solving sessions and possibly can help us deal with this problem. Would you put your personnel to work and see what solutions you can come up with? I have informed other division directors that we may need to use their staff to contribute data and brainstorm ideas. Let me know your final recommendations as soon as possible.

You agree to facilitate a Creative Problem-Solving session to generate some ideas. You put together a small group and begin objective finding.

To begin, you ask the group to defer judgment and list some major concerns in the marketing division. The group generates the following list:

---

1. Recruiting more qualified personnel
2. Improving customer service among international passengers
3. Increasing market share
4. Better predicting customer responses to marketing
5. Developing a marketing slogan

6. Improving manager-subordinate relations
7. Reducing advertising costs
8. Improving target market identification
9. Determining customer preferences
10. Improving focus group procedures

Next, you identify hits. This is a subjective process and varies from company to company and from person to person. In this case, suppose the group identifies items 1, 2, 4, and 9. Items 2, 4, and 9 clearly represent hotspots concerning customers. If the group members agree, they might identify an objective involving customers.

To identify this area, they apply the criteria of ownership, priority, and criticalness. They decide they have ownership over all the hits, since customers are a prime marketing responsibility. Of the hits, they decide that item 2 (improving customer service among international passengers) has higher priority than the other hits, since it is more likely to affect financial profit. (Remember, financial concerns were the priority the vice-president of marketing identified.) It also is critical because the financial position needs improvement to increase market share and ensure organizational survival. Improved customer service may result in more customers (or repeat business) and therefore more profit.

After reviewing the hits and applying the criteria, they decide on the problem statement, "In what ways might we improve customer service for international passengers?" They now are ready to move on to the next stage, fact finding.

Fact Finding

The purpose of this stage is to generate relevant data to improve understanding of the problem. This, in turn, allows you to consider different problem perspectives. To search for data systematically, the group uses the Five W's method. They generate a list of Who? What? Where? When? and Why? questions and answer them as follows:

• *Who are our potential customers?* The flying public. People on business. People on vacation. People combining business and pleasure. Frequent flyers. People visiting families. Males and females. Young and old people. Rich and poor people. People flying on other airlines. *Who provides customer service?* Flight attendants. Ticket counter personnel. Baggage handlers. Catering personnel. Pilots. Ground crew. Travel agents. Baggage claim personnel.

• *What is customer service?* Learning customer preferences. Attending to customer needs. Solving customer problems. Anticipating problems before they occur. Interacting with customers with a positive attitude.

- *Where is customer service most evident?* During flights. When delays occur. At ticketing counters. When any problem affects customers. During peak travel periods.

- *When do most people notice customer service?* When they are ignored. When someone goes out of his or her way to help. When they receive prompt attention. When an employee overlooks a minor policy to help someone in trouble.

- *Why is good customer service important?* It helps attract new customers. It helps retain old customers. Sustained profits depend on it. It helps the company project a positive image. It creates satisfied customers who are more likely to fly with us again.

The group members then converge and identify hits among their fact-finding data. To do this, they underline the most important responses to the questions and list the results:

The flying public
People flying on other airlines
Flight attendants
Ticket counter personnel
Learning customer preferences
Anticipating problems before they occur
During flights
When delays occur
When someone goes out of his or her way to help
When they receive prompt attention
It helps attract new customers
It helps retain old customers
It produces satisfied customers
It helps the company project a positive image

Next, the group examines the hits to see if it might group some together into hotspots. The group members develop the following list:

Employees:

    Flight attendants
    Ticket counter personnel
    When someone goes out of his or her way to help

Customers:

> The flying public
> People flying on other airlines
> Learning customer preferences
> It helps attract new customers
> It helps retain old customers
> It produces satisfied customers

Flight-related data:

> During flights
> When delays occur

Problem Finding

The group now is ready to enter the problem-finding stage to consider a variety of problem perspectives. Restating the problem might unlock a new viewpoint that could lead to many creative solutions. To create these viewpoints, the group examines the fact-finding hotspots and uses the hits to suggest possible problem redefinitions. The group members generate the following list of problems:

In what ways might we (IWWMW):

1. Encourage employees to go out of their way to help customers?
2. Attract passengers who regularly fly other airlines?
3. Attract new customers?
4. Increase international customer satisfaction?
5. Reduce the number of takeoff and departure delays?

Next, they converge and identify hits using the criteria of ownership, likelihood of stimulating many ideas, and freedom from criteria. After analyzing all the statements, they select problems 1, 3, and 4. Of these, they decide that problem 4 is most likely to resolve their objective of improving the airline's financial position. The primary reason for this choice is one of ownership: Their marketing data suggest that the international market is the most unstable. No airline yet has established itself in a dominant market position, as is the case with domestic travel. Thus, they might be able to capture a larger market share and improve their financial position.

Idea Finding

The group now is ready to begin idea finding using the problem, "IWWMW increase international customer satisfaction?" The members start with a purge to list more conventional ideas:

- Install more comfortable seats.
- Offer good entertainment.
- Provide more legroom.
- Train personnel to be more courteous.
- Lower ticket prices.

Next, they select a formal idea-generation technique such as the *two words* method. To implement this approach, they follow these steps:

1. List alternate word meanings for two key words in their problem statement.
2. Examine combinations of two words, one word from each list.
3. Use the combinations to suggest ideas.

For instance, they might focus on the words *increase* and *satisfaction* and set up the technique as follows:

Increase	Satisfaction
Improve	Pleasure
Enlarge	Ease
Enhance	Enjoyment
Renew	Peace of mind
Upgrade	Contentment

Different combinations of these words suggest such ideas as:

- Gourmet food (upgrade—pleasure)
- Seconds on food and drink (renew—satisfaction)
- Free flight insurance (upgrade—peace of mind)
- Vibrating seats (enhance—enjoyment)
- Shortening airport check-in time (improve—ease)

After generating these and other ideas, the group might try another technique such as *brainwriting*. Brainwriting is a brainstorming variation in which a group generates ideas silently and in writing. The steps for this method are:

1. Each group member is given a stack of index cards.
2. Each member writes down one idea per card and passes it to the person on the right.
3. The person receiving a card examines the idea on it for possible stimulation of a new idea.
4. Members write down (on another card) any new ideas suggested and pass the card to the person on the right.
5. After about ten minutes of this activity, the idea cards are collected and evaluated.

Some possible ideas from this technique are:

- Wine-tasting classes
- Videocassette players built into seat backs
- Computers built into seat backs
- Stand-up comedians
- Free popcorn
- Educational seminars
- Motivational speakers
- Theme flights with audience participation (e.g., murder mysteries)
- Free tourism-survival kits
- On-board business card raffles

In this example, the group has generated a total of twenty ideas for improving international passenger satisfaction. Group members now need to converge, identify any hotspots, and select idea-finding hits. For hotspots, they identify:

- In-flight comfort (e.g., more comfortable seats, more legroom, vibrating seats)
- Food enhancements (e.g., gourmet food, free popcorn)
- Educational and entertainment programs (e.g., wine-tasting classes, stand-up comedians)

To select hits from among these hotspots, they decide upon three criteria: cost, ease of implementation, and likelihood of increasing passenger satisfaction. After examining all the ideas and applying the criteria, they reduce the list of twenty ideas to three:

---

1. Vibrating seats
2. Videocassette players built into seat backs
3. Theme flights with audience participation

The group now is ready to move to the next CPS stage and select a final problem solution.

Solution Finding

Solution finding contains two sets of divergent activities. First, the group generates evaluation criteria:

---

1. Cost
2. Time to implement
3. Degree to which current equipment will require modification
4. Effect on routine flight operations
5. Acceptance by airline crew
6. Passenger long-term interest level
7. Ability to interest a broad cross section of passengers

The second divergent solution-finding activity is to improve the ideas from idea finding. In this case, the group members decide the ideas don't need improvement and they move on to convergent solution finding.

Of the seven criteria they generated, the group members decide to delete criteria 2 and 5. They then construct a weighted decision matrix as shown in Figure 2-8. This matrix allows different weighting for each criterion; thus cost may be seen as more important than acceptance of an idea by an airline crew.

The group rates each criterion on importance, using a five-point scale (1 = not very important; 5 = very important). Next, each solution is rated on the degree to which it satisfies each criterion. The lower the number, the less the criterion is satisfied. For instance, vibrating seats were rated a 2 on the criterion of low cost. This means the group believes

Figure 2-8.   Example of a weighted decision matrix.

Criteria	Criteria Importance	Vibrating Seats		VCRs in Seatbacks		Theme Flights	
		Is	Subtotal	Is	Subtotal	Is	Subtotal
1. Low cost	5	2	10	3	15	3	15
2. Equipment modification	5	1	5	2	10	5	25
3. Routine flight operations	4	2	8	3	12	4	16
4. Passenger interest level	4	3	12	5	20	3	12
5. Interest to cross section	3	3	9	5	15	4	12
TOTALS:			44		72		80

vibrating seats will be relatively expensive. (Cost often is a confusing criterion since a low cost will be rated high.) Finally, they multiply the criterion ratings by the ratings for each solution ("is") and sum the products (subtotal). For instance, they multiplied the criteria importance rating of 5 for low cost by the rating of 2 for vibrating seats and recorded a response of 10 as subtotal. Then they summed the products in each column. As shown in the figure, they rated theme flights the highest, closely followed by VCRs, and then vibrating seats. Because VCRs and theme parties are relatively close, they both might be used. In this case, however, the group decides to select VCRs.

Acceptance Finding

It is not enough to select the best solution. Steps also must be taken to ensure the solution can be implemented successfully. This requires consideration of implementation obstacles and ways to overcome them.

A systematic way to ensure effective implementation is to conduct a potential problem analysis (PPA). Although different versions exist, the PPA used here was developed by Kepner and Tregoe and later modified by VanGundy. The steps for conducting a PPA are as follows:

1. Generate a list of potential problems that might hinder solution implementation.

2. Select the most important problems and list possible causes of each.
3. Rate the probability of occurrence of each cause (1 = not very probable; 5 = very probable) and the seriousness of each (1 = not very serious; 5 = very serious).
4. Multiply each probability rating (P) times each seriousness rating (S) to obtain a PS score.
5. Generate preventative actions for each problem cause.
6. Rate the residual probability (RP) that each problem cause still will occur after a preventative action has been taken.
7. Multiply the PS score by the RP score.
8. Develop contingency (backup) plans for causes with the highest PS × RP scores.

An example of a PPA using the VCR is shown in Figure 2-9. There are two problems with three causes each. The group estimates that all the preventative actions will reduce the probability of occurrence of each cause. For instance, equipment failure owing to lack of maintenance is reduced from a probability value of 3 to a 1 after the preventative action of checking the VCRs after every flight. Group members then multiply the PS ratings by the RP ratings to determine which causes should have backup or contingency plans. In this case, the most important area seems to be equipment failure owing to misuse. If built-in "help" functions don't prevent misuse, they suggest a computer diagnostic program that automatically signals potential misuse. If the group wanted, it also could have developed contingency plans for the other, more highly rated causes.

The last acceptance-finding activity involves developing an action

Figure 2-9. Example of a potential problem analysis (PPA).

Potential Problems/Causes	P	S	Preventative Actions	PS	RP	PS×RP	Contingency Plan
1. Equipment failure							
a. Heavy use	4	5	Use industrial equipment	20	2	40	
b. Misuse	5	5	Build in "help" functions	25	2	50	Computer diagnosis
c. Lack of maintenance	3	5	Check after every flight	10	1	10	
2. Passengers don't know how to use equipment							
a. Unfamiliarity	2	3	Show instructional movie	6	1	6	
b. Poor instructions	5	3	Write own instructions	15	1	15	
c. Not user-friendly	5	4	Test with passenger sample	20	2	40	

plan to guide solution implementation. A useful way to structure this plan is to use the Five W's questions of Who? What? Where? When? and Why? For instance, they might ask such questions as: Who will be responsible for implementation? What will they implement? Where will they need to go to implement it? When should it be implemented? The Why? question can be used by asking "Why?" of all the other questions—that is, asking why a particular person (or persons) should be responsible for an implementation activity (who?), why a particular thing should be implemented (what?), why it should be implemented in a particular location (where?), and why one time would be better than another to implement it (when?). This stage concludes with a sequential listing of specific action-plan steps. For instance, the group first might want to survey customers, then contact VCR manufacturers and take bids, consult with engineers on installation problems, rewrite instructions if necessary, and so forth.

After implementation, the only remaining CPS activity is to follow up on the effectiveness of the solution. In this instance, the group would want to know if it has solved the original problem of increasing international passenger satisfaction. If so, the next task would be to relate improved satisfaction with increased revenues from ticket sales. At this point, it is time to put the bean counters to work and leave CPS!

Part II

Creativity Training

3

Facilitating Problem-Solving Groups

Facilitation is one of the most important CPS skills. Skilled facilitators enable groups to work through the CPS process and resolve their problems. They help groups keep focused on their tasks, achieve their goals, and promote productive interactions between their members. Facilitators can be the cement that bonds a group together and ensures productive outcomes.

Unfortunately, many managers are not skilled facilitators. They usually attained their positions on the basis of technical expertise and, perhaps, a little political savvy. Thus, they know more about the content of a meeting than the process. They can contribute technical knowledge and help coordinate others' knowledge. However, they rarely know how to structure group interactions to deal with this knowledge. If they possess facilitation skills at all, they acquired them despite their profession.

Many managers actually may impede problem-solving discussions. Because they overemphasize content, they frequently talk too much, judge ideas prematurely, focus on content to the detriment of process, and withhold decision-making responsibility. In short, they may do more harm than good. Skilled CPS facilitators, on the other hand, structure the CPS process and smooth interactions. They also keep the group on track and see that it keeps its larger goal in sight. Without such help, groups may not be able to solve their problems.

Not every group needs an outside facilitator. Some groups are experienced and skilled enough to solve problems without such help. But such groups probably are an exception. The majority of problem-solving groups require at least minimal assistance.

Facilitator Qualities

CPS group facilitators must possess all the qualities needed for traditional discussion groups but also must have qualities relevant to CPS. For instance, group facilitators in general should possess the following qualities:

General Facilitation Qualities

1. *Self-knowledge.* They understand their strengths and weaknesses relative to group facilitation. Some facilitators excel more at either task or interpersonal behaviors. Those with a weakness in either should be aware of it and strive to improve.

2. *Patience.* Group problem solving is not always a smooth process. Facilitators must be able to tolerate different personalities as well as the unexpected events that occur during group sessions.

3. *Task understanding.* Effective facilitators have done their homework and understand the problem facing the group. They may not be an expert in the problem area, but they know how and where to acquire relevant background data.

4. *Ability to coordinate thinking processes.* Most groups tend to deviate from their assigned task at one time or another. A skilled facilitator can keep a group on track and manage diverse thinking styles.

5. *Well-developed verbal skills.* Facilitators must be verbally fluent, but not excessively. Except in situations where facilitators need to model behavior, they should limit their comments to process issues.

6. *Human relations skills.* People judged to be effective discussion leaders make more positive socioemotional comments than less effective leaders. Facilitators should help participants feel at ease. When group members perceive the facilitator as sensitive to their needs, interpersonal trust and a team spirit are more likely.

7. *Awareness of nonverbal communications.* When we communicate with others, most of our messages are nonverbal. Body posture, leg and arm gestures, and facial expressions are just a few of the ways we communicate nonverbally. A facilitator should be aware of how such communications can contradict verbal ones. In fact, nonverbal messages often are more credible.

8. *High-level communication skills.* Effective facilitators have the ability to articulate issues and express themselves clearly and concisely. Discussions about complex problems require summarizing statements and clarifying questions. They also must express clearly a group's goals

and values. Groups must have a sense of direction, which, sometimes, only a facilitator can provide.

In addition to general facilitator qualities, CPS facilitators should possess a set of qualities relevant to CPS. Most of these are the same characteristics needed for creative thinking. Although they may not need them to solve problems, facilitators should be able to model them for group members.

CPS Facilitator Qualities

1. *Positive thinking.* A positive attitude is especially important for difficult-to-solve problems. Solutions for such problems are not always easy to generate. As a result, you may feel discouraged. Belief in your ability to solve a problem, however, creates a mind-set that you can do it. It you think you can, very often you can.

2. *An open mind.* A primary creativity principle is deferring judgment during idea generation. Because facilitators help encourage ideas (and often record them), they must not react negatively to any ideas proposed. Facilitators who suspend judgment are more effective than those who don't. Also, if a facilitator expresses any displeasure at all with an idea, the proposer may be discouraged from suggesting more.

3. *Basic creative thinking skills.* Effective CPS facilitators should be high in the basic creativity skills of fluency, flexibility, originality, and elaboration. That is, they should be verbally fluent, able to think of categories of ideas and view problems from different perspectives, able to think of novel ideas, and able to add detail and elaborate on an idea. It is especially important that CPS facilitators model these characteristics.

4. *Tolerance of ambiguity.* Creative ideas often emerge from a mess of apparently unrelated and disconnected data. Some people attempt to avoid such ambiguous stimuli and classify problems immediately in black-and-white terms. That is, they try to simplify things as representing either one situation or another. The danger of such behavior is that they may overlook the richness of the data. Apparently unrelated stimuli can provoke unique associations that can lead to unique ideas. If you come to closure too quickly and classify a problem prematurely, you will lose this ability to generate new associations and unique ideas.

5. *Ability to take prudent risks.* Any new idea or behavior requires a certain amount of risk taking. Unique ideas do not develop when you focus on something that already exists. Instead, you must go beyond conventional thinking. And that requires risk taking. Unfortunately, we

risk ridicule in most groups whenever we propose an idea. Most group norms do not encourage "different" thinking. CPS facilitators must encourage such thinking, however, and assume some risks. That is the only way they can expect to help the group generate unique solutions.

6. *Spirit of playfulness.* Most creative ideas don't emerge spontaneously whenever we need them. Instead, we must toy around with a general concept or an ill-formed idea. This playing eventually may lead to a new insight or it may not. However, new ideas never have a chance unless we give them a chance. Playfulness also contributes positively to making a group climate conducive to creative thinking.

7. *Confidence.* CPS facilitators must be confident in their ability to facilitate the CPS process. They must have a thorough understanding of the process and be able to communicate their knowledge to group members. They also must have confidence in CPS to generate creative solutions.

Consultant Dave Morrison has developed a list of CPS facilitator qualities and organized them into three categories: (1) values and mind-sets that contribute to facilitating a meeting, (2) facilitator "skill" attributes, and (3) facilitator "attitude" attributes. With the exception of a few editorial changes the following lists are from his handout *Facilitation Skills:**

Values and Mind-Sets That Contribute to Facilitating a Meeting

1. Believes in the power of groups, in collaboration, and in cooperation.
2. Thinks that all individuals are creative and can contribute.
3. Thinks there is value in all points of view.
4. Only by deferring judgment can an effective, nonbiased search be conducted to solve a problem.
5. Two, three, or four heads are better than one.
6. Effective planning will improve the quality of any meeting.
7. Quantity of divergent thinking will yield quality of thinking.
8. Getting agreement at every step of the problem-solving process will yield maximum buy-in to the outcome.
9. Every individual or group or problem is different. New learning occurs every time a group assembles.
10. A meeting isn't completed until action plans have been made to include the person responsible and date.

*All lists of CPS facilitator qualities are used by permission of Dave Morrison.

Facilitator "Skill" Attributes

1. Can defer judgment (e.g., does not use or allow idea "killer" phrases, writes down everything said when diverging, values all input equally).
2. Can conduct effective "preconsults" (e.g., finds out the client's expectations, restates and clarifies, uncovers the client's desired outcomes, establishes an effective agenda that meets the client's needs, gathers input for the agenda prior to a meeting).
3. Can uncover prior to the meeting if the client has a hidden agenda (e.g., asks, "How would you solve this?" and then tests the client to see how much he or she bought into the solution; constantly probes and listens for hidden agendas, confronts the client if the facilitator suspects the client is using the meeting to convince the participants that his or her solution is best).
4. Can listen and write at the same time.
5. Can ensure that others' points of view are heard (e.g., doesn't cut off people when they talk, doesn't favor management input when diverging, solicits other points of view in meetings, adds to divergence by asking participants to take another point of view).
6. Writes down everything said.
7. Checks with people to ensure they have shared all their viewpoints.
8. Good flip chart pad techniques (e.g., stands to the side, captures full sentences, can decipher own abbreviations).
9. Can talk to the client in terms of process (e.g., "Most of the meetings we will be gathering facts" as opposed to "Most of the meetings we will be discussing safety issues").
10. Ends every meeting with a debrief (e.g., "What worked well? What can we do differently next time to improve?").
11. Shares the agenda at the beginning of the meeting and asks for any additional items.
12. Can control group members and keep them either diverging or converging as appropriate.
13. Listens actively.
14. Can show empathy toward people while remaining objective about the process.
15. Understands role models and can facilitate convergent and divergent thinking.
16. Knows where the group is in any process at all times.
17. Understands meeting roles: client, participants, leader, resources, coach.

18. Knows when and how to step in and out of the facilitator's role.
19. Can avoid discussing content to remain objective and in control of the process.
20. Is able to manage interpersonal conflict among self, others, and meeting participants.
21. Allows people to make decisions based on facts they uncover or discover in conjunction with information provided by authority figures.
22. Can sense mood shifts in a group and deal with them.
23. Can explain the process to the client and answer relevant questions.
24. Constantly displays effort to help the client (e.g., periodically checks with the client).
25. Can get the client to listen to participants (can confront clients when they disagree with other participants and find out why).
26. Establishes who the client is, or knows who owns the problem.
27. Can get people back on track.
28. Recognizes the limited scope that can be accomplished in a given meeting.
29. Can confront the client without making him or her mad and doesn't embarrass the client.
30. Is capable of staying focused on the client's objective.
31. Gives participants process options when the group leaves the formal agenda.
32. Strives to gain commitment to action.
33. Can get everyone involved; builds confidence of each person in the room.
34. Gives everyone an equal opportunity to participate.
35. Can turn every situation into a learning process.
36. Can tap the experience and knowledge of the group to articulate points.
37. Always leaves a meeting with the specific next steps written down.

Facilitator "Attitude" Attributes

1. Has a positive outlook on events, people, and processes.
2. Values others' points of view, opinions, and different values.
3. Is in tune and comfortable with being in a process role versus a content role.
4. Values the learning experience balanced with the importance of outcomes instead of just being focused on outcomes alone.
5. Is confident enough to participate actively.

6. Is energetic.
7. Has a certain confidence that he or she can and will help the client.
8. Is not intimidated easily.
9. Values debriefing.
10. Cares about people's personal needs.
11. Tells the truth. Says, "I'm not comfortable with that." Or is willing to "call it like it is."

Facilitator Guidelines

An important facilitation skill is the ability to structure the problem-solving process. Considerable academic research supports this conclusion. For instance, some researchers found that structuring behaviors (e.g., amplifying ideas, maintaining goal orientation) influenced perceptions of decision quality more than group-member involvement or behaviors affecting social interactions. In another study, discussions facilitated by leaders using a structuring style were judged significantly better than those led by nonstructuring leaders. And others found that students had a statistically significant preference for a more complex, five-stage problem-solving process (a "Creative Problem-Solving Sequence") over a simple, three-stage process. Other studies support similar conclusions.

There are a number of guidelines facilitators can use to structure the CPS process. The following list includes suggestions for the general CPS process and for specific stages. The guidelines are based on my own experiences in facilitating CPS groups, some academic literature, and the contributions of Sid Parnes in his book *A Facilitating Style of Leadership*.

General Guidelines

1. Obtain necessary equipment and supplies well in advance of meetings. For equipment, consider at least one overhead projector and screen, although two would be better: With two projectors, you can use one screen to review previous ideas or to record material for an idea-generation technique; you can use the other screen to record new ideas. Many facilitators prefer overhead projectors to flip charts for a number of reasons: You can write sitting down; transparencies often can be photocopied directly, while flip chart paper must be transcribed; and transparencies are easier to sort through than large sheets of paper. A disadvantage is that flip chart papers can be placed all around a room, while a projector limits you to the number of projectors available.

An even better idea-processing arrangement is to use a computer with outlining software that has a split-screen capability (e.g., Grandview for IBM and compatibles and MORE for Macintoshes). A computer can be attached to an LCD panel that sits directly on the overhead projector and shows the computer screen on the larger screen. Computers have at least two major advantages over flip charts. First, you can edit electronically. It is relatively easy to sort the ideas into categories automatically, make numerous changes (e.g., add, delete, modify), and evaluate ideas by electronic voting and then rank-order the results automatically. Second, and not unimportant, typed data on a computer screen are a lot easier to read than most handwriting!

Common supplies include flip charts, masking tape, markers (or jumbo crayons), index cards (for note-taking and brainwriting sessions), pens and pencils, and writing tablets. You also might consider using a tape recorder to ensure that no ideas are left out or no misunderstandings result owing to interpretations in wording. A disadvantage of tape recorders is that they are time-consuming to transcribe since so much information must be filtered out. If you use a tape recorder, consider one with a speech-compression feature.

2. Establish ground rules with the group before generating any ideas. The most important rule is to separate idea generation from evaluation. Other brainstorming rules also apply: Quantity breeds quality—try for as many ideas as possible; the wilder the better; and try to "hitchhike" on (add to or modify) others' ideas.

3. Create an informal atmosphere. Idea generation is not a formal activity. You should encourage informal interactions among the group members. Sid Parnes suggests that if everyone is comfortable, a group even might sit on the floor with flip chart paper in the center.

4. During divergent activities, remind participants to really stretch their thinking to generate as much data as possible. There are two ways to draw out more ideas. One involves setting a quota of ideas. Thus, you might tell the group to try for twenty ideas. Then when they reach this number, ask them to try for five more. If they continue to generate ideas easily, ask them to think of another five. If you use the quota method, be careful that your quotas—especially the first one—are realistic. Otherwise the group may burn out early. A second way to stimulate ideas is to set a time limit. For example, ask the group to think of as many ideas as possible in ten minutes, then have them try for another three minutes, and so forth until they run out. Research has shown that people often generate their best ideas during the later portions of an idea-generation session, so don't be afraid to ask the

group members to keep trying, even if they initially appear to have run dry.

5. Model appropriate CPS behavior. Be certain to defer judgment on new ideas and retain an open mind at all times. You also should be aware that your facial expressions can give away a lot about your attitudes. We sometimes say something positive but indicate with our facial expressions that we actually feel the opposite. Thus, even if you don't think an idea is very good, try not to let it show in your face!

6. Concentrate on listening carefully. To demonstrate your understanding, use reflective listening and paraphrase what you think you heard.

7. Become comfortable with silence during idea generation. Tell the group that brief periods of silence are okay and quite natural during most problem-solving sessions. They usually indicate people are thinking about what they heard or are trying to think of something new to add. Silence typically is a problem in most groups only at the beginning of an idea-generation session. At this time, people may feel uncomfortable getting started. If you think the silence has lasted too long, ask an idea-spurring question such as, "How would [a famous movie star] handle this situation?" Or you could add one of your ideas to see if it might stimulate some others. However, try to avoid suggesting too many ideas. You need to maintain some separation between the roles of facilitator and group member.

8. Monitor the amount of time available for different activities and remind the group of time constraints. This caveat is especially important if you plan to evaluate the ideas later. Groups often become so involved in idea generation that they neglect to allow sufficient time for evaluation. This is not necessarily bad, however. If a group is on a roll and generating many ideas, you may want to let it continue and use the entire time. You then could evaluate the ideas later if there are no prior constraints such as project deadlines.

9. If the session lasts more than an hour, encourage the group members to walk around. Research has shown that such movement can stimulate thinking.

10. Never assume that people understand how to use a technique, even if they say they do. Monitor the group closely and provide feedback—positive feedback if the members are doing well and corrective feedback if they need help.

11. Try to avoid vote taking during convergence. A much higher quality solution is likely if ideas are discussed thoroughly. Vote taking should be reserved for when little time is available.

12. Remember, you are not expected to be an expert on every subject. Your role is to facilitate and not to generate ideas. You are a catalyst to help the group use its expertise to bring out ideas.

13. Monitor the CPS process continuously. The group members' primary role is content; yours is process. Remind the group whenever it gets off track and needs to move on. Be conscious of flow. It is your job to ensure the group achieves its objective of resolving the problem.

Objective-Finding Guidelines

1. Try to avoid using the word *problem* during objective finding. Instead, use such words as *concern, challenge, opportunity,* or *situation.* The word *problem* has a negative connotation that can create a negative climate at the outset.

2. Make it clear that objective finding is an optional stage of the CPS process. If a target area already has been identified, the group should move to the next stage.

3. To elicit objective areas, use the checklist of stimulators suggested by educators Noller, Parnes, and Biondi in their book *Creative Actionbook*:

> What would you like to do, have, accomplish?
> What do you wish would happen?
> What would you like to do better?
> What are your unfulfilled goals?
> What angered you recently?
> What would you like to get others to do?
> What takes too long?
> What is wasted?
> What is too complicated?
> In what ways are you inefficient?
> What would you like to organize better?

4. Encourage participants to defer judgment when listing data. It is important to identify all possible objective areas. Too much criticism or analysis of every objective as it is suggested will reduce the number of potential areas identified.

5. To help the group select an objective area, have members use the criteria of importance, commitment to work on it, and likelihood of productive outcomes.

Fact-Finding Guidelines

1. Provide examples of how to use the Five W's technique.

2. In his book *A Facilitating Style of Leadership*, Sid Parnes suggests the following questions to prompt fact-finding data:

What do we know about this situation?
What is and isn't happening?
Who is and isn't involved?
Where and when is and isn't this taking place?
How and why is and isn't it happening?

3. Stress that the group should seek more than one W question (i.e., more than one Who? What? Where? When? Why? question). Encourage the members to suspend judgment and generate as much data as possible for each question.

4. Note that the group should focus on describing the situation and not on what "should be." The members' feelings about a current situation also can be just as important as factual data.

5. The same fact-finding data often will appear as responses to different questions. This repetition should not cause trouble as long as there are many different responses to all the Five W's questions. The objective of fact finding is to draw out all relevant data. If some of these data occur more than once, it should not be a concern. The important thing is that the group has identified the data.

6. Allow the group to finish fact finding once it has increased its understanding of the situation sufficiently to deal with it constructively.

Problem-Finding Guidelines

1. Problem-finding statements should contain some indication of ownership. Encourage the group to use the statement, "In what ways might we (IWWMW). . . ?" Avoid statements such as, "How might the manager in Department *A* motivate his employees?"

2. Ask the group members to list all the IWWMW statements they can think of before they use responses to the fact-finding questions to stimulate statements.

3. The group also can try thinking of wishes to generate IWWMW statements. For instance, someone might wish that a floor could clean itself. This wish could be changed into the statement, "IWWMW better clean floors?" or "IWWMW eliminate the need to clean floors so often?"

4. Never allow the group to include criteria in a problem statement. Encourage the participants to modify a statement such as, "IWWMW improve a light bulb at a cost of less than one dollar per bulb?" The reference to cost is a criterion that should not be included. Instead, suggest they set this criterion aside for possible use during solution finding.

5. Watch out for problem statements that contain two different problems. The group can generate ideas only for one problem at a time. It will have to choose which problem to work on first; the members can't work on both at the same time.
6. If the selected problem statement seems too narrow, suggest they try the "Why" method to broaden the statement.
7. If the group can't decide among two or three problem statements, remind the members that it really may not make much difference. Research has shown that if a problem has been redefined many different ways, the ideas generated during idea finding probably will deal with all aspects of the problem.
8. Ask the group to phrase the problem concisely. Suggest that the participants state it as a telegram.

Idea-Finding Guidelines

1. Before beginning idea generation, remind the group about the importance of deferring judgment.
2. Do not allow group members to ask questions about the ideas generated. This is a form of judgment and can impede the flow of ideas. If group members ask questions, suggest they save them for evaluation during convergence.
3. Do not spend time during idea generation deciding if an idea is similar to one already proposed. Go ahead and write it down. You can consider idea duplication later.
4. Use a variety of idea-generation techniques. What works well for one person or group may not work so well for another. Experiment with the individual and group idea-generation methods described in Chapters 7 and 8. Include several techniques based on unrelated stimuli (e.g., analogies, picture stimulation).
5. Many ideas often are vague or too general. For instance, an idea for a new type of candy might be to make it unique. Because it is so vague, this idea actually becomes a problem itself. That is, the problem is to generate ideas to make the candy unique. Or it may be that the idea is too general and needs to be broken down into more specific categories of ideas. However, wait until convergence to modify these ideas; otherwise, you will violate the principle of deferred judgment.
6. To encourage more ideas after the group has run dry, ask the members to pick two or three of the worst or silliest ideas. Then have them use these ideas (by modifying or adopting them) to generate more practical ideas. This exercise also will illustrate the value of deferring judgment.

Solution-Finding Guidelines

1. Unlike the other CPS stages, solution finding has two divergent activities. The first is to generate ways to improve the idea hits selected in idea finding. Note that ideas are the raw material of solutions. These ideas often must be transformed into a more practical form. Of course, if the ideas are judged workable, you can skip this activity. The second divergent solution-finding activity is to generate decision-making criteria. (Although criteria are used throughout the CPS process, most of these are implicit. Solution finding makes these criteria explicit.)

2. Parnes suggests the following general evaluation checklist to stimulate criteria:

> Effect on objective
> Costs involved
> Tangibles involved (materials, equipment)
> Moral or legal implications
> Intangibles involved (opinions, attitudes, feelings)
> Likelihood of causing new problems
> Difficulties of implementation and followup
> Repercussions of failure
> Timeliness

3. Don't try to force a decision matrix on the group. Such a systematic approach is not always needed. A matrix may represent overkill for some situations, such as those in which the choices are relatively clear-cut. Decision matrices are more useful when the choice among alternatives is not so clear or when the group needs to reach consensus.

4. If you use a decision matrix, stress that quantitative totals are not absolute decision indicators. You do not have to select the solutions with the highest score. Instead, the numerical totals can help guide you in making a choice. It is perfectly acceptable to accept a lower-rated solution; however, be sure you have thoroughly considered all possible criteria when making a decision.

Acceptance-Finding Guidelines

1. To improve the odds of successful idea implementation, researchers Scott Isaksen and Donald Treffinger, in their book *Creative Problem Solving: The Basic Course*, recommend using "assisters" and "resisters." To generate lists of each, they suggest considering people, things, locations, times, reasons, and steps.

2. Use solution-finding criteria to suggest ways to overcome implementation obstacles.

3. Use the Five W's (Who? What? Where? When? Why?) to consider implementation issues. For example, Who should implement the solution? What should be implemented? Where should it be implemented? When should it be implemented? Then ask "Why?" for each of these questions (e.g., Why should this person implement the solution at a particular time and place?).

4. Parnes offers the following general implementation questions:

What might I do to gain acceptance?
What other advantages might there be?
What additional resources might help (individuals, groups, money, materials, equipment, time, authority, permission)?
Who might contribute special strengths or resources?
Who might gain from the idea?
Who might need persuasion?

5. Never leave acceptance finding unless at least the first step of the action plan has been clarified. This will help create momentum and ensure that the plan will be given some attention. If it is, implementation will be more likely.

6. Conclude acceptance finding by asking the group members to visualize their plan being implemented. If any new obstacles arise, have the group devise ways to overcome them and then add them to the plan.

Troubleshooting Problems and Solutions

If you spend enough time as a group facilitator, you will encounter problems. Any given combination of people in a group is likely to produce some conflict, misunderstandings, and difficulties in working through the CPS process. The way you handle these problems will determine your effectiveness as a facilitator. Although you can't learn everything you need from reading a book, you can benefit from others' experiences. How you make use of these insights and experiences is, of course, up to you.

This section contains some general troubleshooting hints that should help you in any group situation. These hints are followed by troubleshooting suggestions for specific CPS stages. All of these hints are based on my personal experiences. Many of the general hints are based on the work of consultants Michael Doyle and David Straus, while the others are based on the work of Parnes.

General Troubleshooting

Problem: The group begins to slow down, showing a decline in its energy level.

Possible Solutions:

- Have the group walk around the room.
- Take a break.
- Move on to another idea or topic.

Problem: The group occasionally experiences long periods of silence.

Possible Solutions:

- Do nothing if the group is productive and making progress toward its goals.
- Find out what is behind the silence. If the group is considering a point, leave the members alone; if they appear confused, ask them if you can help.
- If you become uncomfortable, ask the group members what they think they should do next. Wait to see if anyone suggests something. If no one does, offer some alternatives.

Problem: One or more group members tend to dominate most of the discussions.

Possible Solutions:

- Use brainwriting procedures to eliminate verbal interactions (see Chapter 8).
- Say something like "George, you seem to be doing a lot of talking. Let's hear from someone else now."
- Speak to the dominating individual during a break, provide the person feedback on that behavior, and ask him or her to suggest a course of action.
- Ask the group members to speak in turn.
- Limit the amount of time any one person can speak.
- Ask the group members to raise their hands to be called on.

- Have the group toss around a ball. Only the person holding the ball may talk.

Problem: Destructive conflicts arise between two or more group members.

Possible Solutions:

- Acknowledge that a conflict exists and ask those involved to deal with it outside of the meeting.
- Use brainwriting procedures.
- Shift the focus of the discussion to (or maintain the focus on) ideas and not people.
- Establish a ground rule that before anyone can criticize an idea, he or she first must say something positive about it.
- Start the session by noting that everyone's ideas are equal in importance.
- Change seating arrangements so the conflicting parties sit on the same side of the table, but not next to each other.

Problem: Certain "obnoxious" people keep disrupting the group's activities.

Possible Solutions:

- At first, accept the person's actions or words by acknowledging them. For instance, state: "It seems that you don't think we'll ever agree on this problem. Am I correct?" By avoiding evaluation, you can assess your assumptions.
- Acknowledge what you think the person is feeling, without actually agreeing with the content of his or her statement.
- If the problem person makes a complaint that might throw the group off track, defer the issue until later.
- Always begin with the least threatening response. Start with simple acknowledgments and progress through direct confrontations. If necessary, ask the group members if they agree with your perceptions. For example, you might begin by thanking the person for his or her contribution. If that doesn't work, move next to the person and say, "Okay, we've got it!" If that doesn't work, confront the person outside the meeting. Finally, as a last desperate measure, say something like, "I think you're dominating the discussion. What do the rest of you think?"

Problem: The group seems to lose sight of its objective.

Possible Solutions:

- Ask a series of Why? questions to redefine the problem (see the "Why" method described under Problem-Finding Troubleshooting).
- Ask each group member to verbalize his or her perceptions of what the group should be doing.

Objective-Finding Troubleshooting

Problem: The group can't agree on an objective statement.

Possible Solutions:

- Encourage the group members to develop a statement as if they had to send a very expensive telegram. This will help them be economical with their words.
- Substitute a newspaper headline for the telegram message.

Problem: As the group suggests concerns, some members begin offering solutions. These actions slow the objective-finding process and frustrate other group members.

Possible Solutions:

- Suggest they use the solutions to suggest other objective areas.
- Remind the group to defer judgment and continue generating objective areas.
- Take the offenders aside and ask them to "cease and desist."

Problem: The group has trouble generating a sufficient number of objective areas.

Possible Solutions:

- Ask the members to visualize a day in their lives and write down any concerns, challenges, or opportunities they can identify.
- Have the group members generate broad categories of concern in their work lives (e.g., finances, coworkers, bosses, marketing, research). Then have them think of concerns within each area.

Fact-Finding Troubleshooting

Problem: Group members spend time disagreeing about what is a fact and what is an opinion.

Possible Solutions:

- Remind the group that it should defer judgment when diverging during fact finding.
- Note that the distinction between facts and opinions may be irrelevant. What is opinion to one person may be fact to another. The purpose of fact finding is to draw out relevant data to provide new problem perspectives. Thus opinions can provide such perspectives just as readily as facts.

Problem: Most of the facts generated fail to get at the heart of the problem.

Possible Solutions:

- Select an object unrelated to the problem, describe it in detail, and use the descriptions to suggest facts.
- Ask the group to think of similar problems and use the similarities to stimulate additional data.

Problem: Group members don't know when to stop fact finding and move on to problem finding.

Possible Solutions:

- Ask the group if the members have gained any specific, new problem insights. If they have, move on to the next stage.
- See if the same facts keep appearing. If they do, it probably is time to move on.

Problem-Finding Troubleshooting

Problem: Group members resist problem finding because they believe they already know what the problem is.

Possible Solutions:

- Encourage the group members to really stretch their minds and try to generate three new problem definitions.
- Use "What if?" thinking to increase problem perspectives. For instance, ask "What if you didn't know what the problem was? What if you reversed the original definition? What if the 'real' problem was. . . ?"
- If they continue to resist, consider that they may be right. If so, move on to idea finding.

Problem: The group members seem trapped in a narrow problem definition; they fail to consider broader problem implications.

Possible Solution:

- Use the "Why?" method to broaden the problem. Instruct the group
  members to ask "Why?" of their problem and then answer it. Then,
  instruct them to redefine the problem using this answer. Finally, have
  them ask "Why?" of this problem statement and answer it. For
  example, if the original problem is reducing conflict among team
  members, they might ask why do they want to reduce conflict. The
  answer might be to increase team productivity, and the redefined
  problem might be: "IWWMW increase team productivity?" Then
  they might ask why do they want to increase team productivity. Their
  answer to this question might be to make more money. And the
  redefined problem would be: "IWWMW make more money?" The
  group now has broadened the original problem and may select either
  of the two broader definitions if team members wish.

Problem: The group has difficulty generating problem redefinitions.

Possible Solutions:

- Recommend that they substitute different verbs and verb phrases in
  the original problem statement.
- Use the "Get fired" technique: You have five minutes to develop
  three more definitions or you will be fired.

Problem: The group can't agree on the best problem definition.

Possible Solutions:

- Remind the group that there may not be a "best" definition. Any one
  of several definitions may be equally productive, given the amount
  of time the members have spent analyzing the problem.
- Use a structured decision procedure such as a weighted decision
  matrix (Chapter 2) or voting.

Idea-Finding Troubleshooting

Problem: The group begins to run out of ideas.

Possible Solutions:

- Set an idea quota.
- Set a time limit.

- Use brainwriting techniques (Chapter 8).
- Use a variety of other idea-generation methods (Chapters 7 and 8).
- Take a break.

Problem: You are dissatisfied with the uniqueness of the ideas.

Possible Solutions:

- Use idea-generation techniques based on unrelated stimuli (e.g., analogies, picture stimulation).
- Ask the members to think of the most impractical idea and then modify it to create a practical idea.
- Ask the group to think of how someone in another discipline might solve the problem.
- Use guided imagery.
- Take a break.

Problem: A group member keeps criticizing ideas proposed.

Possible Solutions:

- Remind the group of the brainstorming rule of deferring judgment.
- Take a break and discuss the problem with the offender.
- Suggest that the group save criticisms for convergence.

Problem: The group members are uncertain as to when they should stop generating ideas.

Possible Solutions:

- Ask the members if they have produced a variety of problem insights. If so, move on.
- Select several promising ideas and evaluate them against several important criteria. If the ideas satisfy the criteria, move on.
- Examine the ideas to see if many natural categories (hotspots) occur. If the ideas can be grouped into categories, there may be enough diversity to justify moving on.

Solution-Finding Troubleshooting

Problem: You are dissatisfied with solution quality.

Possible Solution:

- Use the solution-finding criteria to improve solution quality.

Problem: Group members can't think of enough evaluation criteria.

Possible Solutions:

- Use analogies.
- Use the Five W's method to prompt criteria.
- Generate a list of solution "musts" and "wants."
- Generate a list of advantages or disadvantages for one idea. Use this list to think of criteria for the other ideas.
- Ask the group members to think of broad categories of ideas; then have them generate criteria within each category.

Problem: Group members are confused about the importance of using weighted decision criteria.

Possible Solutions:

- Use an example with which the group can identify, such as buying a new car.
- Ask an expert in the problem area to provide examples of criteria importance.

Problem: Group members disagree about criterion weights or how to rate ideas.

Possible Solutions:

- Average the idea ratings.
- Encourage the group to achieve consensus (if time is available).
- Obtain expert opinion.

Problem: The group uses a weighted decision matrix and rates two or more ideas as relatively equal in value.

Possible Solutions:

- If time permits, implement all the ideas.
- Flip a coin.

Acceptance-Finding Troubleshooting

Problem: The group wants to implement a solution without considering implementation obstacles.

Possible Solutions:

- Remind the group that the best solution will not help if it is not implemented properly.
- Remind the group that acceptance-finding activities often can reveal ways to improve the solution; thus, they could make successful implementation more likely.

Problem: The group members begin working on their action plan before considering potential implementation obstacles.

Possible Solutions:

- Suggest that their action plan will be better if they consider implementation obstacles first.
- Recommend that each group member generate a list of obstacles, which they then can pool to form a master list.

Problem: The group has trouble generating many implementation obstacles.

Possible Solutions:

- Use Parnes's implementation questions suggested earlier: "What might I do to gain acceptance?" "What other advantages might there be?" "What additional resources might help (individuals, groups, money, materials, equipment, time, authority, permission)?" "Who might contribute special strengths or resources?" "Who might gain from the idea?" "Who might need persuasion?"
- See if the group members can think of examples of implementation obstacles to previous problems; use these to guide generation of new obstacles.

Problem: The group has second thoughts about the value of the solution.

Possible Solutions:

- Have the group review the solution-finding criteria and use them to improve the solution.
- If time is available after implementation, remind the group that adjustments can be made later on.
- Remind the group members that they can't expect perfection in all situations. If the solution they implement turns out to be low in quality, they can learn from the experience.

4

Creative Thinking Exercises

All the tools, techniques, materials, and processes described in this book will help you design and conduct creativity training programs. If you implement your programs well, they should be successful. However, sometimes even the most carefully planned and implemented programs are unsuccessful.

One reason training may not "take" is group composition. Either the individuals or the way they interact can interfere with group creativity. In particular, individuals or groups may not have an internal climate conducive to Creative Problem Solving. From observing and facilitating hundreds of groups, I have noticed that idea-generation techniques frequently are relatively minor factors in a group's creative output. Although techniques can help stimulate thinking, climate seems much more important. This internal climate reflects the capacity of a group to respond receptively to new ideas and to support each other's ideas when they first are proposed. A group with a climate conducive to CPS is more likely to have a satisfying outcome and produce many unique solutions.

In addition to a conducive climate, a group also must be able to view problems from different perspectives and respond creatively to new situations. In fact, this ability contributes directly to group climate. The more finely developed a group's creative thinking abilities, the more conducive its climate is likely to be.

We all possess the ability to think creatively. As human animals, we are born with some creative thinking abilities—it is in our biological makeup to create—but we probably acquired most of our higher levels of creativity. That is, the creative problem-solving abilities we use to solve other than day-to-day problems most likely are learned. Through training and conditioning we have learned to respond to certain situations by custom-designing our responses, creating solutions for nonroutine situations.

Unfortunately, some of us have developed this ability better than others. People we consider highly creative generally seem able to generate creative responses effortlessly: It is part of their "normal" way of responding to life's challenges. If you are not one of these individuals, there is some chance of salvation. Practice with creative thinking can increase your creative abilities. And if you practice enough, you should be able to incorporate some creative thinking abilities into your natural problem-solving style.

If you are a trainer, these exercises can help students incorporate new skills and enhance existing ones, with group problem-solving sessions more productive as a result. The more individuals in a group with enhanced creative skills, the more creative the group's responses will be. Thus most creativity training programs should contain at least one session on creative thinking exercises.

The exercises in this chapter are designed to challenge creative thinking skills. Try each one, look at the sample answers, and then compare your response. Eventually you should learn how to shift focus and do what psychologists refer to as breaking your mental set—the ability to break out of a habitual mode of responding and view something differently or respond differently.

One distinctive feature of these exercises is that there are no correct answers. The exercises demand that you stretch your creative powers and think of many, different answers. Key to this is the ability to test assumptions about the exercises and view them from different perspectives. What are you assuming to be true or untrue that really is not? What information is in the problem and what is not? We often are blocked in our thinking when we assume a constraint exists that really does not.

Another distinctive feature is that a number of creative thinking skills are represented in the exercises. In addition to testing assumptions, many of the exercises test skills of fluency, flexibility, originality, and elaboration. *Fluency* is the ability to generate many ideas rapidly. *Flexibility* is the ability to generate rapidly many different classes of ideas (e.g., different uses for a brick might involve the classes of supporting things and holding down things). Flexibility also refers to the ability to switch viewpoints and view a problem in different ways. *Originality* involves the uniqueness of your responses. If a response is unique to you, then it is original; it does not have to be original to the rest of the world. Finally, *elaboration* is the ability to start with an object or concept and build on it by adding additional material.

The exercises that follow are presented in no particular order—start with any one you wish. You also will find that some will be easier than others. However, some of the more challenging exercises may not be quite as challenging the second time you try them. Although there is a practice effect, you should acquire the ability to approach the exercises more productively over time. You can find some sample responses at the end of the chapter.*

EXERCISES

1. What justification is there for placing these numbers above and below the line?

$$\frac{1 \quad 2 \quad 6}{4 \quad 5 \quad 9}$$

2. How can you add one line to IX and have it result in the number 6?

3. What is the next number that might be placed under the line to fit the series of numbers?

$$\frac{1 \quad 3 \quad 5 \quad 7 \quad 8 \quad 9}{2 \quad 4 \quad 6}$$

4. Which of the figures in Figure 4-1 is most different from the others?

5. What might be improved in a home if straight lines were changed to curved lines? (For example, there might be round windows.)

Figure 4-1. Which figure is most different?

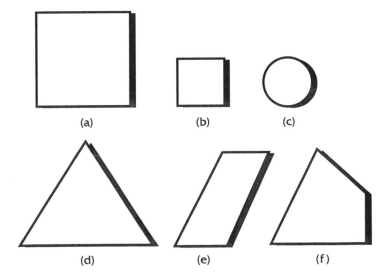

(a)   (b)   (c)

(d)   (e)   (f)

*The first twelve exercises were borrowed from the *Creativity in Action Newsletter* when it was edited by Sid Shore. Many thanks to Sid and his readers for their sample responses. The exercises are used with the permission of The Creative Education Foundation, 1050 Union Road, Buffalo, N.Y. 14224.

6. Draw the following without lifting your pen or pencil from the paper.

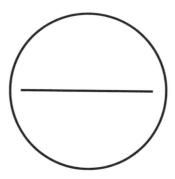

7. What might be the three preceding numbers in this series of numbers?

? ? ? 61 52 63 94

8. Tie a piece of string to a drinking cup's handle. Tie the other end of the string to a doorknob so that the cup is about one or two feet from the floor. Without touching either the cup or the string with your fingers, cut the string with a pair of scissors without allowing the cup to hit the floor.

9. How can you remove spilled salt from a bare table? You are not allowed to blow the salt, fan it, or touch it with anything. And you are not allowed to touch the table, either.

10. Print 1 0 0 0 without lifting your pen or pencil from the paper.

11. A woman was waiting near a bus stop for her husband to pick her up in his car. It suddenly started raining and she had no umbrella, raincoat, or hat and there was no awning nearby to hide under. However, when her husband drove up ten minutes later, she entered the car without a trace of moisture in her hair or on her clothes. How could she have done this?

12. Which of the following items is least like the others? envelope, bag, cup, strainer, barrel.

13. Cut a pie into eight pieces using three or fewer cuts.

14. Roger Price coined the term *droodle* to describe a drawing that at first may not look like anything but later appears as something specific. Look at the drawings in Figure 4-2 and guess what is represented by each. Try to think of more than one response for each drawing.

15. Speak the following words aloud: *joke, joke, joke*. Now what is the white of an egg called?

16. Add one letter at the beginning of the following letters to make a word. *ANY*. What is the word? Now add one letter before the next set

Figure 4-2. Droodle exercise.

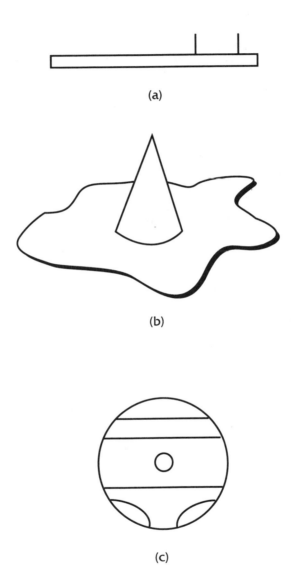

(a)

(b)

(c)

of letters to make a word. *ENY*. What is this word? Was it more difficult to think of the second word? If so, why?

17. This exercise often is used as a game to entertain children on long auto trips. Look for license plates with combinations of three letters, then try to think of words that might contain the letters in the same order. For instance, the combination *DGM* might suggest the words *DiaGraM* or *DoGMatic*. Think of words for these combinations: *FXH, JIW, MZP, ZTE, TJE*.

18. In what ways might you use a table lamp, an ice cream cone, and a pencil to achieve some objective?

19. A man is held in a room with a barred window and a door locked from the outside. Other than himself, the other items in the room are a small wooden table with a matching chair. Because it is winter, the window is closed. The window cannot be reached from the outside. The man is without a belt, suspenders, or shoelaces. The next morning, the person who brings him breakfast finds the man dead, slumped across the table. He discovers a chest wound with a bloodstain on the man's clothes around the wound. The man's shirt is damp with water and there is a small puddle of water on the table. Who killed the victim and how was it done?

20. A car is parked on a straight road facing west. A man climbs into the car and begins driving. After traveling for a while, he discovers he now is east of his starting point. Why?

21. Without looking at it, take out a pen or pencil and draw a picture of the face of your watch. If you don't wear a watch, draw a picture of any clock you look at on a regular basis.

22. How many squares are there in the following drawing?

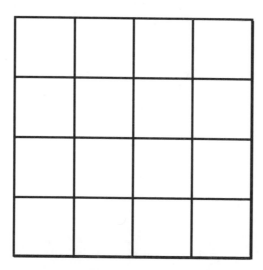

23. Connect the nine dots in the following drawing using no more than four straight lines. You may not lift up your pen or pencil or retrace any lines.

24. Write down your comments for the proposed wheelbarrow design shown in Figure 4-3.

25. What letter comes next in this sequence? *OTTFFSS*

26. What is positive about the following new product ideas?

   a. A glass bowling ball
   b. A cement pillow
   c. A one-foot-long mop handle

27. What's good about the following?

   a. Breaking up with a girlfriend or boyfriend
   b. Completely destroying your three-year-old car in an accident
   c. Not having any friends

28. An open bottle of wine is sitting in the middle of a small rug. In what ways might you remove the bottle without spilling the wine or touching the bottle with any body part or object?

29. Obtain a legal-size sheet of paper and cut or tear a hole in it large enough to walk through.

30. What is similar about the following words? *dime, lamp, keys, floor.*

31. A handy way to memorize any list is to use a mnemonic device. This involves making a sentence out of the first letter of each item on the list. This sentence may not make sense and, in fact, may be more useful if it does not. For instance, you might want to memorize a grocery list

Figure 4-3.   Proposed wheelbarrow design.

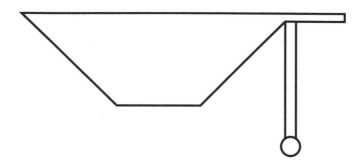

for carrots, celery, potatoes, apples, and bananas. With the letters *CCPAB,* you might construct a sentence such as Can Cynthia Punt and Bat? Try it with the word *create.*

32. Test your powers of originality and write a short paragraph using the following words.

lamp	*bicycle*	*record player*
computer	*bush*	*tiger*
sneeze	*juice*	*cement*
electricity	*chair*	*ice*

SAMPLE RESPONSES AND COMMENTS

1. When written out, the numbers on the top all have three letters (*one, two, six*), while those on the bottom have four letters each (*four, five, nine*). This exercise, like similar ones, requires you to go beyond conventional mathematical assumptions to come up with more than one response.

2. (a) Add the letter *S,* which is just one line. (b) Form a mathematical expression I × 6; this also equals 6. (c) Move the small *v* at the upper half of the X to the left of the I—this results in the slightly modified version of the Roman numeral vI (the remaining portion of the X is irrelevant, since it is not a Roman numeral).

3. (a) 8. The denominator numbers appear to be derived by adding 1 to each preceding numerator number. (b) 30. All the numbers on the top have the letter *e* in them; those on the bottom do not. The next number after the number 9 without the letter *e* in it is 30.

4. (a) Figure a could be the "correct" answer because it has the greatest area within its perimeter. (b) Figure b could be chosen because it is the only one that matches another—the larger square—and has less area than any of the other straight-line figures; it also is the shortest of the straight-line figures. (c) Figure c because it is the only one with a curved line. (d) Figure d because it is the only three-sided figure. (e) Figure e because it is lopsided and would fall over because its center of gravity is off; it also is the most narrow. (f) Figure f because it is the least symmetrical figure.

This exercise is difficult for some people since it is similar to questions found on many IQ tests. Such tests assume one "correct" response. To score high, you must suppress creative perceptions and concentrate on what the test developer wants. One lesson from this observation is that you need to be a flexible problem solver.

5. This exercise tests your fluency skills. If you thought of classes of uses, then you also tested your flexibility skills. Some possible responses:

a. Round house pivoting to follow the sun
b. Round beds to increase even wear of mattresses
c. Round portholes for pet doors
d. Round refrigerator to make reaching for foods easier, as on a lazy Susan (Panasonic now manufactures such a refrigerator)
e. All furniture on wheels
f. Turntable in garage to eliminate need to back out
g. Revolving doors for energy conservation

6. Draw a circle about two inches from the right edge of a sheet of paper, so that you stop drawing at the six o'clock position. Keep your pen or pencil in place at this position. Fold over the paper at the right edge so that the edge covers the right one-fourth or so of the circle. Next, move your pen or pencil in a counter-clockwise direction so that it is at approximately the three o'clock position over the circle. (To do this, you will draw over the folded edge.) Then, complete the figure with a straight line moving from right to left.

7. (a) Reverse the digits and the series becomes: 16 25 36 49. These are the squares of a series of numbers: 4 5 6 7. If we call the "control" numbers for the three preceding terms in the series the next three descending numbers, we see: 3 2 1, whose squares are 9 4 1. Place these latter numbers into the original series by reversing their order: 1 4 9. The series then becomes 1 4 9 61 52 63 94. (b) Each digit is made up of even (e) and odd (o) integers. If the series represents a repeating cycle of odd and even integers, you have:

oe	eo	oe	eo	oe	eo	oe
72	45	18	61	52	63	94

8. This is an excellent exercise for testing assumptions. Once you redefine this problem as how to suspend the cup or prevent it from falling, many solutions should appear. Some examples: (a) Cut the large bow in the knot at either end of the string. (b) Just cut the string a "little bit" so it does not go all the way through. (c) Rest the cup on a large carton, then cut the string. (d) After tying both ends of the string, take the remaining piece, run it through the cup handle, and tie it to the handle again. Since you have to cut only one string, the cup will remain hanging. (e) Flood the room so the cup floats. (f) Take the door off its hinges and lay it flat on the floor before cutting the string. (g) Support the cup on a column of air before cutting the string.

9. (a) Rub a comb on wool fabric to charge it with static electricity. Place the comb next to the salt and it will be attracted by the charge and leap off the table. (b) Take a picture of the table with the salt on it, develop the film, retouch the picture without the salt, and you have "removed" the salt. (c) Shake off the salt with sonic waves. (d) Let someone else remove the salt.

10. (a) Carve the raised numerals 1 0 0 0 on the side of the pencil. Press the numerals on a stamp pad and press them again on a piece of paper. It only takes one impression to print the number. (b) Place a piece of masking tape on the paper. Make a continuous series of loops on the tape that cross over to the paper. Peel away the tape and the number remains on the paper. (c) Wrap one corner of the paper around the unpointed end of a pencil, leaving the point exposed. Print 1 0 0 0 with the pencil point and you will not lose contact between the pencil and the paper—that is, there is no need to "lift" the pencil from the paper to write with it.

11. (a) It rained only on the street next to her. (b) She hailed a cab and waited in it for her husband. (c) A pedestrian with an umbrella stopped and allowed her to share his umbrella. (d) She crawled under a parked car. (e) The rain lasted only a few seconds, allowing her to dry off in a few minutes. (f) She caught a bus, rode it to the next stop, and then returned. (g) She waited in the lobby of a nearby building (the problem said nothing about nearby buildings).

12. The "correct" response to this question is supposed to be the strainer. It is the only one that will not hold a liquid. However, several other choices also are possible. (a) The cup—it is the only one with an easy-to-use handle. (b) The envelope—it is the only one with four vowels. (c) The envelope—it is the only one that begins and ends with a vowel. (d) The barrel—it is the only one held together with hoops. (e) The bag—it is the only one you can crumple up and use again.

13. This is a classic exercise in testing assumptions. Most people have trouble coming up with one solution. However, after you test assumptions,

you soon discover there are an infinite number of solutions! To solve this problem, you need to ask such questions as "What is a cut?" "Do the cuts have to be straight lines?" "What does a piece of pie have to look like?" "What do you have to use to cut the pie?" "Do you have to cut the pie from the top?" After asking such questions, you might think of the types of solutions shown in Figure 4-4. Another solution is to use a knife with seven blades spread out from the center. Stamp the pie once and you have eight pieces. Or cut the pie in half and stack one half on top of the other. Cut this piece in half, stack the pieces on top of one another, and cut them. Or cut the pie into quarters and then slice the pie horizontally through the quarters.

14. Figure a could be a toothbrush with only two bristles or a building with two smokestacks viewed from a distance. Figure b could be the Wicked Witch of the West after Dorothy threw a pail of water on her, or it could be the tip of a missile emerging from a submarine. Figure c might be a navel orange wearing a bikini or a bald person with a long pole strapped to the top of his head.

15. This is an exercise in breaking out of a pattern to solve a problem. If you said *yolk*, you were trapped by the pattern created by repeating the word *joke* three times. The answer, of course, is not yolk but albumen—the white part of an egg. Kind of cracks you up, doesn't it?

Figure 4-4. Cut-the-pie exercise.

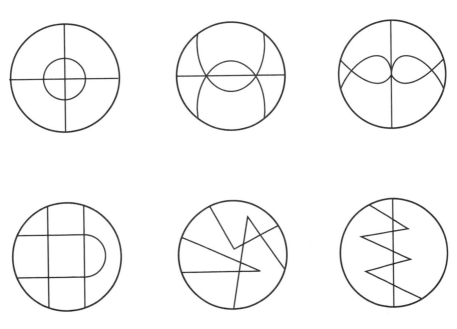

16. Most people think of the word *many* very quickly for the first set of letters. However, some people have more trouble thinking of the word *deny* for the second set of letters. The reason is that the sound of the word *many* creates a pattern. And this is with only one word! As a result, people often search their memories for other words with similar sounds to think of the second word. But the problem cannot be solved unless they break out of this pattern and shift their thinking to allow other sounds.

17. *FXH:* Foxhole, foxhound. *JIW:* Jigsaw, jimsonweed. *MZP:* Marzipan. *ZTE:* Zestiest, zygote. *TJE:* Turbojet, "Trojaned" (as in fooled by a Trojan horse!).

18. (a) Objective: Motivate a child to do her homework. Give her a light to study by, a pencil to write with, and an ice cream cone as a reward if she completes all her work. (b) Objective: Test the braking power of a car at night. Remove the ice cream and place the cone on the highway as a place to begin braking. Spread the melted ice cream on the road surface to mark the amount of skid. Use the pencil to record the final stopping point and use the lamp to see everything.

19. (a) He committed suicide by stabbing himself in the chest with an icicle, which then melted. (He retrieved the icicle by opening the window, reaching through the bars, and breaking off one from the edge of the roof.) (b) A man-eating tiger in the next room broke through a wall and killed the man while he was eating an icicle.

20. (a) He drove in reverse. (b) He made a U-turn (the problem did not indicate that he made no turns—test assumptions!). (c) He kept traveling until he started going around the world and ended up east of where he began.

21. A major creativity skill is the ability to break out of familiar thinking patterns. Our watch faces are very familiar since we look at them so many times during the day; however, we usually do not pay attention to the detail involved. Instead, we just look for specific information—in this case, the time and possibly the date. Most people are very surprised to discover that they cannot remember what their watch faces look like. If this describes you, be careful about becoming trapped in habitual modes of thinking. The next time you look at something as familiar as your watch, try to find at least one thing different or unique about it. This will help you break out of patterned thinking and make it easier to solve your important problems.

22. This is another classic creativity exercise. In school, we are taught to make certain implicit assumptions about problems. In this case, we are taught to assume that the lines in the square can be counted only once. By testing this assumption, many solutions become available. To begin, there are sixteen small squares plus the large outer square; that's seventeen. Next,

there are four 3×3 squares; that's twenty-one. There also are nine 2×2 squares; that's thirty. If you define a square using the small squares as borders, there are even more possibilities.

23. The nine dots exercise is one of the oldest creativity thinking challenges. It is designed to assess your ability to test assumptions. If you had trouble solving it, chances are you assumed you were restricted to the border formed by the square. If so, you limited your solution possibilities. One way to resolve this problem is to use the approach shown in the figure below. This solution assumes the lines can go outside the square pattern and that the lines do not have to intersect on a dot. Another solution is to fold the paper at different angles so all the dots can be connected with one line. Or you could go around the world three times!

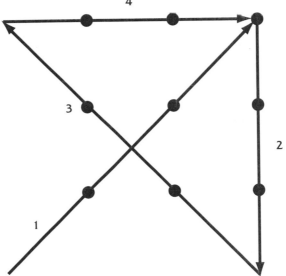

24. This is an exercise in "What's good about it?" When asked to provide comments about something new, most people offer negative criticisms. Whether because they assume that is what is wanted or because they are conditioned to do so, such comments stifle creativity. Although this wheelbarrow design obviously is not practical for most conventional uses, it may have some positive features. For instance, the large hopper means it can carry a lot of material. And, you might add a trap door in the bottom for dumping large loads. The short handle obviously provides no leverage, but it might prompt the idea of a collapsible handle. It could be collapsed for easy storage in small spaces.

25. To the anonymous developer of this exercise, the "correct" answer is E. The first seven letters represent the first letters in the numbers 1 through 7. However, there are other "correct" solutions. You might make a sentence

in which the words each begin with the letters in the acronym—for example, Omar *To Take Fran Franklin Skating Sometime Today*. The answer to the exercise would then be the letter *T*.

26. This exercise tests your ability to maintain a positive attitude in the face of apparently absurd ideas. Not all ideas are well developed when first proposed. Other features also may be impractical. The mark of a true creative thinker, however, is the ability to turn these negatives into positives—to turn lemons into lemonade. Here are some sample responses:

   a. A glass bowling ball: distinctive and unique; easy to find when among other bowling balls; could see through it when holding the ball before rolling it; would make an impressive trophy; could use to tell your "bowling fortune."

   b. A cement pillow: would never need fluffing; would maintain its shape; would last forever; could be used for building construction; would prevent your children from using them for pillow fights.

   c. A one-foot-long mop handle: could be attached to a regular mop handle and used as an extension for hard-to-reach areas; used as a mop for children or short people; recycled as a police baton; designed with interchangeable mop heads for different cleaning jobs.

27. Similarly to exercise 26, creative thinking is shown here by finding positives in apparent adversity:

   a. Breaking up with a girlfriend or boyfriend: no more arguments, don't have to feel so accountable, save money from dating, can spend more time on work or hobbies, can meet new girlfriends or boyfriends, can reflect and learn about yourself, will know how to act differently next time; if upset, can learn how you respond during emotional adversity.

   b. Completely destroying your three-year-old car in an accident: will get a new car, no more repair bills for a while (if the replacement car is new), learn about how car insurance claims are filed; if you just broke up with your girlfriend, you can attract other women with your shiny new car; if you were visibly injured, you may receive sympathy from many people.

   c. Not having any friends: more time for work or hobbies, lower phone bills if friends live out of state, won't have to buy presents for them, won't have to compromise when deciding upon social activities, won't have to put up with their bad habits.

28. The original "correct" solution was to slowly roll up the rug on one side until the bottle slides off. Here are some other possibilities: (a) Attach a very strong vacuum cleaner hose to the bottle and pick it up using

the suction. (b) Have a dog knock it off the rug (*you* were not allowed to touch it). (c) Have a friend pick it up (once again, *you* were not allowed to touch it). (d) Blow strong air at the bottle from two opposing sides; use the two forces blowing against each other to pick up the bottle. (e) Blow foam around the bottle so that it solidifies and forms a stable base; slide the rug out from underneath (this solution assumes that frozen foam is not an "object").

29. You also need to test assumptions to solve this problem. A major assumption is whether the hole needs to be circular and made with conventional means. One solution is to draw lines on the paper as shown in Figure 4-5. Then, cut along the lines and you will create an opening large enough to walk through. Another solution involves testing the assumption about *who* has to walk through the hole. If you puncture the paper with a pencil, you will create a hole large enough for an ant to walk through.

30. (a) All four can be found in at least one room of most houses. (b) They all can be shined. (c) They all can reflect light. (d) People use them all for practical reasons.

Figure 4-5. One solution to the make-a-hole-in-the-paper exercise.

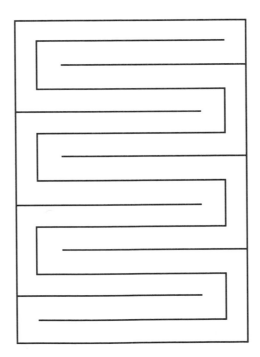

31. Here are some sample responses:
    a. Catch Rabbits Eating At The Entrance.
    b. Could Ralph Exist Although Tom Exists?
    c. Come Remove Extra Attics Tonight, Ed.
    d. Cool Retreats Emit Autos Touching Ecstasy.
    e. Combat Riddles Early At Technical Exacerbation.

32. As he turned on the lamp, he knocked over the computer. She laughed at him as she observed from behind a bush while sitting on her bicycle. Suddenly, a tiger landed on a chair and started dancing to a record player that used no electricity. He drank some radish juice, slipped on the ice, and fell into the cement. She had a sneeze and then laughed again.

5

Designing Creativity Training Courses

A major issue in many companies is whether you can improve problem-solving ability through creativity training. Many managers maintain either you are creative or you are not. Those who think you can't train for creativity usually believe people are born creative, and these managers look for creative ability among existing employees and when recruiting new personnel. They also make a distinction between "creatives" and "noncreatives," thereby stereotyping their employees. Unfortunately, they usually ignore the potential creative contributions of "noncreatives."

In contrast, managers who think it's possible to encourage creativity through training also believe that everyone is creative. However, classifying people as "creatives" and "noncreatives" is artificial. All employees have the potential to make creative contributions; they just need managers to provide them with the resources and opportunities to fulfill their creative potentials. As a result, these managers generally encourage and support creativity training.

Increasing numbers of managers are supporting creativity training, as noted in Chapter 1. Overall, the percentage growth in creativity training has been almost 700 percent since 1985. Businesses now know that to become and remain competitive, they need creative products and processes. Creativity training is one way to achieve this goal.

When you decide to offer such programs, your choice is between in-house training and the services of an external consulting firm. This chapter is intended for those interested in designing in-house creativity training programs.

In-house programs have several advantages over external programs; for example, you can tailor the program to suit your corporate needs.

After all, you understand your needs better than a consultant and are more familiar with available resources. Costs per person usually will be lower, too, which means you can train more people per dollar. And it sometimes may be easier for an internal trainer to conduct follow-up studies.

Some of these advantages are not that clear-cut, however. If you establish a productive working relationship with a consultant, you can inform him or her about your needs. And you can help an external consultant with any followup studies. The major advantage, then, is that in-house programs cost less because you use people on your payroll.

A major disadvantage of in-house programs is that an outside consultant is probably more qualified than in-house trainers. Creativity training is relatively specialized and most personnel do not have the required skills and experience. Unless you have considerable expertise in creativity training, you should consider using a creativity consultant to at least review your training program. It is even better to seek some help in designing your program from the beginning. I've reviewed several corporate programs after they were developed, and making recommendations at this point can be frustrating. It is difficult to do an adequate job if you are not involved in program content and process decisions from the outset.

Another disadvantage of in-house training is that outside consultants are not involved in internal politics and can remain more objective. Turf battles frequently flare up when resource-allocation decisions are made. If your turf is being contested, you are less likely to make objective decisions in regard to it. Outside consultants are not involved in such battles and are less likely to become entangled in interpersonal conflicts as well.

Creativity Training Research

Managers who conduct creativity training can justify their efforts with scientific research. Many studies have been conducted on the effectiveness of the CPS model described in Chapter 2, for example. Results of these studies have been mixed; however, other research leaves little doubt that people can be trained to increase their Creative Problem-Solving abilities. In particular, research has shown that training can increase four primary creativity skills of fluency, flexibility, originality, and elaboration, as measured by the Torrance Tests of Creative Thinking (see Bibliography).

To determine exactly how effective these training programs have been, professors Rose and Lin reviewed the results of forty-six studies, comparing the Osborn-Parnes CPS model to other Creative Problem-Solving approaches. Their results indicate that creativity training accounted for 22 percent of the variance in the participants' creative performance (in other words, about 78 percent of the creative performance probably was due to factors other than the training). These results are impressive since a variance of 22 percent is relatively high in the social sciences. (Whenever you can predict 22 percent of anything, you should be happy!)

Not all of the training programs produced equal results. For instance, there were differences in effects for originality, with some programs producing higher average originality scores. However, the most significant result may be that the Osborn-Parnes CPS model had the greatest impact on creative behavior. Rose and Lin concluded that "the use of CPS in education and business should foster more original thinking among practitioners."

Designing Your Training Program

The secret to successful training is planning. The more you think through your program in advance, the easier it will be to achieve your objectives. Thus, it is very important that you fully consider each program component. If you overlook one part, the entire program may fail.

The nine steps that follow will help you plan a CPS training program. They are presented in order, so you should try to follow them as carefully as possible.

1. Develop a working knowledge of the CPS process.
2. Assess and acquire management support for the program.
3. Determine skills and knowledge needed to use CPS.
4. Develop instructional objectives.
5. Decide on the program format.
6. Prepare materials.
7. Pilot-test the program.
8. Conduct the program.
9. Evaluate the program and make needed revisions.

These steps are by no means a fail-safe guide to effective training. You probably will want to customize them to suit your needs. Depending on your level of training sophistication, you even may want to ignore the sequence of activities and use your own design. If so, the sample training programs presented later in this chapter may be useful. These programs contain both training content and process, thus you have the option of using whatever might apply to your design.

1. *Develop a working knowledge of the CPS process.* As a trainer, you need to have basic familiarity with the CPS process. The material in Chapter 2 provides most of the information you need. If you want more in-depth knowledge, consult the publications in the Bibliography.

You also can learn and experience the CPS process by attending one of the CPS institutes sponsored by the Creative Education Foundation (1050 Union Road, Buffalo, NY 14224). Another alternative is to contract with a consultant to present an in-house overview of CPS.

2. *Assess and acquire management support for the program.* Training is a change activity designed to move people from one level of functioning to another. Whenever you need to invest resources to stimulate such change, you need to involve management.

There are at least two important issues to clarify with management. First, you need to demonstrate that the change effort will be cost-effective. Perhaps the most persuasive statistics are those compiled by the Frito-Lay company. It began a system-wide CPS training program in the 1980s, training thousands of employees in a modified CPS process and then measuring the results. Participants in the program were asked to submit cost-saving ideas. Their data suggested that, over a five-year period, the company reaped cumulative, documented cost savings of almost $600 million!

A second issue to clarify with management is realistic expectations. Not all CPS training programs will be as successful as the one at Frito-Lay. An enormous commitment of money, personnel, time, and other resources is required to achieve such dramatic results. Instead, you should stress that incremental change is more likely. If you encounter some resistance, suggest a pilot program in a couple of departments. If it is successful, you can expand to the rest of the organization.

You also should communicate that even the best programs may fail in the wrong environment. CPS training will not be effective unless it occurs in a corporate culture supportive of creative ideas. If the climate is not supportive, you even may want to consider deferring the training and instead invest in improving the climate. This can be done through team-building sessions, seminars on creative thinking, and various internal structural changes (e.g., altering the way different departments interact).

3. *Determine skills and knowledge needed to use CPS.* Program design begins in this step. You first have to decide what basic skills and

knowledge are needed to use CPS. These can be organized into three categories: (1) creative thinking obstacles, (2) creative thinking skills and abilities, and (3) Creative Problem-Solving stages. Next, evaluate the CPS skills and knowledge that your prospective trainees possess. Finally, examine the differences between the required and existing skills and knowledge. This will help you determine what, if any, areas to emphasize. Because these skills and knowledge are used to develop instructional objectives, samples are presented in the next section and will not be presented here.

4. *Develop instructional objectives.* Instructional objectives specify the behavioral changes expected to occur during a training program. These objectives should be stated clearly and be observable and measurable. If possible, avoid broad phrases such as "to understand," "to appreciate fully," "to grasp the significance of." Instead, use more specific objectives with phrases such as "to describe," "to identify," "to solve." In his book *How to Survive a Training Assignment*, Ellis notes several advantages to using these more specific objectives:

- They increase the likelihood of meeting the trainee needs.
- Trainees and their managers can determine more readily if a specific program will offer the content needed for the subordinates' professional growth.
- Trainers can decide on the most appropriate instructional and evaluative techniques.
- They make it easier to assess if personal objectives have been achieved.
- They shift the focus from knowledge taken into a program to knowledge trainees leave with.

The following list of objectives is organized using the three categories of creative thinking obstacles, creative thinking skills and abilities, and Creative Problem-Solving stages. Although this list is not comprehensive, it should provide you with a good start.

Identify Creative Thinking Obstacles

- Lack of resources and managerial support
- Functional "myopic" thinking
- Fear of criticism
- General resistance to change
- Failure to use all the senses
- Fear of risk taking
- Difficulty in seeing remote relationships

- Tendency to conform
- Overemphasis on competition or cooperation
- Belief that using fantasy to solve problems is a waste of time
- Fear of failure
- Rigid thinking
- Lack of motivation to implement a solution

Demonstrate Creative Thinking Skills and Abilities

- Deferred judgment
- Openness to new ideas
- Fluency
- Flexibility
- Originality
- Elaboration
- Positive thinking
- Ability to test problem assumptions
- Ability to use imagery and fantasy
- Ability to "toy" with new ideas
- Tolerance of ambiguity

Demonstrate Creative Problem-Solving Stages

- Describe the six-step CPS process. Describe divergent and convergent thinking. Demonstrate appropriate application of divergent and convergent thinking.
- Demonstrate objective finding: Give examples of challenges, concerns, and opportunities. Demonstrate ability to identify objective-finding hits.
- Demonstrate fact finding: Explain Five W's technique. Demonstrate the ability to identify fact-finding hits.
- Demonstrate problem finding: Show how to review fact-finding hits. Demonstrate formulation of problem redefinitions. Demonstrate the ability to identify problem-finding hits.
- Demonstrate idea finding: Describe brainwriting versus brainstorming. Demonstrate individual and group idea-generation techniques. Demonstrate the ability to identify idea-finding hits.
- Demonstrate solution finding: Show generation of evaluation criteria. Demonstrate transformation of ideas into solutions. Construct a weighted decision matrix.
- Demonstrate acceptance finding: Show generation of implementation obstacles. Demonstrate generation of "assisters" and "resisters." Construct a Potential Problem Analysis chart. Construct an implementation action plan.

5. *Decide on the program format.* The next step in the training process is to decide how to present the material to the trainees. There are at least five options: (1) presentation, (2) question and answer discussion, (3) small-group discussion, (4) case study, and (5) demonstration and/or practice. A combination of these options probably will work best.

■ PRESENTATION. The presentation approach is an informal lecture that provides trainees an opportunity to ask questions. Major advantages are that (1) it is a quick way to communicate information, (2) it makes it easy to communicate information to a large audience, and (3) it is good for covering underlying concepts and principles. Major disadvantages are that (1) it places the major instructional burden on the trainer, (2) it creates a "tell me" attitude among trainees, (3) it offers limited opportunities for feedback, and (4) it can lead to information overload and boredom.

■ QUESTION AND ANSWER DISCUSSION. This format helps provide information and stimulate thinking about a topic. It will increase interaction among trainees significantly more than the presentation format. As a result, they are more likely to feel satisfied after the session. Major advantages of the question and answer format are: (1) it transfers most of the learning burden to the trainee, (2) it increases trainee involvement, (3) it provides everyone with immediate feedback, and (4) it helps stimulate thinking and higher-order reasoning. Major disadvantages are: (1) it can result in overreliance on questions, (2) it will not be effective if the audience is not prepared (or not motivated) to respond to questions, (3) it can allow a few individuals to dominate most of the discussion.

■ SMALL-GROUP DISCUSSION. The ideal small group for CPS training and problem solving is five people. (You should limit small groups to no more than six or seven people.) In general, small groups create the most effective learning environment. The advantages of using groups are that (1) group members are more willing to introduce ideas and discuss them, (2) they stimulate peer group learning, and (3) they foster cohesion. The disadvantages are that (1) it is easy for groups to get off track, (2) they can be time consuming, and (3) they increase possibilities of interpersonal conflicts.

■ CASE STUDY. Case studies present trainees with facts about a situation. They then use their knowledge and experience to resolve some identified problem. The major advantages are: (1) flexibility—they can be done at home or in class, (2) they help determine if class material has been understood fully and can be applied to real-world situations, (3) they are easy to integrate with other instructional approaches, and

(4) their use enhances learning through communication of results, in both small- and large-group discussions. The major disadvantages are: (1) case studies can oversimplify some problems, (2) there may be more than one solution to a problem (i.e., solutions other than that intended by the author of the case study), and (3) they require time and effort to develop.

▪ DEMONSTRATION/PRACTICE. This format is an effective way to transfer theoretical insights to practical situations. Students observe a demonstration and then practice what they observe. The advantages are that this: (1) makes learning easier through imitation, (2) promotes self-confidence and skill building, and (3) provides immediate feedback. The disadvantages are that: (1) not everyone learns well from watching others, (2) not all trainees can learn at the same pace, and (3) it requires a skilled demonstrator and someone knowledgeable enough to provide useful feedback.

At the end of this stage, you should have developed an outline for the training session. I have developed a general CPS training model that uses most of the training formats just discussed. There are five steps representing five formats: *Tell* (Presentation), *Experience* (Demonstration), *Show* (Presentation and/or question and answer discussion), *Model* (Demonstration), and *Practice* and *Feedback* (Small-group discussion and/ or practice).

- *Tell:* Overview of the six-step CPS process. The instructor provides a general introduction to CPS.
- *Experience:* An experiential guided tour of CPS. The instructor leads the group through the CPS process with participants working individually on their own work-related problems.
- *Show:* A detailed look at CPS using overhead transparencies. Examples are provided on how specific techniques can aid the CPS stages. This activity provides an opportunity for trainees to ask questions.
- *Model:* A large-group experience with CPS. The instructor uses a problem relevant to the group to illustrate the entire CPS process and techniques to facilitate its stages.
- *Practice* and *Feedback:* Small-group practice. Small groups practice the CPS process using a group-generated problem. The instructor provides feedback to the group and everyone evaluates the process.

A distinguishing feature of this program is its use of repetition to reinforce learning concepts, accommodating different learning styles by allowing the trainees to experience the material in a variety of formats.

6. *Prepare materials.* For this stage you should gather all relevant materials and prepare your presentation materials and handouts. Your presentation materials might include slides and paper-and-pencil tests, creative thinking exercises, and background information on problems for practicing CPS. You also should provide each trainee with handouts detailing instructional objectives, the agenda, and relevant points to learn. Incidentally, the statement of objectives on the handout should be an abbreviated version. The specific objectives listed in step 4 probably could be used as learning points. Thus, your objectives statement for the trainees might read as any of the following:

- To identify creative thinking obstacles
- To demonstrate creative thinking skills and abilities
- To describe the six-step CPS process
- To demonstrate divergent and convergent thinking
- To demonstrate objective finding
- To demonstrate fact finding
- To demonstrate problem finding
- To demonstrate idea finding
- To demonstrate solution finding
- To demonstrate acceptance finding

7. *Pilot-test the program.* You now should be just about ready to implement your training program. Before you start signing people up, however, conduct a pilot test to see if there are any bugs. This dry run will help identify potential weaknesses and allow you to overcome them before beginning a large-scale training program. However, even before conducting the pilot test, consider asking a creativity consultant to review your program. He or she may have many constructive suggestions that could save you trouble later on.

To conduct the pilot test, present the program to at least twenty to thirty trainees; you can obtain some statistically valid results with this number. And you also can test the program with four to six different groups of five people per group. Conduct at least two programs and make them as similar as possible to the real thing. After each program, have the trainees complete evaluation questionnaires. Ask them to rate the quality of instruction, the handouts, visual aids, group exercises, pacing of activities, and any other topics of interest to them. In addition to questionnaires, end each session with a large-group discussion of the overall training program.

8. *Conduct the program.* You now should be ready to implement your program. If the pilot tests went well, everything should go smoothly; however, be wary of unexpected events. It is impossible to

anticipate all that could go wrong—even pilot tests won't help you deal with a missing slide or a broken projector. Be sure you have backups for all essential equipment and supplies.

Perhaps the key to the success of any training program—next to planning—is to ensure that you meet trainee expectations. For this reason, it is important to discuss the objectives and check for understanding. You also should determine if the objectives are in line with the trainees' expectations. If not, you may want to make some modifications.

9. *Evaluate the program and make needed revisions.* You should evaluate your training program to determine its effectiveness. Otherwise, you will not know what worked well and what did not. But do not wait until after you have conducted the first session. Plan your evaluation strategy *before* the program. This is the only way to determine if the training made a difference.

Every training program has implied hypotheses about program outcomes. These predictions are derived from your instructional objectives and imply expected outcomes. Thus, if an objective is to demonstrate fluency (number of ideas in a given period of time), a trainee's fluency rate would be expected to be higher after completing the program.

If a training program meets its stated objectives, it has been effective; if it does not, it has been ineffective. However, there also are two other considerations involved in evaluating training effectiveness: trainee acceptance and appropriateness to the trainee population.

▪ ASSESSING OBJECTIVES. It is relatively easy to evaluate objectives if the practice exercises truly test the identified behaviors. Obviously, some objectives will be easier to evaluate than others. The previously listed objectives that begin with "Identify . . ." can be evaluated with paper-and-pencil tests if you are interested in awareness of obstacles or skills. If you want to evaluate behaviors arising from "Identify . . ." objectives, observe a group. "Demonstrate . . ." objectives for creative thinking require observation, since they involve specific behaviors. The same applies to objectives pertaining to the CPS process; how well trainees use the CPS model can be evaluated only by observing them. A written examination could be used, but it would not be as valid.

▪ EVALUATING TRAINEE ACCEPTANCE. This evaluation measure probably is the least valid indicator of a program's effectiveness. Trainees usually react emotionally more to a program's presentation than to its content. This is fine for you if you are a dynamic presenter, but it still says virtually nothing about effectiveness. Many negative comments, however, may indicate ineffectiveness. And strong negative reactions frequently interfere with learning.

Nevertheless, trainee comments (preferably written) can be valuable for several reasons. Educator and trainer R. L. Ribler, in his *Training Development Guide*, notes that they can alert course administrators to potentially serious problems, give trainees a way to let off steam, and provide data that might correlate with longitudinal data such as long-term job performance or other training programs.

▪ APPROPRIATENESS TO THE POPULATION. Before designing your program, consider how appropriate it is for your target audience. Be especially careful to avoid vague descriptions. Of course, such cautions are of little value after the fact.

To determine if you "hit" the right audience, look for certain signs. For instance, was there an unusually large number of questions? Did trainees make statements suggesting their backgrounds are inadequate to deal with the material? Did you observe much squirming, yawning, talking out of place, and other indicators of discomfort?

The bottom line in evaluating CPS training is whether the trainees can apply the CPS process effectively. If their problem-solving outcomes are no different from their pretraining performance, the program was not successful. However, if they can demonstrate they know how to use CPS, the program was a success.

Sample Creativity Training Programs

Corporate America has conducted formal creativity training programs for almost forty years. It has been only recently, however, that a significant number of companies have provided such training. Moreover, the training now is more intensive and involves more employees at all organizational levels.

Even if you do not want to design your own program, some representative descriptions will illustrate how business has gone about trying to become more competitive through creativity training. Six company programs are reviewed: Frito-Lay, Inc., Hershey Foods Corporation, Instrumentation Laboratory, Johnston Controls, Motorola, Inc., and Texas Instruments.

Frito-Lay, Inc.

The Frito-Lay company in Texas has perhaps the most successful creativity training program. As mentioned previously, it is successful in terms of cumulative, documented cost savings of almost $600 million over a five-year period.

In 1981, Frito-Lay managers were concerned about sales leveling off. To become more competitive and increase sales, they hired a consultant to design and conduct a creativity training program. The consultant worked with management to put together a three-level creativity program.

The first level of this program provides training in the basics for ten to twenty employees. More than 7,000 employees have received this training. During the first half-day, the participants are exposed to a series of creative thinking exercises and taught the importance of appreciating different viewpoints. They also are taught divergent and convergent thinking skills. To teach problem solving, the trainers use an eight-step problem-solving model similar to the six-step CPS process. The second level of their program is a two-day course on how to facilitate a problem-solving meeting. The third level is a week-long program that teaches employees how to train others in Creative Problem Solving (i.e., "train-the-trainers" workshops).

Hershey Foods Corporation

I provided CPS training for approximately fifty Hershey R&D division managers, beginning with the division vice-president and his directors. Throughout the training program, groups of twelve to fifteen managers received two-day CPS training sessions. All available R&D managers were included so they would be familiar with the training to be provided their subordinates. They also would learn the CPS process and presumably apply it to their work-related problems.

All the training sessions were conducted in-house, using facilities at the corporate R&D center. Each session began with a two-hour segment on creative thinking principles and obstacles. This presentation illustrates creative thinking using cartoons, quotes, and experiential exercises. Then I used the training model outlined earlier in this chapter: Tell, Experience, Show, Model, and Practice and Feedback.

A primary focus of this training was generation of new-product opportunities. For instance, one product area concerned developing new uses for cocoa. I helped the group use a variety of different idea-generation techniques to stimulate ideas. For instance, one group generated such ideas as a chocolate pill coating, edible packaging, chocolate-smelling diapers, and a chocolate school paste.

In-house facilitators also were trained in the CPS process. These individuals were designated to help lead subsequent problem-solving sessions. The facilitators received special instruction in how to provide training for each of the CPS stages. (Much of the material in this training program is presented in Chapter 3.)

To help continue the focus on CPS, a creativity room was set up. This room was intended as a place to conduct brainstorming sessions away from the normal meeting room. The room actually was two adjacent rooms with a connecting door. One room was designed as a brainstorming room, with a round table and chairs, flip charts, a whiteboard, and supplies of the Product Improvement CheckList and the Circles of Creativity (see Chapter 9). The other room was set up for more informal interactions, with couches and other comfortable furniture. Plans also were made to include creativity books and sample Hershey products.

Instrumentation Laboratory

Instrumentation Laboratory in Massachusetts designed a two-day, monthly CPS program. The first hour is devoted to warm-up exercises followed by an hour on objective finding. Then two hours are spent on fact finding. During the second day, the focus continues on idea finding, then switches to the remaining stages of solution finding and acceptance finding. The last half of the second day deals with decision making, meeting methods, and an exercise on resolving participant problems using CPS.

The training sessions are conducted by a core team of nine managers who attend a five-day training session conducted by an outside consultant. This group meets regularly to compare notes and refine its training methods.

Johnston Controls

Former Johnston Controls manager Larry Korta conducted a one-half day creative thinking program for managers. He used the following activities and topics: (1) the general nature of creativity, (2) creative thinking obstacles, (3) warm-up brainstorming using an organization-related problem, (4) the philosophy of suspending judgment during divergent thinking, (5) characteristics of creative individuals, (6) characteristics of the creative manager, (7) characteristics of the creative organization, and (8) a video of an orchestra playing Ravel's *Bolero*; similarities between the orchestra and a creative organization were discussed.

Motorola, Inc.

Motorola, Inc., through Motorola University, recently began an intensive creativity training program. One purpose was to relate creativity to the goal of total customer satisfaction. Figure 5-1 shows how creativity serves as the foundation for Motorola's five Key Initiatives.* The company's creativity training program was developed to enhance managers' use of creativity as a tool for achieving these initiatives. Approximately twenty managers (three women and seventeen males) received the initial training to validate the program content. The managers were drawn from a cross section of managers representing seven divisions.

Instructional design intern Ingrid Nowicki used instructional design principles to create an elaborate "learning hierarchy" as the framework for developing the course. Based on the hierarchy, the primary objective was: "Managers will recognize and develop the creative potential in themselves and others by applying the creative process to generate, develop, and champion unique ideas to contribute to the success of Motorola." Given this objective, Nowicki then identified three subobjectives, each leading to the development of a separate learning module. The first module was designed to enable managers to develop their creative potential. Next, the course showed managers how to develop the creative potential in others. The last module taught managers the process of championing unique ideas. The relationship of these modules to the overall objective is shown in Figure 5-2. The objectives for each of these modules were broken down further into enabling objectives that described the course content.

During the design phase of the course, Nowicki used the complete hierarchy to conduct research testing how valuable the proposed content of the creativity program would be to managers. The research used an interview schedule that included open-ended questions and rating scales regarding managerial interest in and perceived value of the training. A five-point rating scale was used (1 = little interest; 5 = most interest).

Owing to its complexity, the complete hierarchy cannot be shown here; however, selected segments are highlighted. Discussion of these segments includes sample evaluation comments from managers who participated in the research. Average scores on the rating scales also are presented.

1. *Managers will define creativity.* As shown at the top of Figure 5-3, managers first were asked to provide their own definitions of creativity. Some of their definitions were, "Giving birth to something new,"

*Figures 5-1 through 5-7 appear through the permission of Motorola, Inc. No rights are granted to the reader to use proprietary information that may be contained in these materials, and the reader is advised to contact Motorola, Inc. regarding any anticipated use of such information that may violate existing enforceable rights.

Figure 5-1. Creativity as the foundation for customer satisfaction.

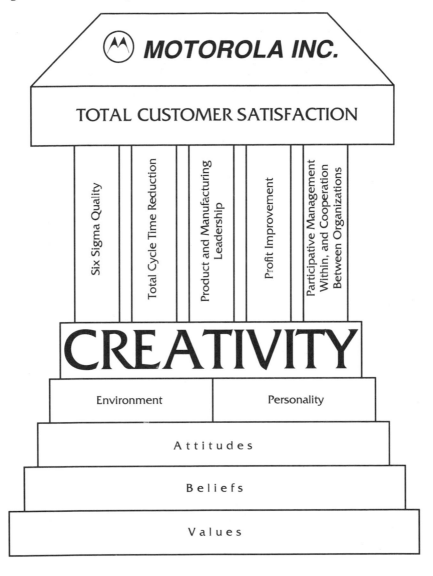

Figure 5-2. Creativity program primary objectives.

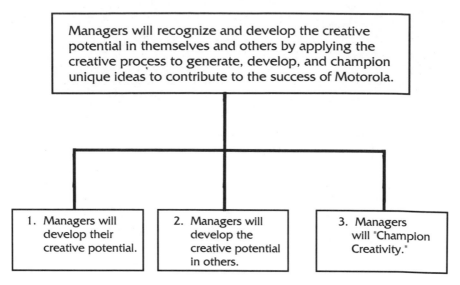

Managers will recognize and develop the creative potential in themselves and others by applying the creative process to generate, develop, and champion unique ideas to contribute to the success of Motorola.

1. Managers will develop their creative potential.

2. Managers will develop the creative potential in others.

3. Managers will "Champion Creativity."

"Thinking without bounds or limitations," "The ability to do original thinking and to turn problems into opportunities," and "Thinking of novel ways of doing things." Further aspects of creativity were discussed as well. This segment received an average value rating of 3.85 and an average interest rating of 4.05.

2. *Managers will identify skills and traits of creativity.* Managers were shown Figure 5-4, which illustrates the variety of skills and traits of creative managers. Examples include good listening, flexibility, deferred judgment, and testing assumptions. When asked how knowledge about skills and traits will benefit them, the managers gave a number of responses: "Responsible for providing a creative environment," "Very important to break down barriers," "Identifying skill levels opens up [the] mind to different ways to be creative," and "A matter of success and achievement for both people and business." The average value rating for skills and traits was 4.60 and the average interest rating was 4.55.

3. *Managers will generate ideas.* This objective is part of a larger objective of demonstrating the Creative Problem-Solving process. Figure

Figure 5-3. Defining various aspects of creativity.

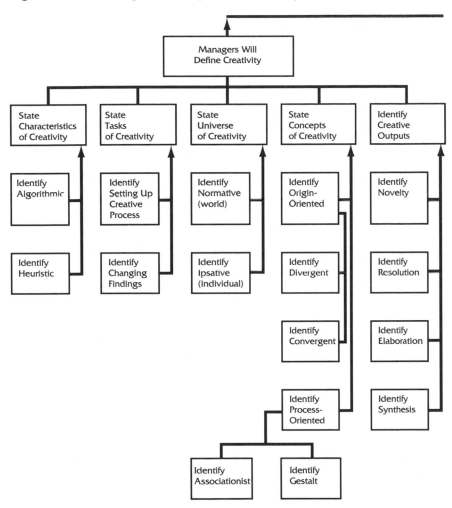

5-5 shows that both analytical (e.g., identify matrix analysis) and creative (e.g., identify analogy) techniques were used. Managers were asked how the process would benefit them and responded that: "Provides a framework for being creative," "Will make me a better manager," "Definition of a process will prevent real creative people from getting

Figure 5-4. Skills and traits of creative managers.

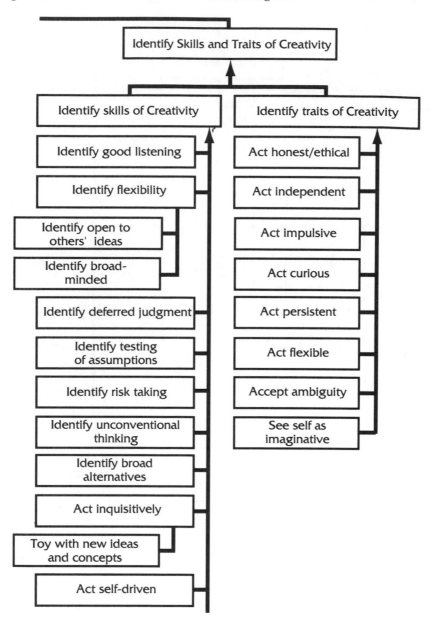

Figure 5-5. Analytical and creative techniques for generating ideas.

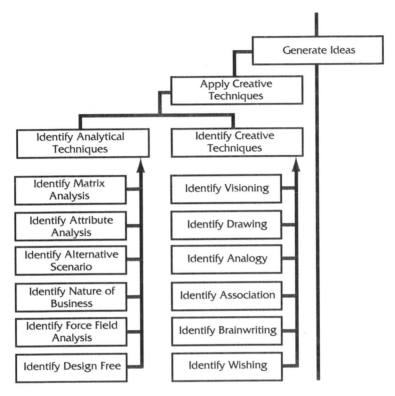

lost and [make] less creative people more creative by following steps," and "Going through it in depth makes [my] own process better [and] stronger to take [the] initiative to be more creative." The average rating of the process was 4.55 and the average interest rating was 4.65.

4. *Managers will identify barriers to creativity.* The managers evaluated the five categories of barriers shown in Figure 5-6: Structural, Social/Political, Procedural, Resource, and Individual/Attitudinal. Comments on the value of this topic included such statements as: "The more people are educated, the fewer will be the barriers," "Being aware of the barriers would be the first step to removing them," "Helps build creativity within the organization and not put barriers up." The average rating of the value of the process was 4.45 and the average interest rating was 4.35.

(Text continues on page 96.)

Figure 5-6. Barriers to creativity.

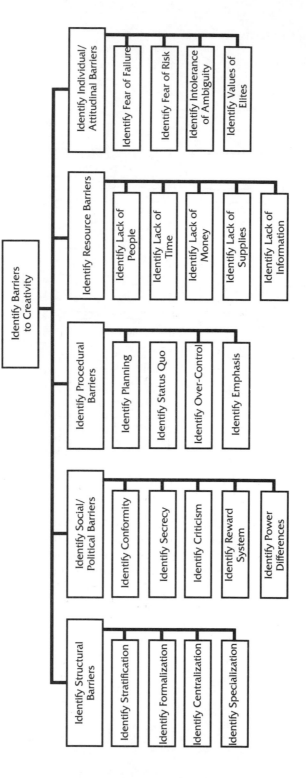

Figure 5-7. Major role assignments of group members.

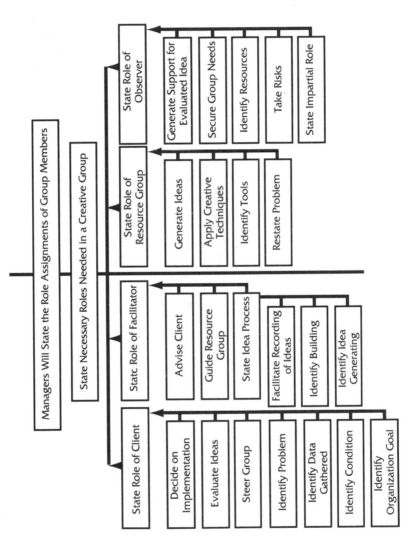

5. *Managers will state the role assignments of group members.* Managers were shown Figure 5-7, which illustrates the four major role assignments of members of creative groups (client, facilitator, resource group, and observer). Comments relative to the value of the role assignment segment included: "Role of observer—most valuable. As manager [we] need to let go," "Assists in creation of a successful team," "This info is truly [the] type of info needed to actually implement techniques. This is guts of course. It's critical to [the] whole process," "It's a much improved system over the one in place now. The role of the observer is very exciting. Could be [an] eye-opening experience." The average rating of the value of the process was 4.10 and the average interest rating was 4.25.

Texas Instruments

TI manager Barb Abrams (at the Colorado Springs division) emphasizes Creative Problem Solving throughout a quality-improvement program. TI's effectiveness teams involve from three to fifteen people who try to improve quality, profits, and creativity. To make these improvements, the teams use a seven-step problem-solving method.

Team leaders are trained during an off-site, four-day workshop. Leaders must go through a training session twice a year to learn problem solving, conflict management, communication, and creativity skills. One exercise Abrams uses involves four or five teams. She asks each team to build a castle from material found in the room. Another team judges the others' products. According to Abrams, such training improves team cohesiveness and increases communication throughout the organization.

6

Conducting and Facilitating Problem-Solving Retreats

Retreats provide a solution for companies that need new ideas but have little time to generate them. I've frequently heard company representatives say, "We'd like to become more creative around here, but we just don't have the time." Traditional staff meetings typically are devoted to "putting out fires" from short-term problems. And when not in meetings, most staff members are preoccupied with personal projects. To become more competitive, however, you must set aside time to focus thinking upon a specific problem. This is especially true for such tasks as company strategy.

The topics of most company retreats are as varied as the people attending them. They commonly focus upon such things as:

- New-product development, including line extensions, new uses for old products, or general product improvements
- Marketing and advertising problems, with a focus on attracting a specific market segment, generating a new marketing theme, or developing an advertising slogan
- General improvement problems, such as improving customer service, moving new product ideas to commercialization faster, streamlining shipping procedures, or recruiting personnel
- Problem identification issues, with an emphasis on selecting priorities
- Strategic planning, including developing or refining a corporate vision, and fine-tuning organizational goals

Retreats have many features in common with Creative Problem-Solving training. They generally use a problem-solving process and focus on some problem related to the organization. They also provide an opportunity for organizational members to interact with others outside their departments. The primary difference, however, is that retreats typically are conducted off-site for the specific purpose of solving a problem. CPS training may or may not be conducted off-site and is not geared toward solving a problem. Instead, the objective of CPS training is to help trainees develop new skills.

Advantages of Retreats

Retreats allow a company to focus on pressing, day-to-day issues or reflect on long-term concerns. More can be accomplished without the frequent interruptions that accompany day-to-day work. By eliminating distractions and concentrating employee resources, retreats provide the ideal opportunity to become task oriented and achieve problem closure.
Some specific advantages of retreats are that they:

- Provide new perspectives on problems. Because individuals bring different viewpoints to a group, problems will be seen in ways more conducive to creative thinking.
- Lend themselves to wrestling with long-term issues, such as matters of strategy.
- Provide a setting conducive to solution consensus.
- Have the potential to initiate enduring organizational changes.
- Foster a sense of cohesion, teamwork, and organizational purpose.
- Are viewed by many employees as a reward for superior performance (especially when they are held in exotic locations).
- Encourage development of new information networks or enhancement of existing ones (especially in interdivisional retreats).
- Increase the odds of successful solution implementation because of a sense of ownership and commitment.

Disadvantages of Retreats

Besides the positive features associated with retreats, there also are several disadvantages, some the result of poor planning, others inherent features of retreats. Among the negative aspects of retreats are that they:

- Involve a certain degree of risk, since success can't be guaranteed.
- Can be expensive if held at an off-site resort with many personnel.

- Increase workloads at the office because of missed time and new problems and solutions generated.
- Can be tiring because of the intense mental effort and the time spent traveling to and from remote locations.
- Sometimes open old wounds or allow renewal of old conflicts (which can be advantageous if handled appropriately).
- Have the potential to create ill will and dislike for retreats if the outcomes aren't viewed as positive. (Such sentiments of dissatisfaction often stem from a lack of followup on decisions made at the retreat.)

Ingredients for a Successful Retreat

Without question, the key to a successful retreat is the planning process, not necessarily the plan. Former president Dwight D. Eisenhower supposedly said, "The plan is nothing. The process of planning is everything." Decisions on who will be involved, what they will do, and when, where, and how they will do it are essential planning ingredients. Planning will not guarantee success; it only makes it more likely. You should view your plan as a working document subject to change.

The following are preretreat guidelines that can reduce aggravation for planners and help make retreats more successful.

Reasons for a Retreat

Decide if you really need a retreat. Problem-solving retreats should be used to help resolve difficult-to-solve problems. Don't use them to resolve routine, mundane problems. Retreats involve substantial investments of resources and should be used wisely.

If you determine that a retreat is in order, clarify the retreat's objectives. Although this may seem obvious, it frequently is overlooked. Decide before the retreat what you want to accomplish and if the retreat is the proper format. Then ask the retreat participants to review the objectives and offer their opinions. If you consider their needs, the retreat should be more successful.

We often learn about life the hard way. I once received a call from a marketing manager of an international corporation. He described a customer satisfaction problem, which we discussed briefly. I later flew to the headquarters to meet with other managers and the divisional vice-president. I spent two hours with the managers and about thirty minutes with the vice-president. When I left I thought I understood the problem clearly.

Some months later, I learned a communication problem existed. While I traveled to the retreat with the vice-president, he shared his perceptions of the problem and the retreat's content. He now wanted to slant the retreat in a different direction. I started to panic since my preparation was geared to my original understanding of the problem. Fortunately, it was a long trip to the retreat site and we agreed that our perceptions were similar and in no way incompatible. As it turned out, the retreat was a success. Always clarify perceptions about your goals well in advance, especially with upper management.

Although there will be exceptions, most retreats should focus on one major objective. Decide in advance if you want the retreat to improve group cohesiveness, plan strategy, or generate new product ideas. There rarely is time to concentrate on several topics, yet management often expects to achieve multiple objectives. Sometimes a retreat will have by-products, such as building team unity; however, don't expect such outcomes unless they are planned from the outset. More retreats or staff meetings may be needed instead.

A limit of one issue per retreat is just about right for one-day retreats involving ten or fewer people. In one of the first retreats I facilitated, management wanted to generate different uses for five products. I divided the fifteen participants into three groups of five each and had them focus on each product in turn. There was constant pressure to move on and deal with the other products. As a result, only three of the products were dealt with in the one and one-half days available. That was my error in agreeing to deal with five products. Some groups may be able to handle that many, but you can't count on it.

To choose an objective, examine your priorities and the needs of the groups involved. Consider a wide range of topics, not just what you think may be the most immediate need. It's easy to overlook a broader issue or to focus too closely on a specific problem. For instance, you first might decide to improve the new-product evaluation process. However, a broader, more appropriate problem might involve clarifying expectations between organizational divisions. Once you have dealt with expectations, the evaluation problem might resolve itself. A rule of thumb is to use a broader topic first if time is available.

Organizational vision and mission are two other issues that often demand attention before a retreat. You might have to clarify your company's desired image and its goals before you can expect any progress. I can recall many problem-solving sessions in which the discussion continually deviated from the problem, turning to the issue of organizational objectives and strategy. For instance, before participants can agree on a new product line, they first have to agree with the company's mission. That is, the individuals and the group must be aligned with the organization. Therefore, it sometimes pays to stop generating ideas and devote time to clarifying perceptions about the organization and where it is headed.

Approval of Upper Management

As with most organizational decisions, you must obtain approval for a retreat from the highest necessary level. Besides simple budget approval, management must understand and agree with the retreat's objectives. Otherwise, the outcome may be ignored or you will face an uphill implementation battle. Of course, prior management approval won't guarantee success, but it will make it easier to gain a fair hearing for the new ideas produced.

Most managers recognize the importance of this guideline. In one organization I worked with, however, a personal conflict caused a manager to overlook it. Although the setting was not an off-site retreat, the incident still illustrates the need for upper-level support: My contact set up an afternoon meeting with a group of upper-level managers to discuss strategic issues. At a meeting that evening, I met the divisional director of worldwide company operations, who had not attended the afternoon meeting. I was somewhat surprised and curious about his absence; however, I just assumed he was occupied by other matters. I later learned he had been excluded intentionally by my contact. Apparently, they had a history of interpersonal conflicts, and excluding the higher-level manager clearly would send a message. Because of this slight, however, the lower-level manager found it difficult to gain support for the project. While it may be obvious what we should do, we sometimes allow our emotions to interfere. Avoid cutting off your nose to spite your face.

An In-House Coordinator

As with any group activity, coordination is needed to plan and conduct a retreat. An official coordinator will make it easier to conduct a successful retreat. His or her duties typically include choosing an outside facilitator, collecting planning data, choosing participants and keeping them informed, making arrangements for physical facilities, and monitoring post-retreat activities. However, don't wait until the retreat to involve a coordinator. The coordinator should be appointed to oversee all retreat activities, beginning with initial planning.

Choose coordinators based on their ability to do the job and relevant experience. (Don't appoint a coordinator if his or her only previous experience was planning the company picnic!) Planning a retreat involves special skills because of its heavy task orientation and its importance to the company. The person you choose should relate to others well and be able to monitor group tasks closely. Other skills include the ability to coordinate many details simultaneously, communicate in a positive manner to encourage commitment, and be aware of the importance of teamwork and ownership of the results.

Although coordinators have an important responsibility, they may not be the best choice to serve as overall retreat facilitators. A different set of skills is needed to design a retreat and see it implemented. Unless coordinators have special expertise in these areas, use an outside person.

An Outside Facilitator

In contrast to in-house coordinators, facilitators have major responsibility for designing and conducting retreats. Facilitators use their problem-solving knowledge to design a retreat best suited to each company's goals. They then execute the plan using their ability to help groups solve problems. In-house coordinators make sure major retreat activities get done; outside facilitators do most of them.

The same person can do both roles, but a case can be made to separate them. Not all in-house coordinators have the ability or time to facilitate a retreat. Outside facilitators also are untainted by organizational politics and offer an unbiased perspective. Someone from the outside thus may be a reasonable and necessary choice.

How do you obtain an outside facilitator? Your peers at other organizations often can suggest qualified individuals. Other possibilities are book authors, consultants, university professors, and contacts at professional conferences. Aside from general references, there are other considerations in choosing facilitators. First, evaluate their philosophy of retreats. If they try to sell you a package approach, approach them cautiously. All retreat situations are different and should be tailored to a company's needs, not to those of the consultant. Facilitators also should be willing to work with coordinators on preretreat planning. Specifically, they should analyze jointly what motivated the retreat and discuss its format.

Another consideration is a facilitator's "tool-kit breadth." There is an old saying that if the only tool you have is a hammer, you will treat every problem as a nail. If a consultant specializes in stress management, for instance, he or she is likely to look for stress-management solutions. A consultant with a broader view and more general approach may be better.

On the other hand, there can be danger in too broad an approach. I once met a woman at a speaking engagement who was a relatively new consultant. She gave me her brochure and asked for my opinion. What I read presented her as a panacea: She was ready to offer training and consulting on organization development, leadership development, team building, stress management, decision making, creative thinking, Creative Problem Solving, conflict management, job enrichment, right- and left-brain thinking, speed learning, negotiation management, performance appraisal, personality assessment, quality circles, and about any other existing behavioral science topic.

A related problem is a weak plan. Retreat success often depends on how much structure you build in—generally the more structure, the greater the likelihood of success—but such structure must be used flexibly. You will have to modify almost any plan. For instance, I frequently schedule more idea-generation techniques than time available. If some groups do not respond well to one technique, I offer backups. Or if I have underestimated the time needed, I bring out a spare technique. The situation is something like cutting a piece of wood to fit an area of defined length. If you make the cut too short, you can't correct it; if the cut is too long, you will have the option of trying again.

Evaluate and Clarify Expectations

Either the in-house coordinator or an external facilitator should assess expectations and clarify misconceptions. This should be done for both organizational decision makers and retreat participants.

In some organizations, high-level managers view retreats suspiciously. Their expectations and understandings may differ from those of the retreat's planners. Managers often believe that individuals are paid to solve problems and retreats are just an excuse to party. I have heard this sentiment occasionally and believe it is shortsighted thinking. A well-planned and coordinated retreat can be productive, and it can be tied directly to long-term effectiveness. Management usually just needs a little convincing.

After assessing expectations, the best way to clarify them is to give a balanced presentation of retreat strengths and weaknesses. (You can find material for such a presentation at the beginning of this chapter.) You make a more convincing argument when you present both pros and cons; otherwise, the person you want to persuade may think you are hiding something. The other person also is more likely to believe he or she controls and owns the decision; therefore commitment to the retreat and its outcome should be higher as well.

Besides the usual rational arguments, many managers respond to the bandwagon syndrome: If everyone else is doing it, maybe we should, too (or at least take a closer look). I don't necessarily advocate this approach, but it may help occasionally. Managers learn other companies are having retreats and decide to follow suit. Monkey see, monkey do.

Although it would be disastrous to overlook managerial expectations, it also would be a mistake to neglect participant expectations. In many organizations, subordinates are not consulted about managerial decisions; thus it is unlikely they would be contacted regarding a retreat's agenda. The high degree of employee involvement in a retreat mandates some participation during planning, however. At least one or two employee representatives should contribute to preretreat planning. If nothing else, give employees a chance to look over the agenda and offer opinions.

Admittedly, widespread participation may not always be appropriate or possible. For instance, if the focus is on broad strategy issues, some companies prefer to limit participation to upper-level managers. You then could include more employees in followup retreats designed to generate ways to implement the strategy.

Issues That Inhibit Creative Thinking

Another preretreat consideration is to ensure that participants have "creativity readiness." That is, participants should be predisposed to creative thinking; there should be no hidden agendas or other issues to deal with before idea generation. For example, many teams need basic team-building skills before they can develop a more creative climate. Such matters as interpersonal trust and cooperation often need attention before creative ideas can be generated. Groups must be able to function as a team before they can exploit their creativity. In one session I facilitated, the participants expressed a need to voice their concerns about a company administrative policy. It was obvious these concerns needed airing before any productive idea generation could take place. Once they were, the members were able to focus their attention on the purpose of the retreat.

A Detailed Agenda

A detailed agenda is a primary planning goal. It should include a sequential description of major activities and the time allocated to each. However, be flexible in your approach. View an agenda as a game plan that can be modified as situations arise. A sample agenda for a one and one-half day retreat is as follows:

RETREAT AGENDA
Veeblefeester Widget Corporation
Dailyshowers Resort

Thursday

7:30–8:30	Breakfast	Chow Chow room
8:30–8:45	Introductions	Ding Dong room
8:45–9:00	Retreat overview, discussion of group assignments	
9:00–9:30	Discuss and clarify the problem	
9:30–10:15	Brainstorming in small groups	Rooms as assigned
10:15–10:30	Break	Caffeine room
10:30–10:45	Pin cards technique	
10:45–11:45	Semantic intuition technique	
11:45–noon	Preliminary idea screening	
Noon–1:30	Lunch	Chow Chow room
1:30–2:15	Stimulus analysis	
2:15–3:00	Product Improvement CheckList	
3:00–3:15	Break	Caffeine room
3:15–3:45	Picture stimulation	
3:45–4:00	Preliminary idea screening	
4:00–4:15	First-day summary and discussion	Ding Dong room

Friday

7:30–8:30	Breakfast	Chow Chow room
8:30–8:45	Evaluation guidelines	

(continues)

8:45–10:15	Idea evaluation	Rooms as assigned
10:15–10:30	Break	Caffeine room
10:30–11:30	Idea refinement and development	
11:30–11:45	Preliminary implementation discussion	Ding Dong room
11:45–noon	Retreat summary and discussion	

I designed this retreat so that idea generation and evaluation would be separated. The participants spend most of the first day generating ideas. They use a variety of techniques such as semantic intuition (see Chapter 8). I also scheduled some time after the morning and afternoon sessions for preliminary evaluation. These "mini evaluation" periods help shorten a long list of ideas, prompt suggestions on how to combine related ideas, and stimulate thinking for more ideas. I set aside the second day just for idea evaluation. During this time, the participants focus on only idea evaluation. This promotes a sense of task completion and may increase commitment to certain ideas. It also can smooth implementation after the retreat.

I also limited the length of the retreat. There is nothing sacred about an eight-hour day. The intensity and concentration called for in retreats often make it impractical to stick to a traditional work schedule. Thus, some groups might benefit from an early finish, but if the groups are energized and seem productive, allow them more time.

Finally, it can be beneficial to stay over at least one night during a retreat. For instance, you might want to schedule informal social activities for the evening. Such experiences promote team building and contribute to a positive problem-solving climate. When I suggested this to a company vice-president, his major concern was that some people would drink so much they would be useless the next day. Although this is possible, you can remind participants to use some restraint.

I conducted a retreat for a chemical corporation that illustrates the positive value of social affairs. The first day was not as successful as we had hoped. There was a lot of negative thinking and an unwillingness to take risks. During an evening social hour, however, several participants loosened up and suggested ideas that later were judged promising by management.

Location

Although not as important as other factors, this matter still deserves attention. If resources permit, consider an off-site location removed from daily distractions. However, the location should be accessible using conventional transportation. If people must be ferried in using two-seater airplanes or portaging with canoes, rethink the location.

Be wary of hotels trying to pump up their convention business. Instead, consider resorts. Although many resorts cater to meetings, seek out those that specialize in conferences—they usually can anticipate your needs and deal with crisis situations. You also can rely on their personnel to arrange details. Always check to ensure things are done correctly, however. Sometimes, simple misunderstandings can create major frustrations. For instance, I've requested rooms with round tables only to find a classroom arrangement with straight rows of rectangular tables. I also usually receive an overhead projector with a spare bulb—but not always. Bulbs do burn out; it happened to me just once and it was a major inconvenience. I now always request a spare.

You also should consider how many meeting rooms are available and their proximity to one another. Ideally, there should be one large room and a separate breakout room for each group. Use the large room to review ground rules, discuss expectations, answer questions, and share ideas. One of the small groups also can use the large room as its meeting room.

Although it often is overlooked, the view from the rooms should be evaluated. Participants can be distracted by beautiful scenery if the view is overwhelming. (The only time scenery was a significant problem in my retreats was when the "scenery" was female. The meeting rooms had glass walls and overlooked a swimming pool. As a result, the two all-male groups in these rooms had dilated pupils for the first several hours of the day.)

Proximity of rooms is important if you have several small groups and only one or two facilitators. I've received excellent aerobic workouts from running up and down stairs to check on groups in different locations! I can do this, however, only with prior structuring of the problem-solving process (and with physical training). And it helps if the groups are self-sufficient regarding process; otherwise, group members become frustrated with the lack of structure and problem-solving progress.

If you use more than two groups and the breakout rooms are distant, use at least one facilitator for every two groups. A one-to-one ratio, however, is better. When multiple groups are used and extra facilitators aren't available, one facilitator will have to oversee the entire retreat. Of course, financial resources and personnel availability could alter these guidelines.

Collect Relevant Data

Most companies need problem data during a retreat. Reports, graphs, and descriptive statistics help illuminate problems. This is especially true during problem analysis, when participants may raise questions that can't be answered easily. They also may have trouble recalling information about certain events.

Although you can't predict with certainty what data you'll need, some preretreat planning can help. Before the retreat, gather relevant reports, charts, data bases, and memos that might prove useful. Ask retreat participants to bring along relevant data. Conduct interviews with people knowledgeable about the retreat topic. However, be wary of collecting too much data. If the primary goal of the retreat is problem resolution, overemphasis on data could lead to "analysis paralysis."

I observed a marketing group that met to generate ideas for an advertising campaign. When someone suggested an idea, the others analyzed it to death. Someone would begin spouting facts and then others joined in with all sorts of demographics. Soon the original idea was forgotten, but as a result, few ideas were proposed and the meeting ended without even one workable idea. Such groups probably are more secure with analysis. At some point, however, they need to break out of this mode and move on.

Computer data bases also can aid in data retrieval if the technology is available on-site. With today's computer programs, there is little need to shuffle through stacks of papers. If a hard disk or floppies are carried to the retreat, data bases and electronically stored reports can be retrieved quickly. Some companies even use a modem at a retreat to access data stored in a headquarters mainframe computer.

Choose and Inform Participants

People attend retreats for a variety of reasons. Usually, they attend because they work in a particular area or have special expertise. Occasionally it's a reward for outstanding performance. If you can select participants, look for those who are highly motivated by the topic, knowledgeable about the problem, and willing to generate and consider off-the-wall ideas.

However, not every group member must be a problem expert. It sometimes helps to include less knowledgeable but more creative individuals. Such "creatives" frequently can enhance a group's creative climate. They can provide the spark needed to achieve breakthrough ideas. And they usually are verbally fluent, are willing to take risks, and suggest somewhat wacky ideas. I remember one retreat in which the group members viewed Charlie as their "creative." They constantly kidded him about his "crazy" ideas and weird sense of humor. However, it was Charlie's group that came up with the ideas favored by management. This outcome probably did not result from Charlie's ideas alone; instead, his behavior (and toleration of it by the other members) created a climate conducive to creative thinking.

Some companies also include as many office personnel as possible. This can help boost morale and multiply idea diversity. (The division of a major airline left only a skeleton staff to cover the office during its retreat.) However, don't force office staff to do just clerical tasks at the retreat. If broad problems are being considered, invite them to participate in idea generation. A lot of creativity goes to waste in companies. When office personnel are included, there is high morale and a climate conducive to creative thinking. These factors make the facilitator's job much easier. Moreover, management benefits from the input of additional people and the commitment that accompanies idea ownership.

After you have drawn up the participant list, keep everyone informed about the retreat. You don't need to tell them every minor detail, but do let them know key decisions as they are made. Create enthusiasm for the retreat by notifying participants about the location and recreational facilities. If any special rewards or side trips are planned, mention them also. As far in advance as possible, provide information on the site, dates, transportation, dress code (typically casual), lodging, and reimbursement procedures.

Groups

Limit groups to five or six people. Don't vary from this guideline, not even if the resort sales personnel say they "always" set up tables for ten people—that just makes their job easier. It's not in your best interests.

In larger groups, participation may be unequal because of cliques, or simply sheer size. Cliques form when interactions among group members become difficult; it's easier to interact with four or five other people than with eight or nine. Unequal participation also can occur; the larger a group, the fewer opportunities to participate. In smaller groups (three or four people), on the other hand, there are fewer resources to draw upon and a dominating individual may emerge.

More important than size, however, is group composition. Whenever possible, don't mix bosses and subordinates. In one retreat, a manager insisted on being in a group with his subordinates. It didn't take long for me to figure out why the group was not generating many ideas. The boss apparently was conducting a new-product idea-generation session the way he conducted staff meetings. He would call on group members by name and ask for their ideas. Then he would criticize each idea as it was suggested. By dominating the discussion and criticizing ideas, he put a damper on the whole process. The subordinates were afraid to suggest any "wild" ideas. Instead, they tried to play it safe and suggested carefully thought-out ideas. It's difficult to think of carefully analyzed ideas and still be spontaneous; as a result, the ideas were few and mundane.

You also should use homogeneous or natural work units only if particular expertise is needed. Natural groups become stilted in their thinking and need fresh input from others. In contrast, groups composed of personnel from different teams can bring new perspectives. For instance, if a problem calls for engineering expertise, a natural work group of engineers may be needed. However, if the problem is more general, interdisciplinary teams will be more effective. For instance, a problem of how to expand a market segment might benefit from diverse views. Of course, there always are exceptions to the group-composition rule. I would not break up a natural work team with proven ability to solve problems constructively.

A mixed group will be better when you want creative solutions. Such groups should vary in gender, personality, general value systems, and backgrounds. This variety can produce the many perspectives needed for creative insights. The only downside is that conflicts may arise because of the differences. You must weigh this possibility against the potential benefits. If interpersonal conflicts are not likely, use a mixed group.

You don't need a psychologist to put together a mixed group. Most managers know their personnel well enough to guide you. Interviews with employees also can validate these perceptions and add others. The objective is to avoid putting together all the "creatives" in one group and the "noncreatives" in another. There may be instances when this approach will work, however. A group of "creatives" might function well for short, intense periods of idea generation; a "noncreative" group might work well for problem analysis and idea evaluation.

One tactic to control conflict or dominating personalities is to form a group with "problem people." Before one retreat, we identified all the troublemakers, malcontents, and obnoxious people and put them together in one group. We then let them fight it out and bother each other. Our attitude was, if they don't produce any useful products, at least they won't bother others. A disadvantage of this approach is that some creative individuals may be excluded. I recommend using this tactic only as a last resort; a skilled facilitator usually can deal with most disruptive behavior.

Many companies frequently use an organizational cross section to form groups—the so-called diagonal slice is a typical approach. Each group contains one or two members from different functional areas throughout the organization. For instance, each group might contain a member from accounting, one from personnel, one from marketing, and so forth. An advantage is that different viewpoints will be represented and broaden the idea base. Another is that group interactions may strengthen organizational links after the retreat. A disadvantage is the loss of problem expertise if the problem is narrow in scope.

Group Facilitators

If you have internal facilitators, use them for the retreat. Try to assign one facilitator to each group; if you can't, one experienced facilitator usually can handle two groups. Sometimes, a single facilitator can deal with multiple groups if they are located near one another and the process is structured and clear to the participants.

Many companies have in-house facilitators who help with training programs and such activities as new-product idea generation. Because of their experience, they need relatively little training—a quick overview of the retreat may be enough. If in-house facilitators aren't available, graduate students from local universities often are eager to gain experience. I have found some graduate students facilitate as well as their more experienced business counterparts. Nevertheless, choose students carefully after observing them work with groups.

Assign facilitators to groups based on their experience and training. Facilitator experience is a prime criterion. I define *experience* as prior involvement in working with groups as a leader; there really is no substitute for it. Training in problem-solving approaches also is important. Not all approaches are the same, however. Your facilitators should be comfortable with the approach you will use; if not, provide training before the retreat.

Assign experienced and trained facilitators to groups needing the most structure and guidance. If conflict is likely, use only experienced facilitators. I usually try to learn which groups will need the most attention and assign facilitators accordingly.

Conducting the Retreat

If you have planned well, the retreat should go smoothly. But things happen that might cause you to revise your plans. You can't predict everything. Most things should be minor, however, if you have foreseen potential problems and your plan is sound.

Here are some guidelines for conducting retreats.

Review Ground Rules

The first task of the facilitator is to review the ground rules. From the outset, you should clarify expectations and establish boundaries of acceptable behavior. If people know what to expect and what the limits are of permissible behavior, they should act appropriately.

The following are some sample ground rules a facilitator might read to a group:

- Separate idea generation from idea evaluation. Try to withhold all judgment during idea generation. Once all ideas have been generated, you will have the opportunity to analyze them. This is most important.
- To benefit from all the resources represented by the group members, limit your comments. Do not be a conversation hog.
- When generating ideas, try to forget potential implementation obstacles. Even wild ideas are acceptable, since they often can be modified or serve as stimuli for other group members.
- Try to stick with the time schedule. However, don't be afraid to deviate if needed. For instance, if one technique helps the group produce ideas, don't stop using it just because the scheduled time has passed. Your facilitator will work with you on this.
- Try to generate as many ideas as possible. The more ideas you think of, the greater the odds are at least one will be a breakthrough.
- Your ideas are just as valuable as other people's. Even if you think an idea is impractical, go ahead and suggest it. It might prompt other ideas.
- Have fun and don't worry about being silly when generating ideas.

You should establish ground rules during planning so participants won't be surprised by them; however, if you can't, explain the rationale for each rule when offered. If there are any participant considerations, discuss and incorporate them as new guidelines if the other members agree. For instance, nonsmokers often request a smoke-free group or a limit on how many people may smoke simultaneously.

Analyze the Problem

Problem analysis is an important retreat activity. Sometimes, retreat success depends on the effort spent in problem understanding and clarification. Without this understanding, ideas may not be geared to the problem. And valuable time may be wasted trying to inform participants about the problem instead of generating ideas.

There are, however, three situations in which you might not need extended problem analysis: (1) if little time is available for the retreat, (2) when you've analyzed a problem extensively before the retreat, (3) if management selects the problem and expects you to use it. None of these situations should preclude problem analysis, however. You can use even ten minutes productively to answer questions or supply clarifying information.

Generate Data

If it has been a while since you discussed the ground rules, review them now. Do this before you generate ideas. Stress the most important rule: Defer all judgment while generating ideas.

You can use several techniques to stimulate and structure idea generation (see Chapters 7 and 8). As mentioned before, I usually schedule more techniques than time available. Among other things, a variety of techniques accommodates different idea-generation styles. If one approach doesn't spark ideas, another may.

This happened during a retreat in which the groups spent forty-five minutes using traditional brainstorming. A member of one group turned to me and asked, "Look at all the ideas we generated! What are we going to do the rest of the day?" I responded that we were going to use other techniques and generate even more ideas. As the day progressed, the ideas continued to flow from this group, regardless of the technique. All the members needed was a little variety in how they approached idea generation.

Techniques that help structure idea generation can also eliminate or reduce the need for skilled group facilitators; however, the groups must be trained properly to use the techniques. Because time rarely is available for such intensive training, facilitators should monitor each group's proficiency.

You also should consider the order in which the techniques are used. The techniques in the sample agenda follow a deliberate order. I schedule traditional brainstorming first, since most people have used it in one form or another. It also serves as a purge activity to rid participants of conventional ideas. Pin cards—the next technique—involve the silent, written generation of ideas on cards passed around a group. It is highly task oriented and establishes a standard of equal participation. The other techniques provide a gradual progression in creativity; that is, they call for more and more remote associations. If any group is uncomfortable with a technique, however, it should try another one.

Control Pacing and Timing

Although planning is the primary determinant of success, control of retreat activities runs a close second. Most of us have suffered through group experiences that can be characterized best as aimless wandering. Avoid this by monitoring each group's activities and supplying structure as needed. One way to supply structure is to control the timing and pacing of activities.

Obviously, the smaller the facilitator-to-group ratio, the better timing and pacing can be controlled. The only exception is in organizations with groups experienced with problem-solving techniques. Their experience often can substitute for facilitator skills, since experience is a form of structure.

To control pacing and timing, observe how groups respond to each technique, then move them from one technique to another based upon their performance. Not all groups respond equally well, any more than individuals do to different teaching or counseling methods. Often, consensus develops within a group that a technique "just doesn't work." At one retreat, a participant responded that "this technique is a red herring." At the very next retreat I conducted, I heard nothing but positive comments about the same technique. Moreover, some groups respond so well to a technique they resist moving to another. In either case, a facilitator should allow the groups to make necessary adjustments.

Technique effectiveness depends on many factors: group climate, problem type, and group-member motivation and experience. If a technique doesn't stimulate ideas, allow the group to move on or return to one that worked well before. But if a group is highly fluent and generates many ideas, don't break the flow and force it to learn another technique. In this case, the group climate will do more to prompt ideas than an imposed technique.

To determine proper pacing and timing, evaluate a group's familiarity with a technique and experience using it. Don't force a technique on a group if the members have little experience or familiarity with it. This is why minimal training is so important; usually a simple explanation, illustration, and short practice session will be enough. The time available also will be an important factor. More complex or time-intensive methods should be reserved for when there is adequate time.

Record Data

Data recording has benefited tremendously from the explosion in computer hardware and software. We now can record group outputs more quickly and efficiently. However, as with most new things, some people resist this technology.

What I hope is not a typical computer-resistance story involves a manager who worked for a large international corporation. He told me that, in his division, the only people who used computers were secretaries (this was about 1986). And they used them only for word processing! Other managers were given computers, but they had no idea what to do with them. Besides, "they had survived so far without them, so there was no reason to change."

This story, in turn, reminds me of a cartoon showing two Egyptian slaves dragging a large stone block behind them. As they plod along, they see a man offering his recent invention, "The Amazing New Wheel," guaranteed to make pyramid building easier. One slave turns to the other and says, "It looks like a good idea, but let's just wait 'til they perfect it." Although we often expect revolutionary change, we usually have to settle for evolutionary change.

Partly because of resistance and partly from lack of awareness, many people continue to rely on tried-and-true recording methods such as newspaper print flip charts, pen markers, notepads, index cards, and masking tape. In a typical scenario, a group facilitator fills a sheet of flip chart paper, tears it off, and tapes it to a nearby wall; the group might modify the ideas or use them as stimuli for new ones. Sometimes a group member or office secretary serves as a recorder and writes down ideas on a notepad; with a recorder, the ideas aren't immediately available as stimuli for other ideas (unless they are transcribed or read aloud).

If a group is fortunate and a facilitator uses a flip chart, members will be even more fortunate if the fortieth idea is written as legibly as the first. Even so, the ideas recorded might not reflect the full meaning intended by the contributor. Ideas often are offered faster than one person can record them. If the rate of contributions is slowed too much, quick-thinking group members may give up. Moreover, once the recorder has listed several ideas, a scavenger hunt frequently develops when the group tries to review a previous idea. Even worse happens, however, when the group tries to cluster the ideas to evaluate them. Because the ideas are scattered around on various flip charts, evaluation is extremely difficult during the same session and more meetings normally are needed.

All this has changed thanks to emerging and existing computer technology. An office secretary or other staff person can record ideas quickly on a computer. And group members usually understand the ideas easily, since no major abbreviations or shortcuts are taken. With large-screen projection of the computer monitor (or multiple computer monitors), group members can view each idea as it is typed. Because it is typed, handwriting no longer is a problem. If members want to review a specific idea, a search command can find the idea quickly. And idea evaluation is even easier. With a simple outlining program, a group can choose high-priority ideas, quickly pull them out of a large list, and group them together automatically. Group members can then vote on ideas and the typist can hit a command key to rank-order the results. Finally, group members can receive hard copies of the session's results before they leave.

What I have just described is only the tip of the iceberg regarding available technology. Recent advances in expert systems and computer neural networks foreshadow even greater data-recording enhancements. Chapters 10 and 11 provide more information on how you can use computers to generate and record ideas.

Evaluate Data

Use a systematic evaluation procedure to ensure all ideas receive a fair hearing. This can be difficult if there are many ideas and you have little time. Many productive idea-generation sessions deteriorate during idea evaluation. Faced with too much to do in too little time, group members feel pressured and choose just any idea to implement. Such an approach rarely results in a high-quality solution.

To overcome this problem, agree upon and stick with a structured evaluation approach. Although these methods vary in complexity, the evaluation process should become more manageable. For example, include a preliminary idea-evaluation segment in the retreat agenda. In the agenda I presented before, group members evaluate ideas after the morning and afternoon sessions. This first screening culls out obviously unacceptable ideas, and it may stimulate thinking for new ideas or modifications of existing ones. To guide this process, use one or two major criteria. For instance, you might eliminate ideas that cost more than $1,000 and call for more than two people to implement.

A second way to structure idea evaluation is to use weighted criteria. In the previous example, cost and time criteria are equal in weight, since no mention is made otherwise; that is, cost and time are equal in importance and both should be used to judge the ideas. Although equal weight may work for an initial screening, more refined analyses call for more refined rating methods. Because people rarely perceive criteria as similar in value, rating procedures should take this into consideration. For instance, when buying a car, most of us believe gas mileage and price are more important than color and seat cover material.

One simple culling approach involves making a list of the advantages and disadvantages of each idea. You then choose ideas with more advantages than disadvantages for further consideration. Another approach is to allocate votes to each group member based on a percentage of the total number of ideas. For instance, if there are 100 ideas and the allocation percentage is 10 percent, each member receives ten votes. The members then allocate their votes any way they want, placing all votes on one idea, dividing them equally among ten ideas, or using any other combination.

Develop Action Plans

The importance of implementation action plans should be self-evident. Unfortunately, because of either time limits or distractions, we often overlook implementation during a retreat. The sun or slopes may be too inviting, or group members simply may burn out from idea generation and evaluation. It is right after idea generation and evaluation that important implementation issues may arise, however. After a retreat, people may be too busy to deal with retreat-generated problems. Nevertheless, you should try to set aside time to deal with implementation.

Consider appointing an implementation monitor and assigning individuals to complete general tasks. If possible, discuss the when, where, and how of these tasks—that is, have the group specify task completion dates, locations, and details. You also might construct an implementation time line to provide an overview of the completion rate of each primary activity; you could develop a more refined schedule later.

Post-Retreat Activities

If you sketched out an implementation plan during the retreat, it should be easy to elaborate upon later. However, just because something is easy doesn't mean motivation and time are available. You may have to find the motivation and make the time to benefit from the retreat. Don't give up now. The five guidelines that follow will ensure that your efforts weren't wasted:

1. *Develop a final implementation schedule.* If you laid the groundwork for implementation during the retreat, a project manager can develop a more formal implementation schedule. Several software programs will simplify this task. Most are based on variations of PERT charts (Program Evaluation and Review Technique), which compute the sequence and duration of various activities. You also can use text outlining and object-oriented graphics programs to design elementary implementation plans. They are easier to learn and much less expensive than high-priced project-management software.

2. *Verify that all plans are implemented as scheduled.* Just having a plan doesn't guarantee it will be implemented. Assign someone the role of implementation monitor. It is important this person be detail oriented and able to oversee several activities simultaneously. The monitor also should be skilled at motivating people to complete tasks and should work well with others.

3. *Keep upper management informed.* This guideline also should be obvious; however, internal political struggles or simple mistakes in communication with management often happen. Therefore, management may believe it is ill-informed about retreat results. This is not good. Upper management probably footed the bill for the retreat and has a vested interest in it. I have attended some post-retreat feedback meetings with upper managers, and they take the results seriously. You should, too.

4. *Provide feedback and involve participants.* Besides general communication complaints, lack of feedback probably is the second most common gripe I hear from employees. Because of the time and effort they invested, you should keep retreat participants informed about outcomes. Most participants are interested in answers to the following questions:

- What decisions were made?
- When will they be implemented?
- Who is responsible for implementation?
- How did upper management react to the overall retreat?

Informing participants is a low-cost activity that yields high dividends. At the least, send a memo with results of the retreat (the most popular ideas) and post-retreat outcomes (what happened to the ideas).

You also might involve some participants in implementation activities. Participants could assume direct responsibility for specific tasks or supply information and opinions. In any event, involvement creates a sense of ownership of a project and increases commitment to it.

Feedback is a two-way street. You also should ask retreat participants their reactions. What did they like best? What worked least well? What should be done to improve the next retreat? How satisfied were they with their groups? How would they rate the performance of the facilitators? These and other questions can help planners improve future retreats.

5. *Begin planning for a followup retreat.* If you don't conduct retreats frequently, a followup may be needed. One issue rarely can be resolved satisfactorily during a short retreat. This is especially true of strategic planning retreats, where there may be unfinished business.

When planning new retreats, consider the results of previous retreats and participant feedback. Although this may seem obvious, we often repeat mistakes. Because of the passage of time or turmoil of current events, we frequently forget what we learned. However, even simple revisions can lead to major improvements. Thus, dig out all retreat evaluation data and use them as a planning guide.

Depending on the problem or topic, conduct followups between six months and one year later. Annual retreats also may be called for to deal with long-term issues. You'll find that followups create a sense of continuity and commitment to resolving organizational problems.

Part III

Idea-Generation Techniques

7

Techniques for Individuals

With some minor modifications, the techniques in this chapter for individuals can be adopted for use by most groups. The only difference is that the group members generate ideas while interacting with one another. The ideas can then be pooled as with traditional brainstorming and evaluated later.

These techniques are described using a three-part format: (1) relevant background information and comments, (2) a step-by-step description, and (3) a sample problem.

The techniques are classified according to their primary use of related or unrelated problem stimuli. Most formal idea-generation techniques use various stimuli to help prompt ideas. In general, these stimuli can be classified as either related or unrelated to the problem—that is, the stimuli may be derived from some problem element or from some source entirely unrelated to the problem. For instance, using a related stimulus to improve a toaster might involve selecting some element of a toaster and modifying it to produce something new. Thus, a toaster's heating element might be used to suggest an idea of a cooled casing for a toaster. To generate ideas using an unrelated stimulus element, you might select a table lamp and use it to prompt ideas. As an example, you might think of the lamp's base and use it to suggest the idea of a toaster on a pedestal. Within the two classifications, the techniques are presented alphabetically, with no implications of preference.

Note that the same problem has been used for several of the examples, so as to illustrate the power of the idea-generation techniques. It is much easier to think of ideas for a variety of new problems than it is for an extended list of new ideas for the same problem. (Problems are repeated in Chapter 8 for the same reason.) The newness of a problem frequently helps stimulate ideas. The more familiar a problem is, the less likely it will prompt ideas. Thus, it is more of a

challenge to generate a large number of ideas for solving an old problem. Idea-generation techniques, however, help overcome this difficulty.

Techniques Using Related Stimuli

Assumption Reversals

Consultant Steve Grossman developed this technique to overcome a
difficulty involved in dealing with logical paradoxes. This occurs when
you see a contradiction between an existing and a desired problem state.
For instance, a logical paradox exists if you are told to reduce your
expenditures by 15 percent but increase your output by 20 percent. To
overcome this paradox, you could try reversing problem assumptions.

Steps

1. Write down all major problem assumptions.
2. Reverse each assumption in any way possible (don't
   worry about the "correctness" of your reversals).
3. Use the reversed assumptions as stimuli and generate
   any ideas suggested.

Sample problem: IWWMW improve a refrigerator?

1. *Write down all major problem assumptions:*

"A refrigerator keeps food cold."
"Opening the door lets out cold air."
"A refrigerator requires electricity to operate."
"A refrigerator is capable of freezing some foods."

2. *Reverse each assumption in any way possible (don't worry about the
"correctness" of your reversals):*

"A refrigerator heats food."
"Opening the door helps retain cold air inside."
"A refrigerator requires no electricity."
"Frozen foods always melt in a freezer."

3. *Use the reversed assumptions as stimuli and generate any ideas suggested:*

- Build in a small microwave oven. ("A refrigerator heats food.")
- Opening the door triggers a boost of cold air until the door is again closed. ("Opening the door helps retain cold air inside.")
- Have a battery-powered backup in case of brief power failures. ("A refrigerator requires no electricity.")
- Install a timed, automatic defroster. ("Frozen foods always melt in a freezer.")

Attribute Association Chains

I developed this technique as a modification of attribute analogy chains (see earlier). The major difference is that attribute association chains use free associations to stimulate ideas while attribute analogy chains use analogies.

Steps

1. List all major problem components and their subcomponents.
2. Read one of the subcomponents and write down the first word that pops into your mind (word association). This word may be entirely unrelated to the previous word.
3. Use this word association as a stimulus and think of another word that pops into your mind. Write down this word. Continue this process until you have listed a total of four or five word associations.
4. Use the word associations as stimuli and generate any ideas suggested.

Sample problem: IWWMW encourage employees to stop throwing litter on company property?

1. *List all major problem components and subcomponents:*

- *People:* wage and salaried employees, supervisors and nonsupervisors
- *Litter:* paper, glass, metal, wood
- *Activities:* walking, driving, sitting, standing
- *Company property:* streets, driveways, sidewalks, buildings, parking lots

2–3. *Read one of the subcomponents and free associate, with one word triggering the next one* (only a few words will be used for this example):

- *Supervisors:* leaders, followers, people, workers, players, games
- *Paper:* scissors, stones, rocks, streams, water, cold, ice
- *Walking:* running, shoes, socks, sweat, equity
- *Streets:* pavement, asphalt, black, white, snow, ski

4. *Use the word associations as stimuli and generate any ideas suggested:*

- Create competitive games among departments, challenging them to pick up litter (from "games").
- Have employees take walks for exercise and carry air blowers to blow trash into special receptacles (from "streams").
- Pay employees for picking up trash (from "sweat" and "equity").
- Place trash receptacles several inches into asphalt pavement to prevent them from being knocked over (from "asphalt").
- Send employees of the most trash-free area on a ski vacation (from "ski").

Exaggerated Objectives

Several idea-generation techniques generate ideas using different problem perspectives. Exaggerated objectives creates these perspectives by exaggerating or "stretching" problem criteria.

Steps

As described by psychologist Robert Olson, the steps for this technique are:

1. List major problem criteria (objectives) that a solution should satisfy.
2. Exaggerate or stretch each criterion (there is no "correct" way to do this).
3. Use each exaggerated criterion as a stimulus to generate ideas.

Sample problem: IWWMW encourage employees to submit ideas to improve the company?

1. *List major problem criteria (objectives) that a solution should satisfy:*

"Will cost less than $1,000 per year to administer"
"Will result in a continual flow of ideas"
"Will involve many personnel"

2. *Exaggerate or stretch each criterion* (there is no "correct" way to do this):

"Cost less than $1,000"—exaggeration: costs over $1 billion
"Continual flow of ideas"—exaggeration: produces no ideas
"Involve many personnel"—exaggeration: requires no people

3. *Use each exaggerated criterion as a stimulus to generate ideas:*

- Costs over $1 billion—pay a bonus to people who submit a certain number of ideas, regardless of the value of the ideas.
- Produces no ideas—make raises contingent upon submitting ideas; no ideas submitted, no raise.
- Requires no people—start a company-wide public relations campaign to advertise the suggestion program.

Morphological Analysis

A systematic idea-generation procedure for problems with many elements, morphological analysis subdivides these elements into subelements. For instance, a fast-food store has as major elements food, customers, cooking equipment, and seating. Each of these, in turn, can be broken down into subelements. Thus, seating could be described as booths, counters, tables, and bars.

Steps

1. List the major problem elements across the top of a sheet of paper.
2. Under each element, list the subelements.
3. Combine two or more subelements, see if the combination suggests any ideas, and write down any ideas suggested. At this point, consider even apparently impractical ideas. They can be refined later on.
4. Repeat step 3 until you have generated a sufficient number of ideas.

Sample problem: IWWMW generate new furniture ideas?

1–2. List the major problem elements across the top of a sheet of paper. Under each element, list the subelements. Major problem elements and their subelements are shown in Figure 7-1.

3–4. Combine two or more subelements; see if the combination suggests any ideas, and write down any ideas suggested. Repeat step 3 until you have generated a sufficient number of ideas:

- A circular, glass television table with the screen facing upward through the center of the table
- A Western-style cork and wood sofa for card playing
- A modern-style plastic chair with storage space under the seat and behind the back

Figure 7-1. Example of morphological analysis.

Shapes	*Kinds*	*Materials*	*Function*	*Styles*
Oval	Chairs	Wood	Sleeping	Chippendale
Square	Beds	Metal	Resting	Shaker
Circle	Sofas	Plastic	Eating	Queen Ann
Rectangle	Tables	Cloth	Sitting	Modern
Cylinder	Dressers	Stone	Storing	Italian
Pentagon	Clocks	Glass	Entertaining	French Provincial
Hexagon	Televisions	Cork	Reading	Campaign
Heptagon	Pianos	Foam	Writing	Primitive
Octagon	Desks	Leather	Thinking	Western
	Chests	Cardboard	Cooking	
	Stools	Marble	Card playing	

- A leather and foam chair for reading and thinking
- A hexagonal stone piano for entertaining

Relational Algorithms

Relational algorithms, developed by educator H. F. Crovitz, generate ideas with unusual combinations of problem elements and "relational" words (prepositions). The idea is based on the creative thinking principle of forced relationships. Two parts of a problem concept are "forced" together with one or more relational words to produce unusual associations. The associations then are used to stimulate new ideas. Supposedly, these unusual combinations provoke unique problem perspectives. Crovitz suggests the following as relational words:

about	at	for	of	round	to
across	because	from	off	so	under
after	before	if	on	still	up
against	between	in	opposite	then	when
among	but	near	or	though	where
and	by	not	out	through	while
as	down	now	over	till	with

I have added the following words to the list:

above	below	except	toward
along	beneath	into	upon
amid	beside	past	within
around	beyond	since	without
behind	during	throughout	

Steps

1. Select two major problem elements.
2. Select a relational word and insert it between the two problem elements.
3. Examine the combination and write down any ideas suggested.
4. Repeat steps 2 and 3.

Sample problem: IWWMW improve a portable radio?

1. *Select two major problem elements:*

- Radio
- Listener

2. *Select a relational word and insert it between the two problem elements:*

- Radio above a listener

3. *Examine the combination and write down any ideas suggested:*

- Put a radio inside of a hat.

4. *Repeat steps 2 and 3.*

- *Combination:* radio after a listener. A "fanny pack" radio.
- *Combination:* radio off a listener. Put a radio inside of a ball, which is tossed at another person.
- *Combination:* radio under a listener. Put a radio inside the soles of jogging shoes.
- *Combination:* radio where a listener. Install portable radio vending machines where joggers run.

Reversals

One often becomes so familiar with a problem that creative solutions are elusive. Reversing the direction of a problem statement frequently can provide new perspectives and suggest new ideas. Many people probably have used reversals to generate ideas and not known it. For instance, consider police operations in which they send invitations to known criminals for a party. Once the criminals arrive, the police arrest them. This reverses the typical approach to law enforcement: Instead of police going out to capture the criminals, they try to get the criminals to come to them!

Steps

1. Reverse the problem statement in any way possible— that is, change the subject, verb, or object.
2. Use the reversed definition to stimulate a practical solution. Although there may not be a logical connection, write down whatever practical solutions come to mind.
3. Repeat steps 1 and 2 until enough ideas are generated.

Sample problem: IWWMW encourage managers to attend a management development seminar?

1. *Reverse the problem statement in any way possible. That is, change the subject, verb, or object:*

- Discourage employees from attending the seminar.

2. *Use the reversed definition to stimulate a practical solution.*

- Cut pay for nonattendance.
- Tell them they won't get promoted if they don't attend.

3. *Repeat steps 1 and 2 until enough ideas are generated:*

- Encourage subordinates to attend a management development seminar. Tell them they may be demoted for nonattendance.
- Encourage managers not to attend the seminar. Offer them the option of taking the seminar as a videoconference.

Two Words

We sometimes have trouble generating ideas because of the choice of words in the problem statement. Simple changes in key words, however, can alter the meaning enough to suggest more ideas. The two words technique helps overcome this obstacle by providing alternate words to consider. Thus, it provides different problem perspectives.

Steps

1. Generate a list of words similar in meaning to the main verb and object in the problem statement (a thesaurus will make this task easier).
2. Select a word from the first list, combine it with a word from the second list, and use this combination to generate ideas.
3. Repeat step 2 until you have examined a number of word combinations.

Sample problem: IWWMW reduce conflict between two departments?

1. *Generate a list of words similar in meaning to the main verb and object in the problem statement.* In this case, the words *reduce* and *conflict* are selected:

Reduce	Conflict
Depreciate	Discord
Diminish	Fight
Lessen	Dispute
Downgrade	Friction
Dilute	Contention
Discount	Disharmony

2. *Select a word from the first list, combine it with a word from the second list, and use this combination to generate ideas:*

- Dilute-Discord: Reduce the number of interactions between the departments.

3. *Repeat step 2 until you have examined a number of word combinations:*

- Downgrade-Discord: Downgrade departmental performance ratings until the conflict diminishes.
- Depreciate-Dispute: Assess fines to departmental members every time they have a public argument.
- Discount-Disharmony: Ignore the conflict and hope the department members can resolve it themselves.

Word Diamond

This technique, which I developed, is a distant cousin of the two words approach to idea generation. Instead of using different word meanings, however, the word diamond uses different combinations of words or phrases in the problem statement. At least four problem words are required, although it also will work with three words. (In this case, the technique might more suitably be called the word triangle.)

Steps

1. Choose four words or major phrases from the problem statement.
2. Place the words in a diamond shape so that each point has a word or phrase.

> 3. Combine one of the words or phrases with another word
>   or phrase and write down any ideas prompted by the
>   combination.
> 4. Combine the word initially selected in step 3 with the
>   remaining two. Use these combinations to suggest addi-
>   tional ideas.
> 5. Repeat steps 3 and 4 until all possible combinations
>   have been examined and all ideas recorded.

Sample problem: IWWMW encourage employees to clean up their work areas?

1. *Choose four words or major phrases from the problem statement:*

- Encourage
- Work areas
- Employees
- Clean up

2. *Place the words in a diamond shape so that each point has a word or phrase.* (See Figure 7-2.)

Figure 7-2. Example of the word diamond technique.

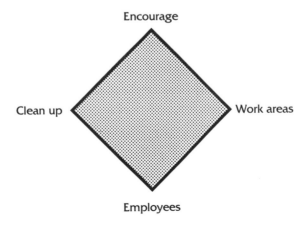

3. *Combine one of the words or phrases with another word or phrase and write down any ideas prompted by the combination:*

- Encourage-Work areas: Make the environment more pleasant by increasing the accessibility of trash receptacles.

4. *Combine the word initially selected in step 3 with the remaining two. Use these combinations to suggest additional ideas.*

- Encourage-Employees: Financially reward cooperative employees.
- Encourage-Clean up: Pay employees a piece rate based on how much scrap waste they dispose of.

5. *Repeat steps 3 and 4 until all possible combinations have been examined and all ideas recorded:*

- Employees-Work areas: Create a sense of ownership so employees will be less likely to litter in their own work areas.
- Employees-Encourage: Form quality circle discussion groups.
- Employees-Clean up: Conduct a contest, and award prizes for the department with the cleanest work area.

Techniques Using Unrelated Stimuli

Analogies

An analogy is a comparison of similarities between like things. In Creative Problem Solving, analogies help provide new perspectives by forcing the user to break away from conventional viewpoints. Analogies are often borrowed from nature; for instance, a new marketing strategy might be likened to the way bees collect honey. Because analogies typically produce unusual perspectives, they often help generate unique ideas.

Although you could generate ideas simply by thinking of things similar to your problem and borrowing concepts, a more systematic procedure is likely to work better.

Steps

1. Decide the major principle represented by your problem.
2. Generate a list of things (analogies) that represent the

major principle. Generally, if your problem involves people, you should think of nonpeople analogies; if your problem involves things, think of analogies involving people.

3. Select one of the analogies. The best analogies frequently are the most unusual or violate some cultural taboo.
4. Describe the analogy in detail, elaborating with action-oriented phrases as much as possible.
5. Use the descriptions to suggest ideas.

Sample problem: IWWMW reduce the number of employees who leave our organization?

1. *Decide on the major principle.* In this case, the major problem principle is retention.

2. *Generate a list of analogies.* Generate a list of things in life that involve retention. Generate your list by phrasing your problem in the following way: Retaining employees in an organization is like . . .

- Building a dam to retain water
- Going to the dentist to keep your teeth
- Trying various "magical" hair tonics to retain your hair
- Building a wall to retain dirt
- Sealing food in a plastic bag to retain freshness
- Fertilizing your lawn to retain the grass
- Keeping the gate closed on a "bucking bronco"

3. *Select one of the analogies.* For instance, you might select the hair tonic analogy.

4. *Describe the analogy in detail.* Trying various "magical" hair tonics to retain your hair involves:

- Checking out the reputation of the manufacturer
- Asking about research studies documenting effectiveness
- Finding out where to purchase the hair tonic
- Traveling to the store (or ordering by mail) to make the purchase
- Reading the instructions on how to use the tonic
- Applying the tonic regularly
- Checking in the mirror to evaluate results
- Writing to the manufacturer to complain about the lack of results

5. *Use the descriptions to suggest ideas.* The final step is to examine each descriptor to see if it suggests any ideas for the problem of employee retention. In this case, the following ideas might be prompted:

- Improve the organization's reputation so employees will feel proud to work there (from "checking out the reputation . . .").
- Conduct exit interviews to determine why employees leave (from "asking about research studies . . .").
- Allow employees to purchase stock or merchandise and services at reduced rates (from "finding out where to purchase . . .").
- Give free local vacations to employees who remain a certain number of years (from "traveling to the store . . .").
- Offer in-house education programs that, when completed, lead to raises (from "reading the instructions . . .").
- Make sure bosses meet with their workers on a regular basis (from "applying the tonic regularly").
- Conduct employee attitude surveys to highlight major concerns and anticipate future problems (from "checking in the mirror . . .").
- Start an employee suggestion program for ideas to retain employees (from "writing to the manufacturer . . .").

Attribute Analogy Chains

This technique was developed by educators Don Koberg and Jim Bagnall. It actually is a combination of two techniques: attribute listing and analogies. In contrast to analogies, which is based solely on unrelated problem stimuli, this method also uses related stimuli. Thus, people who may be uncomfortable with unrelated stimuli alone may find this approach appealing.

Steps

1. List all major problem components (these will vary from problem to problem).
2. List the subcomponents for the major components.
3. List at least one analogy descriptor for each subcomponent.
4. Use each analogy as a stimulus and generate ideas.

Sample problem: IWWMW improve a filing cabinet?

1. *List problem components:* name, material, function, form, parts.

2. *List subcomponents:*

- *Name:* filing cabinet
- *Material:* steel, aluminum, plastic
- *Function:* storing paper documents
- *Form:* rectangular box
- *Parts:* drawers, rollers, handles

3. *List analogy descriptors for each subcomponent:*

- *Name:* paper retainer
- *Material:* hard as a diamond (steel), flexible as a wet noodle (aluminum), moldable as gelatin (plastic)
- *Function:* a battery storing energy
- *Form:* a coffin
- *Parts:* train cars (drawers), roller skate wheels (rollers), lawn mower pull cord (handles)

4. *Use analogies to stimulate ideas:*

- Build in a paper dispenser ("paper retainer").
- Design one drawer as a security drawer for valuables ("hard as a diamond").
- Attach a lamp with a flexible neck ("flexible as a wet noodle").
- Design cabinet shapes using different themes or to reflect different products ("moldable").
- Drawers open and close electronically ("battery").
- Hinged top ("coffin").
- Modular cabinet units ("train cars").
- Wheels on cabinet bottoms ("roller skate wheels").
- Handle pulls recessed into drawer fronts ("lawn mower pull cord").

Modifier Noun Associations

I developed this technique to generate new product ideas. It helps you generate these ideas by combining a noun and a modifier and then free-associating using these combinations.

> ### Steps
>
> 1. Generate a list of nouns and modifiers. Try to include some unusual combinations (e.g., glowing apples).
> 2. Select one combination and free-associate additional modifier-noun combinations from the original combination.
> 3. Use all the combinations as stimuli and generate ideas.

Sample problem: IWWMW improve a portable radio?

1. *Generate a list of nouns and modifiers:* glowing apples, heavy light bulbs, corrosive bed sheets, wicked pickles.

2. *Select one combination and free-associate additional modifier-noun combinations from the original combination:*

- Glowing apples
- Radiant peaches
- Fuzzy elephants
- Hairy trunks
- Fat swimmers
- Flying boats

3. *Use all the combinations as stimuli and generate ideas:*

- A glow-in-the-dark radio (from "glowing apples")
- Insulated storage compartment for fruit and other snacks (from "radiant peaches")
- Radio that makes animal sounds for children (from "fuzzy elephants")
- Novelty radio that grows hair—the louder music is played, the faster the hair grows (from "hairy trunks")
- Radio that floats in water (from "fat swimmers")
- Remote-controlled model ship radio (from "flying boats")

Product Improvement CheckList (PICL)

I developed the Product Improvement CheckList (PICL) as an aid for generating new product ideas. It also has proved useful for generating ideas for a variety of less tangible problems (e.g., marketing and customer service problems). It consists of a poster-size worksheet with

576 idea stimulators organized into four categories: Try To, Make It, Think Of, and Take Away or Add. (A different version of PICL also exists as Circles of Creativity. The stimulator words are arranged on overlapping circles that rotate, allowing comparisons across categories). An abbreviated PICL worksheet is shown in Figure 7-3.

Some examples of stimulators in each category are:

- *Try to:* sketch it, wipe it, tighten it, twist it, build it up, do it backwards, whip it, inflate it.
- *Make it:* soft, transparent, magnetic, portable, disposable, vacillate, zigzag, adjustable.
- *Think of:* escalators, Sir Lancelot, oatmeal, stethoscopes, time bombs, eggshells, disappearing ink.
- *Take away or add:* layers, sex appeal, friction, rhythm, sand, moxie, turbulence, energy, anticipation.

Steps

There are a number of ways to use PICL. Here is the most basic:

1. Select one of the four categories and scan the list of words or phrases.
2. Arbitrarily choose one of the words and use it to stimulate an idea. That is, mentally experiment with the word and see what concept, principle, or action it represents that might be used to prompt an idea.
3. Write down any ideas suggested.
4. Repeat steps 1 through 3.

Sample problem: IWWMW improve a flashlight?

1. *Select one of the four categories and scan the word lists:*

- *Try to:* twist it.

2. *Arbitrarily choose one of the words and use it to stimulate an idea.* "Twist it" suggests ways a flashlight is or could be used.

3. *Write down any ideas suggested:*

- *Twist it:* Make the flashlight handle out of rubber so it can be twisted into different shapes.

Figure 7-3. Sample portion of the PICL worksheet.

WHO . . .

USES IT?
DOESN'T USE IT?
DOES IT MAKE HAPPY?
XXXXX
XXXXX
XXXXX
XXXXX

WHAT . . .

VALUE DOES IT REPRESENT?
ASSUMPTIONS UNDERLIE IT?
IS MOST LIKED ABOUT IT?
XXXXX
XXXXX
XXXXX
XXXXX
XXXXX

WHERE . . .

IS IT USED?
ISN'T IT USED?
COULD IT BE USED?
XXXXX
XXXXX
XXXXX
XXXXX
XXXXX

WHEN . . .

IS IT USED?
ISN'T IT USED?
DOES IT PERFORM BEST?
XXXXX
XXXXX
XXXXX
XXXXX

WHY . . .

IS IT USED?
ISN'T IT USED?
DO PEOPLE USE IT?
XXXXX
XXXXX
XXXXX
XXXXX

PICL—The Product Improvement CheckList

TRY TO   **MAKE IT**

SKETCH IT	STACK IT	SOFT	AGITATE
WIPE IT	PRY IT	HARD	CRYSTALLIZE
POWDERIZE IT	INCREASE IT	QUIET	PETRIFIED
IRRIGATE IT	DECREASE IT	LOUD	GRAINY
FORCE IT	FLUSH IT	THIN	BREAKABLE
ZAP IT	MELT IT	BRIGHT	UNBREAKABLE
SAND IT	SMASH IT	THICK	TEACH
XXXXX	XXXXX	XXXXX	XXXXX
XXXXX	XXXXX	XXXXX	XXXXX
XXXXX	XXXXX	XXXXX	XXXXX
XXXXX	XXXXX	XXXXX	XXXXX
XXXXX	XXXXX	XXXXX	XXXXX
XXXXX	XXXXX	XXXXX	XXXXX
XXXXX	XXXXX	XXXXX	XXXXX
XXXXX	XXXXX	XXXXX	XXXXX
XXXXX	XXXXX	XXXXX	XXXXX
XXXXX	XXXXX	XXXXX	XXXXX
XXXXX	XXXXX	XXXXX	XXXXX
XXXXX	XXXXX	XXXXX	XXXXX
XXXXX	XXXXX	XXXXX	XXXXX
XXXXX	XXXXX	XXXXX	XXXXX
XXXXX	XXXXX	XXXXX	XXXXX
XXXXX	XXXXX	XXXXX	XXXXX
XXXXX	XXXXX	XXXXX	XXXXX
XXXXX	XXXXX	XXXXX	XXXXX
XXXXX	XXXXX	XXXXX	XXXXX
XXXXX	XXXXX	XXXXX	XXXXX
XXXXX	XXXXX	XXXXX	XXXXX
XXXXX	XXXXX	XXXXX	XXXXX

4. *Repeat steps 1 through 3:*

- *Try to inflate it:* This makes me think of blowing up something like a balloon. Make the flashlight buoyant in case it falls into water.
- *Make it transparent:* This word causes me to visualize seeing through a flashlight. Make the flashlight transparent as a novelty, much like transparent telephones.
- *Make it disposable:* This is almost too obvious. Make disposable flashlights.
- *Think of Sir Lancelot:* A knight often used a lance as a weapon. For law enforcement officers, build in a knife or single-shot gun.
- *Think of time bombs:* This makes me think of time ticking away. Include a timer so that the flashlight will turn itself off automatically after a certain time period.
- *Take away or add layers:* Layers cause me to think of something that can be laid on top of something else and possibly removed. Include a variety of interchangeable light filters for the lens.
- *Take away or add anticipation:* The word *anticipation* makes me consider thinking of something before it happens—for instance, thinking of the flashlight turning on before I even touch the switch. Have the flashlight turn on by pressure on the handle.

8

Techniques for Groups

In general, a group will produce more ideas than a single individual. Thus, you should consider using group methods whenever possible. Group methods are indicated when the problem is important, you have sufficient time, and participation of individuals is needed to increase acceptance of solutions and problem ownership.

Of the group techniques described in this chapter, five also can be used by individuals: the KJ method, the lotus blossom technique, picture stimulation, semantic intuition, and object stimulation. However, this flexibility does not necessarily mean they will produce better ideas. The real measure of an idea-generation technique is the creative capacity of the people who use it.

The descriptions that follow are presented in a format similar to that used in Chapter 7: (1) relevant background information and comments, (2) a step-by-step description, and (3) a sample problem. However, no sample problems are provided in instances where pure brainstorming is used. Some techniques rely on only verbal idea generation from group members, while others also manipulate various problem elements (e.g., the use of related and unrelated problem stimuli). As a result, any sample ideas would have to reflect ideas of hypothetical individuals rather than the "mechanics" of a technique. The techniques are presented alphabetically within the two broad categories of brainstorming and brainwriting.

Brainstorming Techniques

Brainstorming techniques refer to methods in which the primary idea-generation method is verbal interaction among group members. The most productive brainstorming groups are those in which the group members conform to the principle of deferred judgment. That is, effective brainstorming groups separate idea generation from idea evaluation.

Force-Fit Game

This technique is an idea-generation approach developed at the Battelle Institute in Frankfurt, Germany. It differs from most other approaches by involving participants in a game. Supposedly this involvement increases their motivation to generate ideas as well as creates a group climate conducive to creative thinking.

Steps

1. Form two groups (A and B) of three to eight people each.
2. Assign one person (not a member of either group) to function as a referee and recorder.
3. The game begins when a member of Group A suggests an idea remote from the problem (or an impractical idea).
4. Group B has two minutes to develop a practical solution to this idea.
5. The referee writes down each solution as it is proposed.
6. The referee awards Group B one point if he or she judges the group was successful in developing a practical solution; if he or she determines the group was unsuccessful, Group A receives the point.
7. Group B next suggests a remote or impractical idea and Group A has two minutes to develop a practical solution to this idea. The referee writes down the solution and awards Group A one point if it is successful in developing a practical idea or Group B one point if Group A was unsuccessful.
8. The game continues for thirty to forty minutes and the group with the most points is declared the winner.

Gordon/Little Technique

Although it may seem contradictory, awareness of a problem can hinder idea generation. Information about a problem obviously is required to achieve a solution; however, it also can cause people to focus on "obvious" solutions (perhaps because of a tendency to stereotype problems and solutions). To counter this tendency to focus on the obvious, creativity consultant William Gordon developed this brainstorming variation, which temporarily suspends information from the problem solvers. Obviously, the problem can be known only to the group leader or facilitator.

Steps

1. The leader describes an abstract definition of the problem and asks the group to generate solutions.
2. After the group generates solutions for several minutes, the leader introduces a slightly less abstract definition of the problem and the group generates solutions to it.
3. The leader reveals the original problem to the group and asks the group to review the solutions to the two previous problems.
4. The group members use these solutions as stimuli to generate solutions to the original problem.

Sample problem: IWWMW improve a portable radio?

1. *The leader describes an abstract definition of the problem and asks the group to generate solutions.* Problem: Think of ways to improve something. Ideas:

- Make it larger.
- Polish it.
- Add more features.
- Use more expensive parts.
- Make it smaller.
- Make it more flexible.
- Make it interchangeable.

2. *After the group generates solutions for several minutes, the leader introduces a slightly less abstract definition of the problem and the group generates solutions to it.* Problem: Think of ways to improve something portable. Ideas:

- Put wheels on it.
- Make it lighter in weight.

- Make it easy to open and close.
- Have lots of pockets for accessories.
- Make it a convenient shape to store in different places.
- Make it easy to pick up.
- Remove features or parts.
- Simplify its operation.

3. *The leader reveals the original problem to the group and asks the group to review the solutions to the two previous problems.*

4. *The group members use these solutions as stimuli to generate solutions to the original problem.* Problem: IWWMW improve a portable radio? Ideas:

- Make it out of stainless steel (from "Polish it").
- Add a spotlight and compass (from "Add more features").
- Make a novelty radio out of rubber so it will bend (from "Make it more flexible").
- Design the portable to function as a component with a larger stereo system (from "Make it interchangeable").
- Add storage compartments for extra batteries (from "Have lots of pockets for accessories").

Object Stimulation

Earlier versions of this method are stimulus analysis and the focused-object technique. Object stimulation is a blend of these methods and also uses the same basic idea-generation principle of unrelated stimuli. The purpose of such stimuli is to present a different problem perspective. In this instance, the unrelated stimuli are objects with no apparent relation to the problem.

Steps

1. Generate a list of concrete objects unrelated to the problem.
2. Select one of the objects and describe it in detail.
3. Use each description as a stimulus to generate ideas.
4. Write down all ideas generated.
5. Select another object and repeat steps 3 and 4.
6. Repeat step 5 until all the objects have been used.

Sample problem: IWWMW reduce the number of employees who leave our organization?

1. *Generate a list of concrete objects unrelated to the problem:*

- Telephone
- Television
- Bicycle
- Automobile
- Microwave oven

2. *Select one of the objects and describe it in detail.* Television:

- Tunes in to many channels
- Different size screens
- Can use a remote control
- Sleep timer
- Portable
- Has a variety of programs
- Volume control

3–4. *Use each description as a stimulus to generate ideas. Write down all ideas generated:*

- Have weekly videoconferences with management to air problems (from "tunes in to many channels").
- Offer a sliding-scale incentive program to retain employees (from "different size screens").
- Have higher management meet periodically with employees from "remote" areas of the company (from "can use a remote control").
- Allow employees to take naps during the day (from "sleep timer").
- Allow employees to work at home (from "portable").

5. *Select another object and repeat steps 3 and 4.*
6. *Repeat step 5 until all the objects have been used.*

Picture Stimulation

Variations of this method have been referred to as visual synectics and Battelle-Bildmappen-Brainwriting. It is virtually identical to object stimulation except that pictures are used as the unrelated stimuli. Either you can give each group member a folder containing pictures or you can show a picture on an overhead projector.

An advantage of this method over object stimulation is that group members are confronted with visual stimuli instead of having to imagine an object. (Of course, this would not be a disadvantage if an actual object is present.)

You should select pictures that contain a variety of stimuli. Don't use pictures containing a lot of people or close-ups of people. Instead, look for pictures of cities, factories, and country scenes. *National Geographic* is a good magazine source.

When you describe the pictures, try to include as much detail as possible. Don't include only physical references such as: "tree, house, car, grass." Instead, also include many action-oriented statements, such as "The river causes the earth to erode."

Steps

1. Select five to ten pictures that are unrelated to the problem.
2. Select one of the pictures and describe it in detail.
3. Use each description as a stimulus to generate ideas.
4. Write down all ideas generated.
5. Select another picture and repeat steps 3 and 4.
6. Repeat step 5 until all the pictures have been used.

Sample problem: IWWMW sell more floor-care products?

1. *Select five to ten pictures that are unrelated to the problem* (only one picture will be used for this example).

2. *Select one of the pictures and describe it in detail.* Picture: a horseshoe magnet.

- Attracts metal
- Made of metal
- Shaped like a horseshoe
- Has two sides

3–4. *Use each description as a stimulus to generate ideas. Write down all ideas generated:*

- Attracts metal. Put metallic flakes on the package to attract customers.
- Made of metal. Make a bright, shiny metal package.

- Shaped like a horseshoe. Package the product in a magnet-shaped package using the theme of a "dirt magnet."
- Has two sides. Put a cleaning product in one side of the package and a wax or shining product in the other side.

5. *Select another picture and repeat steps 3 and 4.*
6. *Repeat step 5 until all the pictures have been used.*

Semantic Intuition

Semantic intuition reverses the normal procedure when an invention is created. Instead of assigning a name to an invention, semantic intuition creates a name and then produces an invention (or idea) based on it. One advantage of this method is that it uses related problem elements but combines them in ways to produce different problem perspectives.

Steps

1. Generate two sets of words related to major problem elements.
2. Select a word from one set and combine it with a word from the other.
3. Use the combination to generate an idea and write it down.
4. Repeat steps 2 and 3 until you have examined several combinations.

Sample problem: IWWMW encourage employees to stop throwing litter on company property?

1. *Generate two sets of words related to major problem elements.*

Things Involved With Employees	Things Involved With Litter
Working	Paper
Playing	Glass
Breaks	Metal
Bosses	Throwing
Pay	Trash cans
Benefits	Wood
Retirement	Picking it up

2–3. Select a word from one set and combine it with a word from the other. Use the combination to generate an idea; write down the idea.

- Require all employees to spend a certain amount of each work-week picking up litter (from "working-paper").

4. Repeat steps 2 and 3 until you have examined several combinations:

- Set up ball-throwing contests during lunch hour and require participants to pick up litter around them (from "playing-throwing").
- Require employees to pick up at least one piece of litter during their breaks (from "breaks-paper").
- Require bosses to pick up litter to set a good example (from "bosses-picking it up").
- Set up a recycling center that pays employees a premium price for litter they sort and turn in (from "pay-picking it up").

SIL Method

This technique was developed at the Battelle Institute in Frankfurt, Germany. The letters *SIL* represent a German acronym that translates in English as "Successive Integration of Problem Elements." It differs from most idea-generation methods in that ideas are generated by progressively integrating previous ideas.

Although individuals initially generate ideas in writing, the SIL method is not really a brainwriting technique. It was classified as a brainstorming procedure since the primary mechanism for generating ideas relies on verbal interactions.

Steps

1. A group of four to seven people silently writes down ideas.
2. Two of the group members read one of their ideas out loud.
3. The remaining group members try to integrate the ideas just read into one idea.
4. A third member reads an idea and the group attempts to integrate it with the one formed in step 3.
5. This process of reading and integrating ideas continues until all the ideas have been read and integrated.

Split-Brain Comparisons

This technique is based roughly on the concepts of analytical and creative thinking. These concepts often are compared rather simplistically with left- and right-brain thinking functions. That is, the left brain hemisphere uses linear, logical, and analytical thought processes, while the right deals more with intuitive, holistic, and creative thought processes. In brain anatomy, the bundle of nerve fibers that joins these hemispheres is known as the *corpus callosum*. The split-brain comparisons technique generates ideas by designing group interactions as a metaphor of brain functioning and physiology. That is, it juxtaposes ideas from creative and analytical groups with an integrating group activity known as *corpus callosum* thinking.

Steps

1. Divide a group of from twelve to fourteen people into two subgroups of primarily analytical and primarily creative thinkers. Divide them on the basis of creative thinking tests or simply by asking them to classify themselves as predominately creative or analytical. One group should contain all analytical thinkers and one all creative thinkers. The groups should be as equal in size as possible. If the creative and analytical thinkers cannot be divided equally, use an approximate division.
2. Physically separate the two groups and ask them to generate ideas to solve a problem. Instruct the analytical group to consider only logical ideas and the creative group to consider only wild, off-the-wall ideas.
3. Terminate brainstorming after about twenty to thirty minutes.
4. Combine individuals from both groups to form one large group (the *corpus callosum* group).
5. Instruct the *corpus callosum* group to select one idea from the analytical group and attempt to integrate it with one idea from the creative group to form a new idea or modification. Continue this activity using other idea combinations until they have generated a sufficient number of ideas.

Sample problem: IWWMW improve a flashlight?

Logical Ideas

- Use a sturdier switch.
- Use a nonbreakable lens.
- Cushion the case.
- Install a battery-life indicator.
- Make it waterproof.

Off-the-Wall Ideas

- The flashlight turns on automatically when it gets dark.
- The light brightens or dims as you wish it.
- You can lengthen the flashlight by pulling on it.
- The size of the lens increases or decreases in response to how much light there is in the environment.
- Throwing the flashlight in the air causes it to turn on automatically.

Integrated Ideas

- The light brightens or dims depending on how much pressure you apply on the switch (from "Use a sturdier switch" and "The light brightens or dims as you wish it").
- Battery life can be increased by spinning the flashlight—the spinning motion activates a small generator inside the flashlight (from "Install a battery-life indicator" and "Throwing the flashlight in the air causes it to turn on automatically").
- Make a glow-in-the-dark case. Squeezing on the case causes it to change different colors (from "Cushion the case" and "The size of the lens increases or decreases in response to how much light there is in the environment").

Trans-Disciplinary Analogy (TDA)

TDA was developed by Henry Andersen, a marketing manager at Mitsubishi Heavy Industries America, Inc. It is based on the notion that new ideas can emerge from anyone at any time. In this regard, Andersen developed the Diamond IdeaGroup, the "multidisciplinary and multinational idea generating, translating, and integrating network serving organizations and individuals worldwide." TDA is a functional translation of the Diamond IdeaGroup. That is, it generates ideas by borrowing perspectives from different disciplines.

Steps

1. Form small groups of at least five people each. Each group should contain people from a variety of occupations.
2. Assign a facilitator to each group.
3. The facilitator asks each group member to select one discipline or activity of special interest to that person. This discipline or activity does not have to be represented by the person's occupation, nor does it have to be a traditional academic discipline. It may even be some activity such as dishwashing or tree trimming. However, the person selecting a discipline or activity should have some familiarity with it (expert knowledge).
4. Each group member selects a central concept from his or her selected discipline and the facilitator lists it on a board or flip chart.
5. After all the concepts are recorded, the group selects one and the individual responsible for it provides a detailed description. (For instance, in one TDA group, a ballerina selected a particular dance movement as her concept. She then described the movement in detail and even demonstrated it.)
6. The group members examine the description and use it to generate ideas. They use each description as a potential idea stimulus.
7. The group then selects another concept and repeats steps 5 and 6.

Brainwriting Techniques

As discussed previously, brainwriting involves the silent, written generation of ideas in a group. The basic brainstorming rule of separating idea generation from evaluation also applies—that is, individuals should defer judgment on their ideas until it is time to evaluate them.

Brainsketching

Most of us use visual images to generate ideas. We often sketch these ideas to help us conceptualize them. The brainsketching technique attempts to capitalize on this ability in a group situation by allowing people to compare idea sketches. This particular brainwriting method originated during discussion in one of my creativity classes. A student conceived brainsketching as a variation of the pin cards technique, a procedure in which idea cards are passed around a group. Brainsketching modifies this procedure by passing around idea sketches.

Steps

1. Each group member individually draws a sketch of how the problem might be solved. No talking is permitted during this activity.
2. Group members pass their drawings to the persons on their right.
3. These individuals modify the original drawings or add comments.
4. This process of modifying and adding to the drawings continues for about twenty to thirty minutes.
5. The group members examine all the drawings and select a final solution or construct a final solution from parts of different sketches.

Brainwriting Pool

This is one of several brainwriting approaches developed at the Battelle Institute in Frankfurt, Germany. It is relatively easy to implement and requires little in the way of leader facilitation skills. Nevertheless, it helps generate a large number of ideas in a short time. The physical setting consists of a group of five to eight people seated around a small table.

Steps

Group members individually:

1. Write down four ideas on a sheet of paper.
2. Place their sheet in the center of the table (the pool) and exchange it for another one.
3. Read the ideas on the new sheet and use them to stimulate new ideas.

4. Write down any new ideas on the sheet and exchange it for a new sheet from the pool when they need additional stimulation.
5. Continue writing down ideas and exchanging sheets for ten to fifteen minutes.

Collective Notebook (CNB)

John Haefele of Procter & Gamble developed the CNB method to generate ideas from a cross section of employees within an organization. A major difference between it and other group idea-generation methods is that the individuals do not meet face to face. Instead, participants write down ideas on their own and then pool them later on. Another major difference is that ideas are generated over an extended period of time, rather than submitted spontaneously in one brief time period. About ten participants usually is enough to generate a sufficient number of ideas.

Steps

The participants:

1. Receive a notebook containing a problem statement and background information.
2. Write down at least one idea every working day for one month.
3. Develop a written summary of their ideas, including a list of their best ones.
4. Return their notebooks to a coordinator, who reviews the ideas, categorizes them, and prepares a detailed summary to submit to management.

Professor Alan Pearson suggests a variation that should increase idea quality. He recommends that after two weeks' time, the participants exchange their notebooks with another preselected participant. They then can use these ideas to stimulate new ideas.

Gallery Method

This approach reverses the basic process of the brainwriting pool or pin cards technique. Instead of moving ideas around for people to examine, the gallery method moves the people around the ideas. It is based on the way people browse around an art gallery to receive stimulation.

Steps

1. Sheets of flip chart paper are attached to the walls of a room (or flip charts on stands are placed around the sides of a room).
2. Group members silently write down their ideas on the sheets of paper (one sheet per person).
3. After ten to fifteen minutes of writing, the participants are given fifteen minutes to walk around, look at the other ideas, and take notes.
4. Group members silently write down any new ideas or improvements upon the ideas of others.
5. After about five to ten minutes of additional writing, the participants examine all the ideas and select the best ones.

KJ Method

The KJ method was developed by anthropology professor Jiro Kawakita when he was at the Tokyo Institute of Technology. He created it as a method for sequential grouping and synthesis of field observations, resulting in a clearer picture of the problem as well as new hypotheses and ideas. New ideas then are triggered by complex associations among other ideas. Although there is some verbal interaction among group members, the primary idea-generation mechanism is brainwriting.

Steps

1. Individuals are instructed to write down ideas on small cards, one idea per card with a goal of 100 cards.
2. Individuals sort the cards into categories of 50 to 100 cards, then 20 to 30 cards, then 10 cards or fewer. The categories should reflect new conceptual categories. These, in turn, help break down rigid thinking and help stimulate new ideas.
3. Individuals write down any new ideas on flip chart paper. These ideas may be related or unrelated to the

problem. They also may be described graphically to increase understanding. A new conceptual picture should emerge after this step.
4. Group members read aloud groups of ideas on their conceptual pictures and write down new ideas prompted by the picture or the discussion.

The KJ method has been used widely in Japan since its development over twenty-five years ago. For instance, Nippon Telegraph and Telephone used it to create a twenty-year technology road map, developing plans for an information network system that showed the conceptual merging of telephone, facsimile, video, and data communications.

Lotus Blossom (or MY Method)

This technique was developed by Yasuo Matsumura, president of Clover Management Research in Chiba City, Japan. The basic approach may be familiar to many Westerners, since it underlies the key concept of Lotus 1-2-3 spreadsheet software. The MY method involves starting with a central theme and then working outward using ever-widening circles or "petals." (In the Lotus 1-2-3 software program, the petals are lined up as windows along the top of the computer screen.) The lotus blossom or MY method starts with a diagram such as the one shown in Figure 8-1. Central themes lead to ideas that themselves become central themes, and so forth.

Steps

1. Each group member is given a lotus blossom diagram with a problem or central theme written in the center.
2. Group members think of related ideas or applications of the idea and write them in the surrounding circles labeled *A* to *H*. For instance, if the problem is superconductivity, the group members might think about commercial applications such as magnetic levitation trains, energy storage, and computer board wirings. Each of these would be written in the circles *A* to *H* surrounding the problem or central theme.
3. Group members use the ideas written in the circles as central themes or problems for the surrounding lotus blossom petals or boxes. Thus, if someone wrote "electrical transmission" in circle *A*, it would become the central theme for the lower middle box.

4. Participants try to think of eight new ideas for the original problem involving the theme in the selected lotus blossom. In this example, they would think of eight new applications for superconductors in electrical transmission, such as high-voltage lines. Each of these ideas is written in one of the boxes marked 1 to 8.

5. This process continues until the lotus blossom diagram is completed. If necessary, expert opinion may be sought.

Figure 8-1. Diagram of the lotus blossom technique.

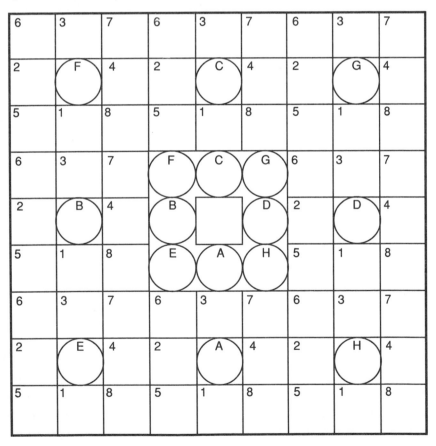

NHK Brainstorming

Although labeled a brainstorming technique, NHK brainstorming actually is a brainwriting variation. The primary idea-generation process
involves silent, written generation of ideas. It does, however, contain
some brainstorming activities. This technique was developed by Hiroshi
Takahashi, of the Japan Broadcasting Corporation (NHK).

Steps

1. Individuals write down five ideas each on index cards
   (one idea per card).
2. The individuals form into groups of five.
3. Each individual explains his or her idea while the rest
   of the group members write down ideas that come to
   mind.
4. All the cards are collected and sorted into categories of
   related themes.
5. New groups of two or three people are formed. The
   groups then brainstorm ideas for the themes and write
   the ideas down on index cards.
6. After an hour or so, each group organizes the new ideas
   by themes and presents them to the larger group. (All
   ideas are written on a chalkboard for all to see.)
7. The participants form new groups of ten people each
   and brainstorm improvements regarding the ideas on
   the chalkboard, one idea at a time.

Nominal Group Technique (NGT)

This technique was developed by management professors Andre Delbecq and Andrew Van de Ven in 1968 as a way to systematically structure
group discussions. Because there is little verbal interaction and decisions
are made quantitatively, consensus can be achieved easily. NGT has all
the advantages of brainwriting and also includes an idea-evaluation
stage. A major disadvantage is that the written ideas are not shared,
thus preventing stimulation from others' ideas. However, new ideas can
be added after the written ideas have been shared with the larger group.

Steps

1. Five to seven individuals write down their ideas without speaking.
2. Each group member orally presents one of his or her ideas without justification or elaboration. The group leader records the idea on flip chart paper (the ideas are numbered sequentially) and the next group member orally presents his or her idea. New ideas triggered by the oral presentations also may be added to the lists. This process continues until the leader has recorded all the ideas—one at a time—from each group member.
3. The leader points to each idea and requests clarifying comments. No evaluation is permitted other than to eliminate duplicate ideas and to correct an idea proposer's intended meanings.
4. Group members receive index cards and rank-order five to nine ideas from among those listed (ratings also can be used but require more time to tally). Group members select their favorite ideas and write down each one on a separate card. They indicate the sequence number of the idea on the upper-left-hand corner of the card. Next, each member spreads out his or her priority cards and places them in order of preference by selecting the most important, then the least important, then the most important of the remaining cards, and so forth. Finally, they record each idea's ranking on the lower-right-hand corner.
5. The leader tallies all the rankings or ratings and presents them to the group. The group examines the results and looks for inconsistencies or peculiar voting patterns. The leader encourages clarification of inconsistencies and solicits any information that might help understand an idea's intended meaning.
6. If a final vote is needed, the procedure outlined in step 4 is followed.

Pin Cards

Pin cards are a close cousin of the brainwriting pool. The major difference is that ideas are passed around to other group members instead of placed in the center of a table. In this regard, the brainwriting pool may have an advantage in offering more idea anonymity than pin cards (if that is a concern). Otherwise, both procedures can generate many ideas.

Steps

1. Five to seven people are given a stack of index cards and seated around a small table.
2. Group members individually:

   - Write down one idea on a card and pass it to the person on their right.
   - Read the idea on each card and use it to stimulate new ideas.
   - Write down any new ideas on a new card and pass it to the person on the right.
   - Continue writing down ideas and passing on idea cards for ten to fifteen minutes.

3. The cards are collected and pinned to a bulletin board, taped on a wall, or arranged on a large table in logical categories for future evaluation.

Part IV

Resource Materials

9

Creativity Training Materials

In addition to the process, techniques, and other elements of CPS, creativity training requires a variety of materials. In this chapter are descriptions of eight types of resource materials: creativity films and videos, audiocassette tapes, games and exercises, newsletters, tests, tools, books, and magazine articles. These materials will help you design training programs, improve your personal creativity skills and abilities, increase your awareness of significant creativity writings, and assist you in evaluating training articles. A brief description is provided for each type of material, except for the books and magazine articles. Whenever possible, prices and ordering information also are provided, although in many instances they were not available. (An attempt was made to obtain up-to-date information; however, there may be instances in which the distribution rights changed during publication of this book.) Inclusion of these materials in no way implies their endorsement. You will have to make your own decisions regarding product quality.

Films and Videos

The Bolero. Conductor Zubin Mehta presents a thrilling rendition of Ravel's *Bolero* and demonstrates teamwork, leadership, communication, and performance. Pyramid Films, Box 1048, Santa Monica, CA 90406. $395; $75 for 30-day rental. 213-828-7577.

Brainstorm. Useful as a session starter. Discusses open-mindedness and receptivity to change. Pyramid Films, Box 1048, Santa Monica, CA 90406. $250; $75 for 30-day rental. 213-828-7577.

The Business of Paradigms. Joel Barker discusses how unwritten rules can have a limiting effect on our organizations. Understanding this limitation can help increase productivity. A best-selling video. Excellence in Training, 11358 Aurora Avenue, Des Moines, IA 50322. $895; $200 for 5-day rental. 515-276-6569.

Changes, Changes. A simple story about building blocks and wooden dolls that illustrates adaptation to change. Events and situations portrayed change as the forms that are constructed with the blocks. Weston Woods, Weston, CT 06880. $60; 20-day rental. 203-226-3355.

Claude. An award-winning animation on the inevitable tension that arises when creativity challenges the existing structure. Highlights the need to encourage those who create in spite of discouragement or lack of understanding. Pyramid Films, Box 1048, Santa Monica, CA 90406. $145; $75 for 3-day rental. 213-828-7577, ext. 308.

Creative Problem Solving: How to Get Better Ideas. This film compares the psychological view of creativity with the common view, studies actions that encourage or discourage creativity, demonstrates how the brain works in the creative process, delineates problem-solving steps and brainstorming, and summarizes management attitudes that encourage creativity in the workplace. Vantage Communications, Inc., P.O. Box 546, Nyack, NY 10960. 800-872-0068, ext. 863.

Creativity in Business. Shows how creativity in the workplace can be learned. Crisp Publications, 95 First Street, Los Altos, CA 94022. $495; $150 for a 5-day rental. 415-949-4888.

Creativity in Management. Comic actor John Cleese discusses how management can create an environment conducive to creativity. Excellence in Training, 11358 Aurora Avenue, Des Moines, IA 50322. $149; no preview. 515-276-6569.

Dot and the Line. An award-winning animation about perceptual differences as illustrated with a dot and a line. Films, Inc., 1144 Wilmette Avenue, Wilmette, IL 60091.

Focus on Tomorrow. A business dilemma concerning the decision to support an old product or introduce a new item. BNA Communications, Inc., 9401 Decoverly Hall Road, Rockville, MD 20850. $495; $175 for 5-day rental. 301-948-0540.

Koestler on Creativity. Noted creativity theorist Arthur Koestler discusses his bi-associative theory of creativity. Based on his book, *The Act of Creation.* Time-Life Films, Inc., Distribution Center, Multimedia Division, 100 Eisenhower Drive, Paramus, NJ 07652.

Machine Story. An animated salute to the history of inventions. Shows how the discovery of primitive tools led to the development of today's space-age technology. Vantage Communications, Inc., P.O. Box 546, Nyack, NY 10960. $125; $95 to rent. 800-872-0068, ext. 863.

Mind's Eye. Shows how assumptions we make can interfere with our perceptions. Michigan State University, Instructional Media Center, East Lansing, MI 48824. $13 rental for 3 days (nonprofit organizations only). 517-353-7850.

P.I.S.T. (Psychological Improvement Situational Training). An outrageous spoof of motivational training programs. An icebreaker to shake up employees and get them thinking about new methods and solutions. Pyramid Films, Box 1048, Santa Monica, CA 90406. $250; $75 to rent. 213-828-7577.

Powers of Ten. This film is an adventure in magnitudes. You start at a picnic by the lake and then are transported out to the edges of the universe and then into the microworld of cells, molecules, and atoms. *Powers of Ten* makes a statement about the importance of keeping proper perspective in any situation. Vantage Communications, Inc., P.O. Box 546, Nyack, NY 10960. $250; $95 to rent. 800-872-0068, ext. 863.

Problem Solvers. People from diverse occupations discuss how they solve problems. Similarities and differences between the occupations are illustrated vividly. Churchill Films, 662 North Robertson Boulevard, Los Angeles, CA 90069. 800-472-7772.

60 Second Spot. Illustrates the teamwork and management of creativity that goes into producing a major television commercial. Pyramid Films, Box 1048, Santa Monica, CA 90406. $225; $75 for 3-day rental. 213-828-7577.

Sonata. Compares two different types of creativity using a metaphor of a skyscraper under construction and a musical composition. Modern Talking Pictures, 1212 Avenue of the Americas, New York, NY 10036. 212-541-7571.

Square Pegs, Round Holes. An animated story about a square peg who thinks he is different from the rest of his environment. He then decides to find his own niche in the world. Film Fair Communications, 10900 Ventura Boulevard, Studio City, CA 91604. $125; $15 for 3-day rental. 818-766-9441.

Up. Uses a hang-gliding metaphor to deal with the paradoxes inherent in a chaotic world. For the manager who must act boldly in an unpredictable environment. Pyramid Films, Box 1048, Santa Monica, CA 90406. $395; $75 to rent. 213-828-7577.

Why Man Creates. This classic film demonstrates how the creative process fuels innovation. Shows where ideas come from and the key ingredients of successful creativity and innovation. Pyramid Films, Box 1048, Santa Monica, CA 90406. 213-828-7577.

Audiocassette Tapes

Defining and Developing Creativity (by Silvano Arieti). This program explores the nature of creativity and its relationship to mental health and illness. Allowed to flower, creativity promotes wellness. Here are the biological, environmental, and cultural factors most likely to inspire creative thinking. One cassette. Vantage Communications, Inc., P.O. Box 546, Nyack, NY 10960. $10.95. 800-872-0068, ext. 863.

From Basics to Breakthroughs: A Guide to Better Thinking and Decision Making (by Roger Firestien). A two-cassette program in which you will experience a personal Creative Problem-Solving process designed to move you from problem to creative action. Creative Education Foundation, 1050 Union Road, Buffalo, NY 14224. $29.95. 716-675-3181.

How to Change Ideas (by Edward de Bono). Dr. de Bono discusses how lateral thinking can pave the way to innovation. One cassette. Vantage Communications, Inc., P.O. Box 546, Nyack, NY 10960. $10.95. 800-872-0068, ext. 863.

Journeys Into Creative Problem Solving. Taps into the "power centers" of your brain. *Success* magazine, P.O. Box 2, Church Hill, MD 21690-0002. $29.95.

Masterthinker: Your Easy Guide to Innovative Thinking (by Edward de Bono). Creativity expert Edward de Bono presents this introductory course on learning new thinking techniques. Includes four cassettes and three books. Creative Education Foundation, 1050 Union Road, Buffalo, NY 14224. $99.95. 716-675-3181.

Masterthinker II: Six Thinking Hats (by Edward de Bono). A complete course with case histories and role-playing exercises. Includes six cassettes and two 96-page workbooks. Creative Education Foundation, 1050 Union Road, Buffalo, NY 14224. $99.95. 716-675-3181.

Power Think: Achieving Your Goals Through Mental Rehearsal (by Roger Firestien). Helps you create a workable system to accomplish your goals and "pro-act" for the future. Uses mental imagery and rehearsal to help you become more successful. Creative Education Foundation, 1050 Union Road, Buffalo, NY 14224. $12. 716-675-3181.

The Right Brain Experience (by Marilee Zdenek). A two-cassette program that provides an overview of right-brain functions and eleven exercises to release the powers of your right brain. Creative Education Foundation, 1050 Union Road, Buffalo, NY 14224. $15.95. 716-675-3181.

SUPER Creativity (by Tony Buzan). An inexpensive, single-cassette program of theory and practical exercises designed to eliminate rigid thinking patterns. By the originator of "Brain Maps." Creative Education Foundation, 1050 Union Road, Buffalo, NY 14224. $9.95. 716-675-3181.

Tapping Into Your Creativity. A program designed to help you find your "childlike brilliance." *Success* magazine, P.O. Box 2, Church Hill, MD 21690-0002. $79.95.

Games and Exercises

C.R.E.A.T.E. A noncompetitive board game designed to improve your creative ability and provide an entertaining experience. The board is divided into four sections that correspond with Creative Problem-Solving stages: Focus (zeroing in on a problem), Incubate (using the power of your subconscious to get an idea), Aha! (gathering an insight or resolving a block), and Action (testing an idea, implementing it, and making it work). Players move toward the finish line by selecting cards that specify different activities. For instance, you might be asked to mimic ink coming out of the pen of your favorite author. "C.R.E.A.T.E." has two unique features. First, players can change the rules as they go along. In fact, if you make a suggestion to change a rule and the group approves, you win an idea token. A second unique feature is that there are no wrong answers. This is because the questions call for creative or thoughtful responses. Examples include: "In what ways is a typewriter like a swimming pool?" "If you could speak only five words for the rest of your life, what words would you choose?" "You pick up tomorrow's newspaper and are amazed by the unexpected news. What do the headlines say?" Throughout the game, criticism during idea generation is discouraged; thus you might be required to list three positive things about being depressed and lonely. Bruce Honig, C.R.E.A.T.E., P.O. Box 3325, Oakland, CA 94609-0325. $29 plus $3 shipping and handling.

Creativity. Consists of ten exercises designed to stretch an individual's creative thinking. The exercises cover such topics as broadening options, vision, maze awareness, perception challenges, developing logic, and improving general problem-solving and creative abilities. All the exercises are timed. If all ten activities are used, the total time required is only thirty minutes. Each creativity kit consists of five booklets and an Administrator's Guide. Education Research, Division of EduSearch, 370 Lexington Avenue, New York, NY 10017. 1–10 kits, $13.95; 11–24 kits, $11.95.

Think Tank. A Creative Problem-Solving board game that emphasizes both rational and nonrational thinking and helps improve team problem solving. One game can accommodate four teams of up to five players each. "Think Tank" offers three types of problems to solve: (1) venture, (2) business, and (3) personal. Each team picks a problem card to play with for the entire game. Players move around the board by answering nine key questions about the problem. Players throw a die to determine which of five idea-generation techniques they will use. Once a team has completed all twelve squares on the board, it is given evaluation criteria to select the best problem solution. Teams present their solutions to other teams, which vote on the best solutions. The team with the largest number of votes wins. Marian J. Thier, 200 East 57th Street, Suite 12G, New York, NY 10022. 212-688-5246.

Newsletters

"CreativeMind." Examples of departments include "Tips, Methods & Techniques," "Theory of Creativity in Business," and "Computerized Creativity Aids." Sample articles: "Random Stimulation: The Toy Chest," "Editorial: Train or Support Creativity," "Inspired History, the Origin of the Washing Machine." P & L Create, 300 Valley Street, #304, Sausalito, CA 94965. One year—6 issues—$29.

"Creativity in Action." Each issue contains a feature article such as "The Yin and Yang of Creativity: East Versus West." Regular departments include "Creative Solutions" (examples of creative solutions from the news), "News & Notes," "Puxxles" (creative thinking exercises with more than one solution). Other recurring departments are: "Meeting Management," "Computer-Aided Creativity," and "Acceptance Finding." Creative Education Foundation, 1050 Union Road, Buffalo, NY 14224. $49 for 12 issues per year.

"The Innovator." This newsletter carries articles that reflect the mission of Creative Learning International: "Ideas, Tools, Techniques, and Training for Developing Creativity." Each issue reviews the latest in creativity research and applications. Regular features include interviews, book reviews, creativity software reviews, a column on "Future Gazing," brainstorming tips, creativity-related products and tools, and an idea-generation advice column. Creative Learning International, P.O. Box 160, Neenah, WI 54957. $50 for 6 issues.

"Mind Play." Covers a fairly wide range of topics pertaining to creativity and innovation. Regular features include articles on mind mapping and "mental gymnastics" (creative thinking exercises). Examples of previous articles include: "Ethics: Bottomline Issue?" "Rebuilding a Baseball Club," "Corporate Renewal," and "Possibility Thinking." Occasional features include interviews and book reviews. 10677 Esmeraldas Drive, San Diego, CA 92124. 619-541-1846. $36 for 6 issues.

"New Sense Bulletin." Emphasizes right-brain thinking. Includes a variety of articles and tips on becoming a more creative thinker. P.O. Box 42211, 4717 North Figueroa Street, Los Angeles, CA 90042.

Tests

Consequences (P. R. Christensen and J. P. Guilford). Measures ideational fluency (divergent production of semantic units) and originality (divergent production of semantic transformations). Sheridan Psychological Services, Inc., P.O. Box 6101, Orange, CA 92667.

Expressional Fluency and *Ideational Fluency I* (P. R. Christensen and

J. P. Guilford). Both of these instruments measure the ability to diverge and generate ideas. Sheridan Psychological Services, Inc., P.O. Box 6101, Orange, CA 92667.

Fluency I (P. R. Christensen and J. P. Guilford). Measures divergent production of semantic relations ("the ability to produce efficiently ideas bearing prescribed relations to other ideas or to produce alternate relations"). Sheridan Psychological Services, Inc., P.O. Box 6101, Orange, CA 92667.

Kirton Adaption-Innovation-Inventory (M. Kirton). Assesses the extent to which people either work within the boundaries of a problem to produce a novel solution (Adaptors) or approach a problem by redefining it and working toward a transformation (Innovators). *Journal of Applied Psychology 61* (1976), 622–629.

Making Objects (S. Gardner, A. Gershon, P. Merrifield, and J. Guilford). Measures divergent production of figural systems. Subjects are given a collection of simple figural elements and told to construct certain objects using them. Sheridan Psychological Services, Inc., P.O. Box 6101, Orange, CA 92667.

Myers-Briggs Type Indicator (MBTI) (I. Myers and K. Briggs). Based on Carl Jung's theory of psychological attitudes, functions, and types. Measures introversion and extroversion as well as a preference for perceiving and judging or for thinking and feeling. Consulting Psychologists Press, Palo Alto, CA.

New Uses (R. Hoepfner and J. P. Guilford). Measures the degree of "functional fixedness." Sheridan Psychological Services, Inc., P.O. Box 6101, Orange, CA 92667.

Preference for Idea Generation (M. Basadur). Provides an indication of a preference for ideation during problem finding and problem solving. *Journal of Applied Behavioral Science 21* (1985), 37–49.

Product Analysis Scale (S. P. Besemer). Evaluates creative products in terms of novelty, resolution, and elaboration and synthesis. Helps devise ways to improve creative solutions. In S. G. Isaksen (ed.). (1987). *Frontiers of Creativity Research: Beyond the Basics.* Buffalo, N.Y.: Bearly Ltd. See also I. O'Quinn and S. P. Besemer. (1989). *Creative Product Analysis Semantic Scale: Development, Revision, Reliability and Validity Testing.* Unpublished manuscript, State University of New York at Buffalo.

Remote Associates Test (S. Mednick and M. Mednick). Assesses the ability to see relationships between seemingly mutually remote ideas and form them into new and useful combinations. Houghton Mifflin Co., 2 Park Street, Boston, MA 02129.

Sketches (A. Gershon, S. Gardner, and J. Guilford). Evaluates figural fluency—the ability to produce efficiently a variety of figures in response to specifications. For instance, the test taker is asked to make unrecognizable figures recognizable. Sheridan Psychological Services, Inc., P.O. Box 6101, Orange, CA 92667.

Torrance Tests of Creative Thinking (E. P. Torrance). Perhaps the most famous series of creativity instruments. Uses pictures or words to measure fluency, flexibility, originality, and elaboration. Scholastic Testing Service, Inc., 480 Meyer Road, Bensenville, IL 60106.

Utility Test (R. Watson, P. Merrifield, and J. Guilford). Evaluates the ability to think of new and unusual uses for familiar objects based on as wide a variety of attributes of the objects as possible. Sheridan Psychological Services, Inc., P.O. Box 6101, Orange, CA 92667.

Word Fluency (P. Christensen and J. Guilford). Measures the ability to produce words rapidly that fulfill certain letter properties. Sheridan Psychological Services, Inc., P.O. Box 6101, Orange, CA 92667.

Tools

The Circles of Creativity. A variation of the Product Improvement CheckList (PICL) described in Chapter 7. It consists of several hundred stimulator words and phrases organized into categories of "Try to . . ." "Make It . . ." "Think About . . ." "Add or Take Away. . . ." The words are on a ten-inch square with a rotating disk at the center containing two pointers and two die-cut rectangles. As you turn the disk, words appear under the cutouts and at the ends of the pointers. A "Try to . . ." pointer rotates on the disk and points to a circle of words surrounding it. To use it, you rotate the disk randomly and use any of the stimulus words selected. See Figure 9-1 (which has been reduced in size to fit on the page). VanGundy & Associates, 1700 Winding Ridge Road, Norman, OK 73072. 405-321-1309. $19.95.

The Creative Whack Pack. Contains sixty-four idea-stimulating cards based on Roger von Oech's book, *A Whack on the Side of the Head.* Each card contains a thought-provoking statement, quote, motivating phrase, or suggestion for stimulating new ideas. Creative Learning International, Customer Service, P.O. Box 160, Neenah, WI 54957. 800-955-IDEA. $12.95.

Idea Volley Bulb. For brainstorming, this is a giant, inflatable light bulb made of durable vinyl. Group members can pass it around so that whoever holds the bulb must come up with an idea. Or individuals can write ideas on the bulb and pass it on to stimulate the thinking of other members. It comes with an instruction guide and suggested activities. Creative Learning International, Customer Service, P.O. Box 160, Neenah, WI 54957. 800-955-IDEA. $24.95.

The MindsEye Courier. It is well known that certain brain-wave activity levels are associated with specific states of consciousness. Our

Figure 9-1. The circles of creativity.

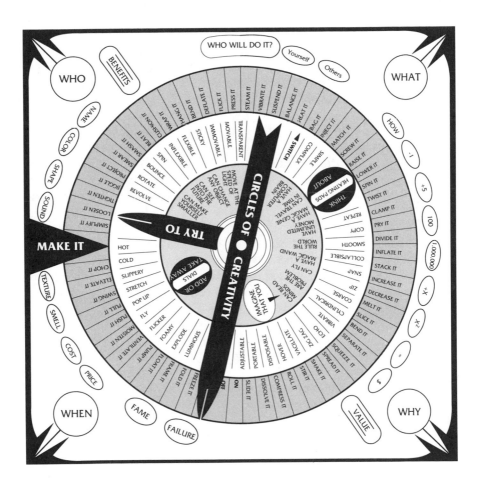

normal waking state is known as the beta range (13+ Hz pulses per second); relaxation and meditation are in the alpha range (9–12 Hz); deep relaxation and mental imagery are in the theta range (4–7 Hz); and sleep is in the delta range (1–3 Hz). The MindsEye Courier is designed to target your brain-wave patterns electronically so that you can access the alpha and theta states. If you can tune in to these states at will, you should think more clearly and produce more creative solutions. When you lower your defenses, ideas should flow more freely. A headset emits sounds and eyeglasses flash lights that help reset your brain waves. It also includes a power pack and input jack for use with cassette or compact disc players. Companion devices, also sold by Synectic Systems, can plug into IBM and compatible computers. Synectic Systems, P.O. Box 95530, Seattle, WA 98145. 206-632-1722. $395.

The Pocket Innovator. Creative Learning International president Gerald Haman invented the award-winning Pocket Innovator to improve creative thinking and solve problems quickly. It combines a creative process with key words to stimulate new ideas. All of this is contained on 150 plastic, color-coded, hand-held cards. The reverse sides of the cards contain the Ideas Library, a collection of useful creativity enhancers, affirmations, and quotations. The creative development process contains seven stages: (1) preparation, (2) investigation, (3) transformation, (4) incubation, (5) illumination, (6) verification, and (7) implementation. Key words are included to stimulate your thinking and help accomplish each stage. A user's guide and instructional audiocassette also are included. Creative Learning International, Customer Service, P.O. Box 160, Neenah, WI 54957. 800-955-IDEA. $49.95.

The Pocket Persuader. Similar in design to the Pocket Innovator, in that it uses plastic, color-coded cards. The latter will help you get ideas, while the Pocket Persuader will help you gain acceptance and support for them. As part of the Persuasive Advantage System, the Pocket Persuader guides you through six stages of the persuasive process: (1) preparation, (2) situation overview, (3) solutions, (4) features and benefits, (5) agreement, and (6) quality service. It also contains sections on persuasive words and buying motivators and objections. The Persuasive Advantage System includes the Pocket Persuader, a user's guide, instructional audiocassette, and planning worksheets and examples. Creative Learning International, Customer Service, P.O. Box 160, Neenah, WI 54957. 800-955-IDEA. $99.95.

Post-It Keynote Pads. A Keynote is a six-sided Post-It note designed to link ideas during brainstorming sessions. As an example of one activity, a leader can write down several key words, one per note, and place them on a wall. Group members then use each key word as a stimulus and place ideas (written on Keynotes) in clusters around the key words. Creative Learning International, Customer Service, P.O. Box 160, Neenah, WI 54957. 800-955-IDEA. $23.80; 20 pads per bundle, 25 sheets per pad.

The Product Improvement CheckList (PICL). PICL was described in Chapter 7 as an idea-generation tool that uses almost 600 stimulator words, phrases, and questions to prompt new ideas and product or process improvements. The words and phrases are listed on both sides of a large worksheet on durable paper. Users randomly select a word and free-associate with it to think of new ideas. The words also can be combined randomly with problem-related words and the combination used to stimulate ideas. Both individuals and groups can use it to stimulate thinking. VanGundy & Associates, 1700 Winding Ridge Road, Norman, OK 73072. 405-321-1309. $10 each, quantity discounts also.

Books

Some of the books listed in this section may or may not be included in the Bibliography. This list is not exhaustive; there are many other books related to creativity. However, it should provide you with a good start for researching the topic of creativity. The books are organized into six categories: The Brain, Creative Problem Solving, Visualization and Imagery, Advanced Reading, Innovation and Business Management, and General Creative Thinking.

The Brain

Blakeslee, T. (1976). *The Right Brain*. New York: W. H. Freeman.

Buzan, T. (1974). *Use Both Sides of Your Brain*. New York: Dutton.

Edwards, B. (1986). *Drawing on the Artist Within*. New York: Simon & Schuster.

Ferguson, M. (1979). *The Brain Revolution*. New York: Bantam.

Russell, P. (1970). *The Brain Book*. New York: Hawthorn.

Zdenęk, M. (1983). *The Right-Brain Experience: An Intimate Program to Free the Powers of Your Imagination*. New York: McGraw-Hill.

Creative Problem Solving

Bransford, J. D., and B. S. Stein. (1984). *The IDEAL Problem Solver: A Guide for Improving Thinking, Learning, and Creativity*. New York: W. H. Freeman.

Brightman, H. J. (1980). *Problem Solving: A Logical and Creative Approach*. Atlanta, Ga.: College of Business, Georgia State University.

de Bono, E. (1985). *De Bono's Thinking Course*. New York: Facts on File.

————. (1970). *Lateral Thinking: Creativity Step by Step*. New York: Harper & Row.

Geschka, H., U. von Reibnitz, and K. Storvik. (1981). *Idea Generation Methods: Creative Solutions to Business and Technical Problems*. Columbus, Ohio: Battelle Memorial Institute.

Isaksen, S. G., and D. J. Treffinger. (1985). *Creative Problem Solving: The Basic Course*. Buffalo, N.Y.: Bearly.

Koberg, D., and J. Bagnall. (1991). *The Universal Traveler*, 7th ed. Los Altos, Calif.: William Kaufmann.

Miles, L. D. (1971). *Techniques of Value Engineering and Analysis*, 2nd rev. ed. New York: McGraw-Hill.

Mudge, A. E. (1971). *Value Engineering*. New York: McGraw-Hill.

Osborn, A. F. (1963). *Applied Imagination*, 3rd ed. New York: Scribner's.

Rawlinson, J. G. (1981). *Creativity, Thinking and Brainstorming*. New York: Halsted.

VanGundy, A. B. (1987). *Creative Problem Solving: A Guide for Trainers and Management*. Westport, Conn.: Quorum.

————. (1984). *Managing Group Creativity: A Modular Approach to Problem Solving*. New York: AMACOM.

————. (1987). *Stalking the Wild Solution: A Problem Finding Approach to Creative Problem Solving*. Buffalo, N.Y.: Bearly.

————. (1988). *Techniques of Structured Problem Solving*, 2nd ed. New York: Van Nostrand Reinhold.

Visualization and Imagery

Bry, A., with M. Bair. (1978). *Visualization: Directing the Movies of Your Mind*. New York: Barnes & Noble.

Gawain, S. (1978). *Creative Visualization*. Mill Valley, Calif.: Whatever Publishing.

Khatena, J. (1984). *Imagery and Creative Imagination*. Buffalo, N.Y.: Bearly.

La Berge, S. (1985). *Lucid Dreaming*. Los Angeles: Tarcher.

McKim, R. H. (1972). *Experiences in Visual Thinking*. Monterey, Calif.: Brooks/Cole.

Advanced Reading

Allen, J. (1975). *As a Man Thinketh*. Marina del Rey, Calif.: DeVorss.

Bohm, D., and F. D. Peat. (1987). *Science, Order, and Creativity*. New York: Bantam.

Harman, W., and H. Rheingold. (1984). *Higher Creativity*. Sausalito, Calif.: Institute of Noetic Sciences.

Hunt, M. (1982). *The Universe Within: A New Science Explores the Mind*. New York: Simon & Schuster.

Kneller, G. (1965). *The Art and Science of Creativity*. New York: Holt, Rinehart & Winston.

Parnes, S. J. (1992). *Sourcebook for Creative Problem Solving*. Buffalo, N.Y.: Creative Education Foundation Press.

Perkins, D. N. (1986). *Knowledge as Design*. Hillsdale, N.J.: Lawrence Erlbaum Associates.

————. (1981). *The Mind's Best Work*. Cambridge, Mass.: Harvard University Press.

Taylor, C. W., and F. Barron (eds.). (1963). *Scientific Creativity: Its Recognition and Development*. New York: Wiley.

Weisberg, R. W. (1986). *Creativity, Genius and Other Myths*. New York: W. H. Freeman.

Innovation and Business Management

Albrecht, K. (1987). *The Creative Corporation*. Chicago: Dow Jones-Irwin.

Clark, C. (1980). *Idea Management: How to Motivate Creativity and Innovation*. New York: AMACOM.

Drucker, P. (1985). *Innovation and Entrepreneurship*. New York: Harper & Row.

Garfield, C. (1986). *Peak Performers*. New York: Avon.

Kepner, C. H., and B. B. Tregoe. (1981). *The New Rational Manager*. Princeton, N.J.: Kepner-Tregoe.

Ray, M., and R. Myers. (1986). *Creativity in Business*. New York: Doubleday.

Roth, W. F., Jr. (1985). *Problem Solving for Managers*. New York: Praeger.

Tatsuno, S. M. (1990). *Created in Japan: From Imitators to Innovators*. New York: Harper Business.

Waitley, D. E. (1986). *Winning the Innovation Game*. New York: Berkley.

General Creative Thinking

Adams, J. L. (1979). *Conceptual Blockbusting: A Guide to Better Ideas*, 2nd ed. New York: W. W. Norton.

————. (1986). *The Care and Feeding of Ideas*. Reading, Mass.: Addison-Wesley.

Agor, W. (1984). *Intuitive Management*. Englewood Cliffs, N.J.: Prentice Hall.

Arieto, S. (1980). *Creativity: The Magic Synthesis*. New York: Basic.

Brown, B. (1980). *Supermind: The Ultimate Energy*. New York: Harper & Row.

Campbell, D. (1977). *Take the Road to Creativity and Get Off Your Dead End*. Niles, Ill.: Argus Communications.

Cohen, D. (1977). *Creativity—What Is It?* New York: M. Evans.

Davis, G. (1981). *Creativity Is Forever*. Dubuque, Iowa: Kendall-Hunt.

Groch, J. (1969). *The Right to Create*. Boston: Little, Brown.

Hanks, K., and J. Parry. (1990). *Wake Up Your Creative Genius*. Nyack, N.Y.: Vantage Communications.

Jones, K. (1985). *Designing Your Own Simulations*. New York: Methuen.

Litvak, S. B. (1982). *Use Your Head*. Englewood Cliffs, N.J.: Prentice Hall.

Madigan, C. O., and A. Elwood. (1984). *Brainstorms and Thunderbolts: How Creative Genius Works*. New York: Macmillan.

Nierenberg, G. I. (1982). *The Art of Creative Thinking*. New York: Cornerstone Library (Simon & Schuster).

Olsen, R. W. (1980). *The Art of Creative Thinking*. New York: Barnes & Noble.

Osborn, A. (1964). *How to Become More Creative*. New York: Scribner's.

Rico, G. (1983). *Writing the Natural Way*. Los Angeles: Tarcher.

Robbins, L. B. (1985). *Waking Up in the Age of Creativity*. Santa Fe, N. Mex.: Bear.

Stein, M. I. (1984). *Making the Point: Anecdotes, Poems & Illustrations for the Creative Process*. Buffalo, N.Y.: Bearly.

VanGundy, A. B. (1983). *108 Ways to Get a Bright Idea*. Englewood Cliffs, N.J.: Prentice Hall.

———. (1991). *Training Your Creative Mind*. Buffalo, N.Y.: Bearly.

Vaughan, F. (1979). *Awakening Intuition*. New York: Doubleday.

Von Oech, R. (1986). *A Kick in the Seat of the Pants*. Menlo Park, Calif.: Creative Think.

———. (1982). *A Whack on the Side of the Head*. Menlo Park, Calif.: Creative Think.

Wertheimer, M. (1945). *Productive Thinking*. New York: Harper & Row.

Wujec, T. (1988). *Pumping Ions: Games and Exercises to Flex Your Mind*. New York: Doubleday.

Magazine Articles

As with the books in the previous section, the list of magazine articles is not exhaustive. (Academic research articles are not included since this book is written for the practitioner.)

Agor, W. H. (1983–84, Winter). "Using Intuition to Manage Organization." *The Bureaucrat*, pp. 49–52.

Beckett-Young, K. (1987, October). "Thinking Well." *Elle*, p. 356.

Brown, R. L. (1979). "Can Daydreaming Solve Training Problems?" *Training/HRD*, 16(6).

"B-School Buzzword: Creativity." (1977, August 8). *Business Week*, p. 66.

"But We've Always Done It That Way." (1979, November). *Leadership*, p. 69.

Calano, J., and J. Salzman. (1989, July). "Ten Ways to Fire Up Your Creativity." *Working Woman*, p. 94.

Case, J. (1989, June). "Sources of Innovation." *INC.*, p. 29.

Cherry, K. (1990, March 6). "Japanese Are on the Cutting Edge of Creativity." *Mainichi Daily News* (Tokyo).

"Creativity: The Renewable Frontier." (1984). *Human Potential*, 1(4).

de Bono, E. (1972). "The Virtues of Zig Zag Thinking." *CHEMTECH*, 1(1), pp. 10–14.

DeGarmo, S. (1989, November). "Leap Over Mountains." *Success*, p. 2.

Delaney, G. (1987, January–February). "Generating New Ideas in Your Sleep." *New Realities*, pp. 48–49.

Elliott, W. A. (1987). "Creativity and Enterprise." *Vital Speeches of the Day*, 53(20), pp. 637–640.

Englebardt, S. L. (1988, February). "Are You Thinking Right?" *Reader's Digest*.

Fishman, S. (1986, June). "Fads: Cashing In on Crazy Ideas." *Success*, pp. 44–50.

Foegin, J. H. (1990, January). "Encourage Employees to Dream." *HR Magazine*, p. 104.

Galagan, P. A. (1989, June). "Creativity and Work." *Training & Development Journal*, p. 23.

Gardner, M. (1985, April). "Brain Bogglers." *Discover*, pp. 87–90.

Garfield, C. (1987, April). "Peak Performance in Business." *Training & Development Journal*, pp. 54–59.

Gates, M. (1989, July). "Can IBM Innovate?" *Incentive*, p. 22.

————. (1989, September). "Can 'Play at Work' Spur Creativity?" *Incentive*, p. 13.

————. (1989, September). "Managing Creativity." *Incentive*, p. 181.

Geber, B. (1990, May). "How to Manage Wild Ducks." *Training*, p. 29.

"Get Rid of Tired Ideas With Brainstorming." (1979, May). *Leadership*.

Goldring, N. (1990, February 5). "Broadening the Circle." *Advertising Age*.

Goldstein, M. (1985, November). "Management on the Right Side of the Brain." *Personnel Journal*, pp. 40–45.

Gordon, J., and R. Zemke. (1986). "Making Them More Creative." *Training/HRD*, 23(5), pp. 30–45.

Gunther, M. (1989, January). "Boosting Your Output of Good Ideas." *Popular Science*.

Guterl, F. V. (1987, October). "Art of Managing Creativity." *Business Month*, p. 34.

Hathaway, N. (1987, June). "15 Great Creative-Block Busters." *New Woman*, pp. 54–58.

Hickman, C. R., and M. Silva. (1985, September). "How to Tap Your Creative Powers." *Working Woman*, p. 26.

Hines, T. (1985). "Left Brain, Right Brain: Who's on First?" *Training & Development Journal*, 39(11), pp. 32–34.

Holden, C. (1987, April). "Creativity and the Troubled Mind." *Psychology Today*.

"Increasing Productivity Through Creative Thinking." (1986). *Productivity*, 7(5).

Jablin, F. M. (1981). "Cultivating Imagination: Factors That Enhance and Inhibit Creativity in Brainstorming Groups." *Human Communication Research*, 7(3), pp. 245–256.

Joseph, J., and A. Hall. (1985, February). "Japan Focuses on Basic Research to Close the Creativity Gap." *Business Week*, pp. 94–96.

King, P. (1989, December). "Creativity's Sacred Sources." *Psychology Today*.

Konh, A. (1987, September). "Art for Art's Sake." *Psychology Today*, p. 52.

Kozlov, A. (1989, October). "Breaking the Cycle That Stifles Innovation." *Psychology Today*.

Lynch, D. (1986). "Is the Brain Stuff Still the Right (or Left) Stuff?" *Training & Development Journal*, 40(2), pp. 23–25.

Mason, J. G. (1958, January). "How to Develop Ideas." *Nation's Business*.

Miller, W. C., and T. Pearce. (1987–88, Winter). "Synergizing Total Quality and Innovation." *National Productivity Review*, p. 34.

Mitchell, R. (1989, April 10). "Masters of Innovation." *Business Week*.

"Mix Skepticism, Humor, a Rocky Childhood—and Presto! Creativity." (1985, September). *Business Week*, p. 81.

"Murphy's Newest Set of Laws." (1981, April). *Western Association Newsletter*.

"Ned Herman: A Brainy Kind of Guy." (1987, December). *Training*, p. 103.

Page, B. and R. T. (1989, September–October). "Creativity in Turbulent Times." *The Futurist*, p. 25.

Policliff, S. P. (1985, March). "In Search of the Elusive Aha!" *New Age Journal*.

Prince, G. (1978, November). "Putting the Other Half of the Brain to Work." *Training*.

Rehder, R. (1985). "Stifling Innovation and Change." *Training & Development Journal*, 39(7), pp. 60–62.

Rosenfeld, R., and J. C. Servo. (1984, August). "Business and Creativity." *The Futurist*.

Rossiter, C. (1984, July). "Four Steps to Creative Insight." *Human Potential*, pp. 8–11.

Scott, G. G. (1989, November–December). "Making Effective Decisions Through Brainstorming." *Manage*, p. 34.

Smith, E. T. (1985, September 30). "Are You Creative?" *Business Week*, p. 80.

Stiansen, S. (1988, March). "Boot Camp for Ideas." *Success*, p. 58.

"The Innovators." (1989, October 2). *Newsweek*, p. 34.

Tucker, R. (1985, October). "Ten Proven Methods for Hatching Brilliant Ideas." *Republic*.

VanGundy, A. B. (1980). "Try These Creative Problem-Solving Techniques in the Classroom." *Training/HRD*, 17(12), pp. 32–35.

Waitley, D. E., and R. B. Tucker. (1987, May–June). "How to Think Like an Innovator." *The Futurist*, p. 113.

Wallace, D. (1989, September). "Creative Muscle." *Success*, p. 63.

Welles, C. (1983, March). "Teaching the Brain New Tricks." *Esquire*, pp. 49–54 passim.

Wieder, R. S. (1983, November). "How to Get Great Ideas." *Success*, pp. 29–31 passim.

10

Computer Software for Individuals

Computer-enhanced creativity may seem misnamed—we usually don't associate computers with creativity. After all, if creativity distinguishes humans from machines, a computer cannot make us more creative. Or can it?

Apparently, many software developers and users think so. In the last few years, they have developed programs to enhance Creative Problem Solving (CPS) and creative thinking. Although such programs can't make us more creative, they can enhance our ability to analyze, synthesize, and process problem information. The more efficiently we can do this, the better we can solve problems creatively.

The program descriptions that follow are by no means exhaustive. Not all programs for Macintosh and PC computers are included, and by the time this book goes to press, there undoubtedly will be even more programs available.

There may be some question as to what constitutes creativity software. Some programs clearly fall into this category, since they structure the CPS process; others, however, are more indirectly useful. For instance, you can use outlining programs to record, process, and present ideas; however, they weren't designed just for that purpose.

I have categorized computer-enhanced creativity software in five ways: (1) CPS programs, (2) outlining and presentation programs, (3) thesaurus programs, (4) incubation programs, and (5) groupware programs (described in Chapter 11). Each program description includes an address, phone number, price, availability for Macintosh or PC computers, a brief description, and general comments.

Creative Problem-Solving Programs

The primary purpose of these programs is to enhance CPS efforts. Their most distinguishing feature is their ability to structure the CPS process; that is, they guide you through a series of steps to arrive at a solution. Unlike books on CPS, computer software allows more systematic interaction. The software structures your interaction so you don't have to question what to do next. Some of the programs offer more flexibility than others. You'll have to decide which ones best suit your problem-solving style.

CPSE (The Creative Education Foundation, 1050 Union Road, Buffalo, NY 14224. 800-447-2774; 716-675-3181. $50. MAC)

CPSE is based on the popular Creative Problem-Solving process developed by Osborn, elaborated and refined by Parnes, and more recently modified by Isaksen and Treffinger. It uses a HyperCard shell, so it is relatively easy to move about from one card to another.

The program first guides you through some general questions and asks you to list relevant information on each card. Then you can move to a more structured set of cards (Problem Solving 2) that asks for more specific data. This activity uses the CPS stages developed by Osborn and Parnes.

After describing your feelings about a situation, you list data according to what you know and need to know about the situation (fact finding). Then you list IWWMW problem statements, select the most important one (problem finding), and write down ideas to resolve it (idea finding). Next, you list evaluation criteria and fill in information for a decision matrix (solution finding). Finally, you list steps for implementing a plan of action. The program helps guide you by asking you to think of the Who? What? Where? When? Why? and How? questions. A third set of cards presents a more detailed look at the overall process.

Comments. The HyperCard interface makes this program extremely easy to use. You don't need much familiarity with computers once you are in the program. However, this simplicity also may be a weakness. CPSE is not well implemented and may not offer much advantage over following steps in a book and writing responses on paper. HyperCard enables users to skip around a program without regard to order. However, CPSE presents the CPS process as more or less sequential or linear. This was not the intention of the original CPS developers.

There are also other problems with the program. It is relatively confusing to use (e.g., no guidance is provided on how to use fact-finding data to stimulate problem statements; reference is made to IWWMW statements, but the acronym is not defined as it should be). There is virtually no documentation. Also, there are several instances of awkward wording and, unfortunately, at least one rather important typographical error: The name of the founding father of CPS is spelled "Osborne" instead of "Osborn." One addition that could strengthen CPSE substantially is techniques to facilitate the CPS stages. For instance, it might be helpful to include different idea-generation techniques for idea finding.

If you want a low-end, very basic CPS program, you might give CPSE a try; the price certainly is right. However, if you want a more sophisticated Macintosh program that runs on HyperCard, MindLink (see later in chapter) is a better choice—if you can afford it.

C.R.E.A.T.I.R. (IdeaPlex, Inc., 602 Alleghany Street, Blacksburg, VA 24060. 703-231-7307. $35,000. PC)

C.R.E.A.T.I.R. (Computer Resources Enlisted to Activate Triggers for Innovative Responses) is a complete hardware and software CPS system. It is a hypermedia process that uses computerized encyclopedias on CD-ROM disks, and audio, video, and even aromatic stimuli. C.R.E.A.T.I.R. uses these resources to help analyze a problem, generate ideas, and develop implementation plans. There are six problem-solving steps: (1) problem description and analysis, (2) key word selection to describe the major goal, (3) generation of ideas, (4) idea screening through importance ratings, (5) idea packaging and evaluation, and (6) reporting on each step in the process.

Comments. The nice thing about a full-system CPS environment is that it does everything for you. With both hardware and software in place, all you have to do is show up and begin working. The program guides you through each step using the latest technology and a variety of aids to prompt problem analysis and idea generation. The strengths of the C.R.E.A.T.I.R. are its relative ease of use, vast data base of stimuli, variety of stimuli, and ability to structure and guide the CPS process. The use of CD-ROM encyclopedias and aromatic stimuli are innovations in computer CPS.

An obvious disadvantage of such a full-system environment is its cost; $35,000 is a lot of money for a problem-solving tool. Of course, it could pay for itself with just one good idea. If you use C.R.E.A.T.I.R., it might amount to overkill for some problems, however. You might obtain similar results with the Idea Generator Plus ($195), IdeaFisher ($595), or MindLink ($499). True artificial intelligence is not likely in the near future. CPS programs don't provide us with creative solutions; they only help us think of solutions we already know or formulate new ideas based on what we know. Is the extra thirty-some thousand dollars worth the difference? Yes, if you can afford it. But if you can, you probably could afford to buy all the other CPS programs as well.

IdeaFisher (Fisher Idea Systems, 2222 Martin, #110, Irvine, CA 92715. 714-474-8111. $595. MAC/PC)

One way our minds generate ideas is through association. We think of one thing, which leads to another and then another. Unfortunately, our minds are limited in their ability to think of all possible associations. If there were no limits on how much information we could recall, our thinking would become pretty cluttered. Our minds also are limited in the ability to recall information on some topics.

IdeaFisher now has changed this situation, and it offers potential for extending the limits of human associative thinking. IdeaFisher is the brainchild of Century 21 Real Estate cofounder Marsh Fisher. He noticed that our minds can store information well but have trouble recalling it. We just can't think of everything we know on demand. A computer, however, can recall what it knows on command.

IdeaFisher is a sort of combination hypertext/data base/thesaurus program. It contains 387 broad "topical categories," 61,000 idea words and phrases, and over 705,000 direct idea cross-references. There are three major components used to solve problems and generate ideas: QBank, IdeaBank, and Notepads.

QBank. This component contains almost 6,000 questions divided into three categories:

1. *Orientation-clarification* questions help identify and clarify goals. The program provides specific questions for writing a story or script, a new product or service, a name or slogan, a marketing strategy, an advertisement, or a solution to general problems, and for adding user associations.
2. *Modification* questions help transform potential ideas into more interesting concepts. Over twenty-four categories of questions are included, such as action-motion, combining-synthesizing, increasing-adding-expanding, emotions-attitudes-behaviors, and size-weight.
3. *Evaluation* questions help assess goals and ideas using twelve criteria categories. Examples are: taking stock-midproject review,

attractive, interest-appeal, feasibility-practicality, efficiency-ef-
fectiveness, and implementation.

After you use QBank, IdeaFisher produces alphabetic lists of key
words and phrases from your answers. This feature makes it easy to
target important and relevant data.

IdeaBank. The second major component of IdeaFisher, IdeaBank,
contains 28 major categories of words, 387 topical categories, and over
61,000 words and phrases. The net effect is a subject-matter hierarchy
with general categories at the top and specific information at the bottom.
Examples of major categories include: actions-motions, clothing-jewelry-
grooming, materials-chemicals-gases, and sports-recreation-hobbies.
Each of these categories is subdivided into subcategories. Thus, the
action-motion category is subdivided into such categories as bend-flex-
fold and bubble-gurgle-fizz. The topical categories section contains
words and phrases organized into such titles as kinds, people-animals,
and things-places.

One useful program feature is comparison. It enables you to compare two sets of information simultaneously. For instance, suppose you
were writing an ad for Red Label Scotch and wanted to generate ideas
to market the product. You could open one computer window to show
different types of red (e.g., auburn, dusty rose, ruby) and another
window to show people associated with red (e.g., Lucille Ball, Red
Buttons). Comparing combinations between the categories then might
prompt marketing ideas. Thus you might design an ad using a Lucille
Ball look-alike.

Notepads. An Idea Notepad and a Question Notepad are used to
record thoughts and keep track of ideas. In addition, these features
make it easy to trace development of an idea.

To illustrate how you can use IdeaFisher, consider a problem of
developing a new sock product that people can wear all summer long.
Begin with QBank, choose orient-clarify, and open the category for
developing a new product. You then type responses to such questions
as: "Does the audience or customer fit a particular category?" Next, you
can use the appropriate command to extract a list of key concepts from
your answers. Copy selected words from this list to the Idea Notepad
and use them to develop a more refined strategy. Then select one key
concept such as "socks," display a list of topical categories, and select
one such as push-pull-repel. Next, select section titles to show idea
words and phrases associated with push-pull-repel. One of these is
varieties-examples (things that repel). Open this category and notice
that the list contains such items as *insect repellent, mosquito coil, riot gear*.
Review this list for stimulation and you may have an insight. For
instance, you might think of putting insect repellent on socks.

Comments. Development of IdeaFisher consumed an exceptional amount of effort (over 200 people), money (over $3.5 million), and time (twelve years). The result is a breakthrough creativity product that is useful for about any creative activity. It is a major step toward overcoming limits of the human mind in prompting unique associations. Thus its most important strength may be its ability to help us think of ideas we might not have considered otherwise. Although it is not on HyperCard, its format is similar to hypertext. That is, you can skip from one category or activity to another without the restrictions of a hierarchical outline. This feature makes it easy to compare associations and form new associations.

At least one research study has evaluated the effectiveness of IdeaFisher. Professor David Watson at the University of Hawaii predicted that people using IdeaFisher association lists would work longer at a creative task and produce more ideas. He randomly assigned the study participants (mostly graduate students) to an experimental group (with association lists) and a control group (without lists). He asked them to think of catchy phrases to go with a T-shirt design. The results indicated that the participants using the lists worked significantly longer than those not using the lists (an average of 77.8 minutes versus 54.8 minutes). Those using the lists also produced significantly more ideas (an average of 87.4 versus 63.7). He didn't assess idea quality, but there usually is a positive relationship between quantity and quality.

Although the strengths of IdeaFisher clearly outweigh its weaknesses, there are a few. Its all-text interface will be unappealing to most Macintosh users accustomed to graphic user interfaces; PC users, however, will find the interface pretty conventional. Some other minor problems: It requires some effort to learn and achieve a degree of proficiency; the filters are a nice feature, but finer discriminations between associations might be more useful; it consumes 7 megabytes of hard-disk space, and the program may be overwhelming for someone who just wants to brainstorm a few ideas. These objections are relatively minor, however, when compared to the program's potential for generating unique ideas.

Idea Generator Plus (Experience in Software, 2000 Hearst Avenue, Berkeley, CA 94709. 800-678-7008; 415-644-0694. $195. PC)

The Idea Generator Plus follows the general CPS process, although it uses three broad stages instead of six:

1. *Describe the situation.* There are three activities in this stage: Describe the situation, list the desired goals, and describe the people

involved. To complete these activities, the program prompts you to develop a clear problem statement, list and rate the importance of goals, and describe people needed to help resolve the problem. The program then generates a summary report.

2. *Generate ideas.* During this stage, the program asks you to defer judgment and use a variety of techniques to generate ideas. Techniques included are: Consider similar situations, examine metaphors, think of how someone else might solve the problem, pretend each goal is the only one (this prevents premature problem closure), reverse the problem goals and think of ways to achieve them, focus upon the qualities of people who might hinder solution achievement, and make the most of your ideas by transforming ideas you previously considered useless. After you have generated all ideas, Idea Generator Plus asks you to conduct a preliminary evaluation and revise, modify, or generate any new ideas stimulated. The program then generates a summary report for this stage.

3. *Evaluate the ideas.* During the last stage, the program helps you select the most promising ideas. Three activities are involved: Choose ideas to evaluate; rate the ideas using the goals; and evaluate costs, benefits, and effects upon people. The program also generates a summary report at the end of this stage.

Throughout the entire problem-solving process, Idea Generator Plus uses your responses to formulate more specific questions to answer. Although the program doesn't use artificial intelligence, this questioning procedure creates the illusion that it does. For instance, a real estate company asked how it might make a certain profit within two years. The company indicated that one of its goals was to "hire new brokers." Idea Generator Plus then asked the company how it could generate more high-priced sales. The company responded that it could "contact more top executives." The program next asked the company how it could do this, and it responded that it could contact business associations and country clubs. The company used these responses to develop a recruitment plan. This plan involved sending letters to business associations and social clubs asking them to encourage their children to consider a career with the company.

One nice feature of the program is its ability to format data as files that you can transfer by "hot links" to personal information managers (e.g., Lotus Agenda, Grandview, and IBM Current), outlining programs (e.g., MaxThink, Ready!), decision support systems (e.g., Decision Pad, BestChoice3), and word processors (e.g., WordPerfect, Microsoft Word).

Comments. The Idea Generator Plus was one of the first current-generation CPS software programs. Its ability to structure the CPS process has made it popular with people in diverse areas. For an MS-DOS program, it is user friendly and requires relatively little computer sophistication to master. Other important strengths are the use of a variety of idea-generation aids, the use of weighted decision criteria during evaluation, and the ability to return to previous stages of the process to make revisions.

The manual provides excellent documentation including easy-to-follow instructions and troubleshooting questions and answers. Customer support is a priority of the Experience in Software company; you'll find support staff willing to help with any problems. The company priced the program competitively at $195, which should make it difficult to pass up if you are looking for a PC-based CPS program.

Idea Generator Plus does have a few limitations. Perhaps the greatest is the potential of limiting creative thinking by setting goals early in the process. The program instructs you to be as specific as possible when setting these goals, since you may use them later as criteria. However, if you are not careful, this process could place unnecessary constraints on idea generation. Another program weakness is the lack of an illustration showing how to work through the entire process. An example continued through each stage would have been helpful. Finally, some may find the program too structured and believe that it inhibits their creative thinking. If this is a function of the MS-DOS command environment, a graphical user interface such as found on Macintosh systems or Windows 3.0 could alleviate this problem. Others may resist structuring creativity simply because they resist any forms of structured or imposed thinking.

Despite these disadvantages, this program has much to offer. This is especially true if you must purchase an inexpensive, PC-based CPS program—which the Idea Generator Plus is.

Idegen + + (FinnTrade, Inc., 5874 Doyle Street, Suite 11, Emeryville, CA 94608. 415-547-2281. $495. MAC/PC)

The first version of Idegen + + was created by Finnish professor Vikko Virkkala in 1982. The current version was developed in 1990 by a European team of experts who wanted to commercialize Professor Virkkala's computer-aided Creative Problem-Solving process.

The Idegen + + program is divided into five modules: (1) Ideas, (2) Evaluate, (3) Sort, (4) Print, (5) Idea Pad. All of these modules are listed as on-screen menu options.

The Ideas phase begins with problem clarification to help identify a

problem. It then moves on to use "distant models," "general principles," and a "modification checklist." Distant models are words that
help create new and imaginative connections with a problem. These
ideas can be relatively wild and help spark other, more practical ideas.
Next, you can use five problem-solving principles to provide additional
input:

1. How to use available knowledge and how to decide if you need
    more information
2. How to analyze the problem situation
3. How to obtain participation in reaching your goal
4. Determining the ideal goal that you envision; if anything was
    possible
5. Determining the higher-level goal, your ultimate purpose in
    solving the problem

The final activity in the Ideas phase is the modification checklist. This
device asks you to examine your ideas from a variety of perspectives
and dimensions. The result should be additional clarification and illumination.

The second phase, Evaluate, helps you assess your ideas using a
series of four questions. This phase also guides you in assigning idea
priorities for the next two phases: Sort and Print.

Sort, the third phase, is designed to clarify the best and worst ideas.
This will enable you to decide which ideas to pursue further.

The fourth phase is Print. It allows you to print your ideas directly
to your printer or import them to a word processor. Once your ideas
are in a word processor, you can modify the words, correct errors, and
condense data. The result is a polished list of preliminary ideas that you
can use for presentations or brainstorming in groups.

The last phase, Idea Pad, provides a convenient way to jot down
ideas that may occur suddenly. You then can use them later during a
regular Idegen + + session.

Comments. A major strength of Idegen + + is its use of distant
models, or unrelated stimuli to help generate ideas. The variety of
phrases should help you think of many unique ideas. The program's
emphasis on first generating wild ideas and later modifying them also
is a major advantage. Idegen + + does not quite have all the bells and
whistles of some of its competitors, such as MindLink, but it is easier to
navigate than MindLink. And it may be priced a little too high. However,
it is well executed in the Macintosh version (the only version reviewed
here) with its use of HyperCard.

MindLink Problem Solver (MindLink, Inc., Box 247, North Pomfret, VT 05053. 802-457-2025. $299. MAC/PC)

The synectics approach to CPS developed by creativity consultants William Gordon and George Prince is one of the most well-known and practiced problem-solving models. MindLink Problem Solver (referred to hereinafter simply as Mindlink) is based upon major synectics principles and concepts. Perhaps the most important of these is the use of "triggers" to stimulate ideas. Triggers force together a concept or thought unrelated to a problem and attempt to provoke unique ideas through this combination. Repeatedly forcing connections provides new perspectives that should multiply the number and quality of ideas.

Implementation of this connection-making operation is accomplished through a HyperCard-based, four-step problem-solving process: (1) problem identification and definition, (2) wishing exercises and idea generation, (3) development of ideas into solutions, and (4) action plans for implementing solutions. MindLink provides two ways to use this process: Guided Problem Solving and Problem Solving.

Guided Problem Solving takes you through a series of specific activities: Describe the problem, list wishes, use triggers to get more wishes, select one interesting wish and generate ideas to achieve it, use more triggers and list resulting ideas, select one interesting idea, develop a potential solution to the original problem, list pluses and concerns about the solution, develop options around the concerns, and list the remaining steps for solution implementation.

The second option, Problem Solving, is similar to Guided Problem Solving but offers more flexibility and a more extensive search for solutions. Problem Solving begins with a description of the problem and follows with worksheet cards for developing wishes, ideas, builds (idea additions/enhancements), and solutions. While using each worksheet, you can open up triggers to stimulate more data. The program stores the results of each worksheet. You then can refer to them later to deal with any incomplete thoughts left on the worksheet.

MindLink also contains two other major components: an idea "gym" and an idea-generation tool. The purpose of the gym is to help you limber up your mind before beginning problem solving. It also can serve as a break from thinking about your problem. It contains a series of self-paced creative thinking exercises, grouped into units of four exercises each. The idea-generation tool is sort of a shortcut approach to CPS. It contains a collection of electronic cards, each of which includes a place to describe your problem, a space to list ideas, an idea trigger button to prompt ideas, and a print button to print results.

Comments. MindLink takes full advantage of the HyperCard interface and provides an extremely user-friendly environment. Most users should be able to navigate the program easily, with little reference to the manual. However, unless you are familiar with the synectics approach, you should read the manual, especially the section written by George Prince. In it, he clearly describes the rationale behind the synectics approach.

Perhaps the greatest strength of the program is its flexibility. Unlike other programs, MindLink does not restrict you to one, structured approach. Instead, you can choose from the idea-generation tool for simple, unstructured problem solving, the Problem Solving component for more complex and unstructured problem solving, or the Guided Problem Solving tutorial for an in-depth, structured approach. And, with a few exceptions, the HyperCard format makes it relatively easy to move around from one card to another.

Another major strength is MindLink's ability to help turn wild ideas into more practical problem solutions. The idea triggers help prompt unusual associations and unique ideas. Although you have to think of the ideas, the program makes it easier to do so.

The strength of the HyperCard environment also is a weakness of the program. Switching between some cards can be slow—sometimes slow enough to lose the free flow of ideas. However, a more serious problem with the HyperCard format is that it can be difficult (if not impossible) to start if you just exited from a previous card. (You can reset MindLink at the Hello card using a Command 3). Inexperienced users also may find it difficult to move between other cards (although inexperienced users of MS-DOS programs may find them even more daunting). Mastering the triggers also can take some practice for inexperienced users. The examples provided, however, help somewhat.

MindLink deserves consideration as a flexible, full-function Creative Problem-Solving tool. It doesn't have the data base capabilities of IdeaFisher, but the potential of its triggers for sparking unique ideas should not be overlooked. And even though the HyperCard format can be slow and sometimes awkward, it is much more intuitive to use than PC-based programs.

The Solution Machine (The Gemini Group, R.D. 2, Box 117, Bedford, NY 10506. 914-764-4938. PC/MAC)

The Solution Machine uses the synectics approach to Creative Problem Solving. It guides you through a series of questions and activities for different problem-solving stages. It also provides numerous "connect-a-phors" to use in making fanciful connections between some unrelated stimulus and your problem. Both the PC and MAC versions are in a DOS format.

To illustrate the steps in using the Solution Machine, its developer, Kenneth Finn, utilizes an example of a fictional Mello-Pops line of candy. Sales are flat and the company is looking for creative solutions:

1. *Describe the problem freely (generate definitions).* The program begins by prompting an employee task group to generate several problem statements. For instance, "How to make Mello-Pops sell better," "How to package Mello-Pops more attractively for the customer," and "How to increase interest in Mello-Pops." The group selects its favorite statement and moves on to the next step. In this case, it selects: "How to package Mello-Pops more attractively for the customer."

2. *Describe the problem in an action statement.* The next task is to describe the problem in the form of several action statements. These statements begin with "How to? . . ." and have four parts: (1) *the action,* the thing you want to do; (2) *the object,* a thing or person you want to change; (3) *the qualifier,* the kind of action change you want; and (4) *the end result,* the result you expect will follow. The program even provides examples of each (e.g., action words include *build, increase,* and *improve*) and prompts the user in order. For instance, the Mello-Pop company team might develop the following statement: "How to package (*the action*) a Mello-Pop (*the object*) more appealingly (*the qualifier*) so that people will buy more (*the end result*)?"

3. *Rate the problem for difficulty.* The Solution Machine now asks the group to rate the problem for difficulty. This serves as a benchmark to assess the probability of achieving workable solutions. It also can use the rating capability to evaluate solutions at any time. It uses a 10-point scale and rates the problem as 9.

4. *Introduce and develop an imaginary situation.* The Solution Machine generates ideas with "connect-a-phors"—unrelated stimuli that create different problem perspectives. The program, however, first presents an imaginary situation such as, "A musical robot analyzing a house with a piece of rope." The group visualizes the imaginary situation and describes it in detail (e.g., "The robot is round with music coming from the inside. It sounds like a music box. He uses the rope to climb to the roof of the house. He does this because he is thinking of buying the house."). Then the group uses these situation descriptions as stimuli to generate ideas.

5. *Generate ideas using "connect-a-phors."* After the group has described the imaginary situation in detail, it searches for "connect-a-phors" to stimulate ideas. The program reminds the group of its problem, "How to package a Mello-Pop more appealingly so that people will buy more." The program then asks, "If we were to solve our

problem the same way the robot is solving his, how might we do it?"
Group members suggest such ideas as, "We could give out musical
jump ropes." Next, the Solution Machine prompts the group to think of
ideas using each of the key words in the "connect-a-phor." For instance,
music suggests the idea of adding music to the package displays.

6. *Refine the "connect-a-phors."* The computer displays a numbered
list of ideas. The group reviews the ideas and looks for practical
solutions. In this case, the group selects an idea involving a robot-type
dispensing machine. However, it still remains open to other ideas.

7. *Evaluate the ideas using the plus/minus inventory.* The plus/minus
inventory lists the pros and cons of every idea and considers each
separately. (This approach is different from the traditional method of
listing the pros and cons and then adding up each column.) The
emphasis is on keeping all the positive elements of a solution—even the
"good" parts of a bad idea. All these elements then are available as idea
stimulators to improve the solution.

For instance, the group might list pluses of a robot dispenser as, "It
would get attention" and "It would make it easy to locate Mello-Pops in
the store." Minuses might include, "The dispenser would be expensive
to design and make" and "It would have high maintenance costs." If
the minuses outweigh the pluses, the group is guided in overcoming as
many minuses as possible. It even may want to generate new problem
definitions to help remove these obstacles.

At the conclusion of the program, the group can print out a record
of its session. After examining this summary, it may decide to generate
more ideas. If so, it can select from such techniques as reversals,
opposites, the quick technique, and adjectives. All ideas generated with
these techniques can be filtered through the plus/minus inventory and
evaluated with the original ideas.

Comments. The Solution Machine is a clever program for developing unique problem solutions. Its strengths lie in its ability to force the
user to view a problem from a variety of perspectives. Its approach to
analogies ("connect-a-phors") is creative and should prompt many
ideas. Moreover, its overall implementation is useful for structuring the
CPS process. Its major disadvantage—especially for Macintosh computer users—is its DOS interface. It is awkward to move around the
program and there is little flexibility in returning to previous stages, as
with MindLink.

Recommendations

Of the programs reviewed, IdeaFisher, Idea Generator Plus, and
MindLink are the most useful. It is difficult to categorize one of these as

best, since they all have good and bad points. IdeaFisher is a good choice because of the depth and breadth of its data base for developing associations. Macintosh users, however, may find its interface a little unfriendly. Its format also doesn't follow a conventional CPS process; nevertheless, it is an extremely powerful program. MindLink also is an excellent choice because of its ease of use. The idea triggers help prompt ideas, and it provides several options for structuring the CPS process. The Idea Generator Plus also is a good program that closely follows the CPS process. If cost is a consideration, it is an excellent choice for PC users. Idegen + + and the Solution Machine are good second choices; of these two, Idegen + + is the program of choice. The Solution Machine is not implemented as well as the top-recommended programs and could benefit most from addition of a HyperCard interface. Although it is well implemented and uses a HyperCard interface, Idegen + + lacks some minor features and is a little overpriced. C.R.E.A.T.I.R. is a well-conceived program, but its cost probably is prohibitive except for corporations.

Outlining and Presentation Programs

Programs in this category help record, edit, and process data during different problem-solving stages. You can move data around easily and regroup them for analysis. Several of these programs also have presentation capabilities.

There are a few limitations in regard to this section. Not all available programs are included in this category; space limited the number of programs, some companies wouldn't provide review copies, and I am more familiar with and have greater access to Macintosh programs.

ACTA Advantage (Symmetry, 8603 East Royal Palm, Suite 110, Scottsdale, AZ 85258. 800-624-2485. $129. MAC)

This is a Macintosh desk-accessory outlining program. This means you can develop an outline within any program application without leaving it. You then can paste the results into a word processing program or more powerful outlining program.

Comments. ACTA Advantage is intuitive and easy to use. Its availability as a desk accessory makes it an attractive tool for recording and organizing ideas, when compared to more expensive outlining programs. It doesn't have all the features of more powerful programs, but its relatively low price makes it a good choice.

CA-Cricket Presents (Computer Associates, 10505 Sorrento Valley Road, San Diego, CA 92121. 800-531-5236. $495. MAC/PC)

CA-Cricket Presents is an integrated presentation program that includes a text editor and tools for drawing and making graphs and tables. It includes an ACTA outlining processor and presentation templates designed by artists. It also contains such features as an "electronic light table" for arranging frames, "speaker's notes" for building a frame-by-frame script, and a "video presents" aid for viewing presentations on your computer. It also includes most special presentation effects.

Comments. Although this program provides outlining capabilities, its greatest strength is presentations. It makes good use of graphics and the templates are especially useful.

Calliope Plus (Innovision, P.O. Box 1317, Los Altos, CA 94023. $99. MAC)

Calliope Plus is a unique visual outlining tool for recording, linking, and arranging ideas. It is based on a three-stage creativity process: Expansion, Contraction, and Refinement. During the first stage, Expansion, you type in ideas as quickly as you can think of them. Unlike other outlining programs, however, the program represents ideas as light bulbs with associated text (text windows accompany each light bulb). During the Contraction stage, you organize the ideas by discarding the least useful ones. Then you can link the ideas together to provide more cohesive concepts. The links provide information on the flow of ideas. This can be especially useful for project planning. Finally, during the Refinement stage, you can print and save the linked ideas.

Comments. The unique interface of this program makes it fun and interesting to use. Its ability to visually present ideas provides an easy way to conceptualize relationships between ideas as well as a flow of events. It also is easy to rearrange the concepts into different clusters representing different relationships. Although interesting to use, Calliope Plus has limited features, such as an inability to scroll within the text screens and the small number of ways to display and manipulate ideas.

Comment (Deneba Software, 3305 N.W. 74th Avenue, Miami, FL 33122. 305-594-6965. $99.95. MAC)

Comment is a desk-accessory, electronic equivalent of 3M's Post-it notes. It allows you to attach notes electronically to any document and will open them when you scroll past the location or on command. There are four different types of notes. Posted Notes are like Post-it notes, in that you can attach notes containing text or graphics to any document. Window Notes are like Posted Notes, except you attach them to an entire window instead of to a specific location in a text document. Scratch Notes are not attached to anything and Time Notes keep track of appointments and reminders. For CPS, Comment is useful in its ability to add free-form comments to any document. You can attach a visible marker and display the notes whenever desired. This simple procedure allows you to create hypertext-like documents without using more complicated software.

Comments. Comment is an easy-to-use desk accessory that will allow you to add notes about your ideas during brainstorming. The result will be a less cluttered appearance and an efficient way to process ideas. However, if you plan to "hide" much text, MindWrite might be a better choice. Of course, this would require you to buy another word processor. The advantage of Comment is you can use it with your existing programs, including graphic programs and spreadsheets.

Fair Witness (Chena Software, 905 Harrison Street, Allentown, PA 18103. 215-770-1210. $495. MAC)

In Robert Heinlein's *Stranger in a Strange Land*, there is a profession known as a Fair Witness. This occupation requires someone to perform like a supergrade notary; such a person is trained to observe events and details and then describe them later with perfect recall. The Fair Witness software program is a computer version of this occupation. Like a good notary, Fair Witness helps record, organize, and present information. However, it is difficult to categorize it as a particular type of software. In fact, Fair Witness may represent an entirely new software category.

Although it is similar to an integrated software package, it just does not quite fit the standard definition of such packages. It's an outliner, but not quite. And it's a personal information manager, but not quite. And they've also thrown in some project management and presentation tools. Because of this confusion, Chena Software coined a new term to categorize Fair Witness: "work processor."

Information can be presented in a number of ways. There is an outliner view that makes it easy to record and develop your thoughts, much like conventional outlining programs. If you want a less structured outliner, you also can use the free-form view, which you later can change into a flowchart.

You begin using Fair Witness by creating ideas in an outline format (this is the more structured approach). The program makes it easy to arrange and rearrange all your ideas. Next, you can group ideas into categories (or bins) set up at the bottom of the screen. These bins make it easier to see what else you need to do. So far, the program functions like a conventional outliner. At this point, however, you can begin a more detailed process. First, you can attach information to your ideas. You do this by creating an information chart that consists of a series of spreadsheet-like rows and columns. (You even can attach sounds to the columns.) The columns can contain notes, names, tasks, pictures, numbers, dates, or titles. Finally, you can use a ratings column to tally votes and scores for idea lists. You have a choice of several procedures ranging from simple ratings to weighted averages of many voters over multiple criteria.

Comments. Fair Witness is a unique program that may set a trend for future information-management applications. Both individuals and groups will find it useful for brainstorming. Although most advanced text outliners can help generate and record ideas, Fair Witness also helps with idea evaluation and implementation. And it allows users to process information more efficiently than many outliners. Thus, it probably comes the closest to providing features found in a CPS software program, yet its outlining functions give it a flexibility found in few CPS programs. About the only weakness of the program is that it will take a while to master all its features—however, this is a weakness shared by other powerful programs.

Grandview (Symantec, 10201 Torre Avenue, Cupertino, CA 95014. 408-253-9600. $295. PC)

Grandview is the PC-equivalent of MORE, also published by Symantec. It is primarily an outlining tool that can help record and organize information using word processing and cross-referencing features. It provides connections to Lotus Freelance Plus and Harvard Graphics, allowing you to construct presentations from Grandview outlines. A built-in calendar helps you track due dates and schedule appointments.

In addition to dates, you also can assign items such as priority or person to the headlines in the outline. Each outline can have up to twenty user-defined categories. For example, your project outline might have columns showing assignments for a date, people involved, and budget categories; a to-do list might have columns showing assignments for the date, priority, and status categories. With its file-linking capabilities, you can share information between Grandview files; thus you could link a master schedule with an individual to-do list. File linking also allows you to connect files within a network. You also can export outlines to WordPerfect and other word processors.

Comments. Grandview is a powerful PC outlining tool that also combines word processing features. It is relatively easy to learn the program's basic outlining procedures. Project planning features may be a little more difficult to learn but will prove valuable when mastered. An advantage of Grandview is that you can run it as either a memory resident or a stand-alone application using less than 20K of RAM. In the memory resident mode, you have instant access to all program features without leaving another application. Grandview doesn't have the drawing and presentation features of MORE, so it is not a full-function, integrated program. This is not necessarily bad, since there are advantages to a more narrow focus. Moreover, you can link Grandview outlines to presentation programs and achieve the same result.

Idea Tree (The PC Arcade, 276 Morehouse Road, Easton, CT 06612— also available from Mindware in Minneapolis, MN—$2.95, 5.25-inch disks; $3.95, 3.5-inch disks. Minimum 2-disk order. PC)

The Idea Tree is a shareware, visual outlining program designed for PCs. It is similar to the Macintosh-based Calliope program in that it allows you to view your thoughts graphically. Unlike Calliope, however, it displays your ideas in a tree structure. You also can export notes to a word processor.

Comments. The Idea Tree interface can be a little awkward to use for some functions; however, pull-down menus simplify many operations. The Idea Tree will be especially useful for problems that can benefit from a hierarchical ordering of concepts; problems that require more open-ended thinking may be less appropriate.

Inspiration (Ceres Software, Inc., 2520 S.W. Hamilton Street, Portland, OR 97201. 503-245-9011. $249. MAC)

Inspiration is based on Tony Buzan's concept of mind mapping (a.k.a. brain mapping or idea mapping). Mind mapping is an alternative outlining process that rejects traditional linear outlines. When drawing a mind map, you begin with a central concept and then add topics and subtopics in a branching fashion until you have included all your thoughts. The result looks something like a bundle of nerve fibers.

With Inspiration's diagraming technology, you can construct mind maps electronically. It also allows you to take advantage of many special features available only with a computer. You select a predrawn symbol, add text, select another symbol, add text to it, and continue until you have listed all your ideas. (As you add subtopics, you often think of related topics, which become new subtopics.) You then can arrange the symbols in any pattern desired and connect them with lines. The result is a diagram representing a flow or pattern of related concepts.

Inspiration is more than a graphic diagraming program, however. It also lets you create a conventional text outline. You also can switch easily between the graphic and text views. Changes made in one view automatically are made in the other.

Comments. Inspiration is intuitive and easy to use. It is easy to switch between the two formats. The variety of symbols and patterns available allows creative expression in outline design, and the visual format may enable you to conceive of relationships among ideas more readily. The documentation is excellent; it does a credible job of explaining all of the program's features and some shortcuts. On the downside, Inspiration may not be for you if you have trouble thinking visually (or don't like to). It lacks advanced features found in more powerful text outlining programs. Selecting and manipulating symbols can be distracting if you only want to list data. If you want a simple outlining program, try ACTA Advantage—it's a desk accessory and is about half the price of Inspiration. If you like to think visually, however, give Inspiration a try.

MaxThink 90 (MaxThink, Inc., 2490 Channing, #218, Berkeley, CA 94704. 415-540-5508. $89. PC)

Conventional outlining programs use an analytical thinking process in which they break down topics into subtopics. This process helps organize your thoughts using a hierarchy. MaxThink 90 also helps organize your thoughts, but it helps you think, too. Unlike many conventional outliners, MaxThink focuses on higher-order thinking processes such as synthesis, analysis, and evaluation.

To promote higher-order thinking within an outline, MaxThink supports several innovative functions. For instance, it will scramble a list to spur new ideas and rotate a list one topic at a time to evaluate the effects of presentation order. It also will order topics randomly and allow you to sort disorganized ideas in a special bin. The latest version of MaxThink contains hypertext features that allow you to cross-link webs of knowledge. This capability makes it easier to jump to different locations and explore information in more powerful ways.

Comments. MaxThink is a well-designed, cleverly implemented program. Its developer, Neil Larson, is a forward-looking thinker who tries to stay one step ahead of current word processing technology. He has succeeded in MaxThink. The current version has so many features that he can't add many more without increasing memory size. A network version also is in the works that will permit group outlining. For the price and what it offers, MaxThink is an exceptional value.

MindWrite (Delta Point, 200G Heritage Harbor, Monterey, CA 93940. 408-375-4700. $195. MAC)

MindWrite is unique among the programs in this section, since it is a full-function word processing program. What makes it truly different, however, is its seamless integration of word processing and outlining. You can record ideas in any order and then organize them quickly using MindWrite's outlining features. You don't have to open a desk-accessory or cut-and-paste text to an outlining program. MindWrite integrates both functions within one program. In fact, you can reorganize topics with the mouse, eliminating the need for cut-and-paste operations. You also can collapse text to focus attention on the total document. Some other features are: unlimited document windows, built-in spell checking and proofreading, text importation from other word processing programs, auto-renumbering of labels, automatic revision tracking, selective word counts, a cumulative clipboard, and sophisticated search and replace functions.

Comments. MindWrite is a "best buy" program, considering that you get integrated, full-function word processing and outlining capabilities for only $195. It is relatively easy to learn to use and the documentation is excellent. If you do much word processing and outlining, MindWrite should speed up your writing. It also should enhance idea recording and processing during brainstorming sessions. You can elaborate on the ideas after the sessions and easily reorganize your thoughts.
MindWrite doesn't have all the bells and whistles of a full-fledged outlining or presentation program such as MORE. If you want such features, you will have to pay more. Another alternative is to use low-cost outlining-only programs such as ACTA Advantage or MaxThink.

However, if your primary needs are for word processing and outlining, MindWrite is the best choice.

MORE (Symantec, 10201 Torre Avenue, Cupertino, CA 95014. 408-253-9600. $395. MAC)

MORE is an extremely powerful program that contains outlining, word processing, desktop presentation (including on-screen slide shows), and financial charting. It is ideal for CPS, either for individuals or with groups. You can record, process, and edit ideas electronically, mark priority ideas, and group them automatically with a single keystroke. You also can rearrange ideas easily and narrow them down to the most important ones. In groups, you can record quantitative ratings from each member, sum, and then rank-order the ideas automatically. Finally, you can present your best ideas using advanced presentation features. Among other features, MORE contains over 100 presentation templates, extensive text editing capabilities, a master chart for laying out an entire presentation, a chart tutor for guidance on preparing transparencies and slides, and advanced drawing and graphic tools.

Comments. This latest version of MORE makes it a formidable competitor among Macintosh outlining and presentation programs. Its capabilities are powerful for what started out as a relatively simple outlining program. The documentation is extensive and well done; the publishers even include many tips on how to communicate more effectively. It is difficult to fault this program. For some users it may be too powerful and thus overwhelming. It is a rather daunting task to learn all of its capabilities. However, you really don't need to for relatively simple outlining tasks. MORE is overpriced as a simple outliner, but it offers much more in presentation features.

Persuasion (Aldus, 411 First Avenue South, Seattle, WA 98104. 206-628-2320. $495. MAC)

Persuasion began as a drawing program. As a result, it has many powerful drawing features for creating professional presentations. Although you can create outlines, they are somewhat limited. Other features include powerful charting, multiple master slides for each presentation, flexible output (you can print outlines, notes, handouts, and slides), a slide show mode (in which slides can be blown up to fit the screen), a spelling checker, easy formatting style sheets, and a number of templates.

Comments. Persuasion is a popular, highly acclaimed program. It is relatively easy to learn and has just about any presentation feature you could want. Its only disadvantage (in this category) is its lack of more complete outlining capabilities. However, it wasn't designed as an outliner, so it really can't be faulted.

PowerPoint (Microsoft Corp., One Microsoft Way, Redmond, WA 98052. 800-426-9400. $395. MAC/PC)

PowerPoint is a desktop presentation program with extensive graphic capabilities. You can produce both color and black-and-white slides, include notes about each slide on "notes pages," and provide handouts to audience members, all from the same slide. Major features include complete word processing functions with special presentation formatting features, templates, a slide show function to rehearse presentations, a spelling checker, built-in color schemes with gradated backgrounds, an interface to the Genigraphics company for professional slides, automatic slide design features (e.g., moving, resizing, pattern filling), importation of text and graphics from other programs, and a complete set of drawing tools.

Comments. PowerPoint is an easy-to-use, full-feature presentation program. It provides everything you need for professional-looking presentations. The documentation is excellent; the manual is a bound book with color illustrations and Microsoft provides a useful quick-reference guide. The only major disadvantage of PowerPoint is that it doesn't have outlining capabilities. You can, however, import outlines from MORE.

Recommendations

The best Macintosh outlining program in this category is MORE; the best PC program, MaxThink. Grandview, however, also is a good selection for PCs, although it is more expensive. If your budget is tight, ACTA Advantage is the choice for Macintosh users, the Idea Tree for PC users. Macintosh users also might consider MindWrite, since it is intermediate in cost between ACTA Advantage and MORE. While its outlining capabilities are more limited, you do get a good word processing program. Although not an outliner, you might consider Comment as an alternative to MindWrite. It provides the same hypertext-like capabilities as MindWrite, although it is more limited.

Fair Witness is in a category by itself. It has many of the same features offered by MORE plus additional capabilities for idea evaluation, presentation, and implementation. It also costs about $100 more than MORE, however. If you use CPS and brainstorming frequently, Fair Witness is the better choice; if your outlining needs are more modest, MORE is better.

After the above programs, you might consider Calliope Plus and Inspiration (unless, of course, money is no object). Both provide a novel way to create outlines and link concepts. Calliope Plus, however, has more limited features; of the two, Inspiration is more powerful and useful. You also might choose Persuasion as an outlining program, but only if your major need is for presentation capabilities.

Of the presentation programs reviewed, you might choose Persuasion; however, the advanced presentation features in MORE, Power-Point, and CA-Cricket Presents make them attractive choices also. If cost is important, choose MORE. Not only is it $100 to $200 less expensive than some of the others, but it also has advanced outlining capabilities.

Thesaurus Programs

Thesaurus programs help define problems by suggesting alternative words. They also can stimulate ideas by evoking different associations. Sometimes, simply changing a single word in a problem statement can prompt new ideas.

Big Thesaurus (Deneba Software, 3305 N.W. 74th Avenue, Miami, FL 33122. 305-594-6965. $99.95. MAC)

Big Thesaurus displays over 1.4 million combinations of synonyms, antonyms, and related, compared, and contrasted words. It contains over 100,000 words, making it the largest thesaurus desk accessory. It is organized by meaning rather than part of speech and includes a separate definition for every meaning group.

Comments. This program is fast. The average access time is less than one second. It supports multiple "lookup" windows open at the same time and replaces words without loss of font or format information. Other nice features are that it permits unlimited cross-referencing and remembers the last twenty searches.

Headliner (Salinon Corporation, 7424 Greenville Avenue, Suite 115, Dallas, TX 75231. 214-692-9091. $195. PC)

Headliner is a specialized thesaurus-type program designed to help write advertising slogans and titles, newsletters, radio or TV spots, magazine articles, and speeches. It uses twenty-five data bases that contain over 33,000 common or clever expressions, idioms, proverbs, quotations, songs, movies, book and TV titles, and a variety of slogans. It will search for key words or sound-alike words, substitute new phrases, match for acronyms or rhymes, retrieve and edit text retrievals, create new expressions with a built-in editor and save them in a electronic notepad, and check alliterative constructions and profanities in multiple languages.

Comments. This is a powerful, relatively easy-to-use program. If you need creative slogans and use PCs, this could be the program for you. Like IdeaFisher, it speeds up the process of search for key words and related expressions. For the money, it is an excellent value.

Inside Information (Microlytics, Inc., 2 Toby Village Office Park, Pittsford, NY 14534. 716-248-9150. $119. MAC)

This Macintosh desk accessory organizes the English language in a rather nontraditional way. Instead of grouping words in categories of meanings, it uses 7 general classes: nature; science and technology; domestic life; institutions; arts and entertainment; language; and the human condition. Each of these classes contains 20 subclasses, 125 categories, and 700 subcategories. Categories are defined by subject matter (e.g., chemistry, law, music), common property (e.g., colors, tools, verbs of motion), or specific usage (e.g., insults, slurs, epithets). You can explore categories in three ways: (1) outline view, which lists information vertically, (2) graphic view, which shows data in a series of boxes, and (3) tree view, which presents a pyramid of knowledge. A unique reverse dictionary allows you to type in descriptive words and then view appropriate terms and definitions. This is handy when you can't think of a word but know what it means. For instance, if you type in *stock and profit*, it will suggest such words as *arbitrage* or *inside information*. Another feature is electronic bookmarks that you can insert to recall important entries instantly.

Comments. Because of the unique way it organizes information, Inside Information is a powerful aid for stimulating new ideas. Its desk-accessory format and intuitive user interface make this program extremely easy to master and use. Microlytics also publishes the *Random House Dictionary*, available on floppy disks. It provides the same features as Inside Information and allows file exchanges between the two programs.

Language Master (Franklin Electronic Publishers, Inc., 122 Burrs Road, Mount Holly, NJ 08060. 609-261-4800. $99. MAC/PC)

Language Master provides dictionary definitions for 80,000 entries and includes 1.4 million responses for 40,000 thesaurus entries. The dictionary contains definitions, usage notes, and hyphenation information. The thesaurus contains synonyms, antonyms, related and compared words, and contrasted words divided into groups sharing a common meaning and part of speech.

Comments. Language Master is not as powerful as Spelling Coach Professional (see later). However, it offers many similar features at almost half the cost.

NamePower (Decathlon Corporation, 4100 Executive Park Drive, #16, Cincinnati, OH 45241. 800-648-5646. $149. MAC)

NamePower is designed to help you create unique names on the Macintosh. It has two modes: alphabetic with random letters, and words and word parts. Alphabetic with random letters allows you to select anywhere from three to eight letters for a name. You then select the positioning of vowels and consonants and you even can choose certain letters for a position. For instance, suppose you want to create a name with the feel of *Acura*, but you want it to have an American flavor. To start, select a five-letter name and indicate you want the first two letters to be *A* and *M*. Next, code the program to produce the last three letters as: vowel, consonant, vowel (like the last three letters in *Acura*). The screen shows AM121 (1 = vowels, 2 = consonants). NamePower then takes over and quickly produces a large number of options. If you want, you can make minor changes and produce another list with similar characteristics. Each change will result in a completely different set of potential names.

The second mode, words and word parts, contains a data base of thousands of words and word parts organized into 100 categories. The categories include noun or adjective descriptors such as financial, modern, astronomy, health, and high tech. To use this mode, you can select up to three categories. NamePower then lists every possible combination of names generated from the category lists. Some names produced with this mode include *AmeriQuest*, *InterWest Bank*, and *ElderShoe*. You also can add your own data base of words related to your project and mingle them with the NamePower names.

Comments. At the time of this writing, a review copy of NamePower was not available. The program literature suggests it may be a useful program for Macintosh users. While it may not have all the features of Namer (a PC program), it should be relatively easy to use. The two naming modes should work well and the data base should be especially effective. Combining your own words with those of NamePower will produce unique associations. Although people in advertising and related fields will benefit from this program, others in any creative field also should find it handy.

Namer (Salinon Corporation, 7424 Greenville Avenue, Suite 115, Dallas, TX 75231. 214-692-9091. $195. PC)

Namer is a specialized electronic thesaurus, similar to Headliner (see earlier). It is designed to help advertising, marketing, and others develop names for new products, services, or companies. It contains eleven name creation methods, organized within over twelve data bases of key words. It categorizes over 10,000 name parts by industry and connotation. It also includes a naming thesaurus and user's guide, and functions for data base editing and file creation. Namer can learn your name preferences and check for obscenities in five languages.

Comments. This program is very useful for generating names. It should enhance your creative thinking abilities much as do IdeaFisher and Headliner. The user interface should be integrated better to eliminate the need to exit one data base to switch to another. Other than this problem, Namer is a cost-effective thesaurus program for IBM and compatible computer users.

Spelling Coach Professional (Deneba Software, 3305 N.W. 74th Avenue, Miami, FL 33122. 305-594-6965. $195. MAC)

Spelling Coach Professional is a desk-accessory, 188,000-word spelling checker, 85,000 word-definition dictionary, and 100,000 word thesaurus. The thesaurus is another Deneba product, Big Thesaurus, and contains over 1.4 million synonyms, antonyms, and related, compared, and contrasted words. It also has many other features such as legal, technical, and medical dictionaries, interactive spell checking, custom alert sounds, user-definable hot keys, and sequential spelling error corrections as they occur or as they are displayed in a list.

Comments. This is a powerful, easy-to-use program, especially for a desk accessory. Although the dictionary and spelling checker may not be as useful for idea generation as the thesaurus, this program is a well-integrated package. The spelling checker is a little slow compared to some other programs, but the thesaurus is first rate.

Word Finder (Microlytics, Inc., 2 Toby Village Office Park, Pittsford, NY 14534. 716-248-9150. $59.95. MAC/PC)

Word Finder contains a large, 220,000-word synonym thesaurus and a smaller thesaurus with 120,000 synonyms. It works as a desk accessory on the Macintosh and is easy to open and use. Don't expect to find a traditional thesaurus. The program groups synonyms together alphabetically as nouns, verbs, or adjectives. You can replace words instantly by double-clicking on the synonym.

Comments. This is an excellent thesaurus. Its developers even recognize the potential of thesauri for stimulating ideas: "If you are searching for a creative idea, the words presented on the screen also can help launch you into a new perspective." The words in Word Finder are more up to date than those found in a hardcover thesaurus. For the price, this program is an excellent value.

Writer's Dreamtools (Slippery Disks, P.O. Box 1126, Los Angeles, CA 90069. 213-274-3600. $35 per stack or $79 for 3 stacks. MAC)

Writer's Dreamtools consists of three HyperCard stacks that provide an innovative set of writing aids. The first stack, Events Day-by-Day, includes over 3,700 births and deaths of famous people, over 3,400 of the most important events in history, and the feast days of every saint and holidays of every country around the world. The events stack also contains information on politics, government, aviation, business, publishing, industry, war, sports, art, and music. The second stack, Cliches & Catch Phrases, contains over 12,500 entries alphabetically indexed with over 1,700 key words. Slang Thesaurus, the third stack, includes over 20,000 (mostly X-rated) slang expressions with key words for easy searching.

Comments. Advertisers, copywriters, speech writers, journalists, and many other kinds of writers will find this program invaluable. The Cliches & Catch Phrases and the Slang Thesaurus will be especially useful for general idea generation. The HyperCard format makes it easy to move around within each stack. Computer novices should be able to use this program with little difficulty. At $79 for all three stacks or $35 for a single stack, Writer's Dreamtools is worth purchasing.

Recommendations

There probably is no one best program in this category. Some programs are more useful for specific occupations. For instance, Namer, Name-

Power, Headliner, and Writer's Dreamtools are ideal for people in advertising, marketing, and journalism. Inside Information presents information in a way unique to traditional thesaurus programs. However, traditional programs such as Big Thesaurus, Spelling Coach Professional, Language Master, and Word Finder can do an adequate job of stimulating ideas.

Incubation Programs

Incubation programs attempt to leverage and enhance the mind's intuitive abilities. Unlike previous programs, they don't contain stimuli for direct idea stimulation; however, you may find that more subtle forms of stimulation can provoke useful ideas. Only two programs are included in this category.

MindSet (Visionary Software, P.O. Box 69447, Portland, OR 97201. 503-246-6200. $39. MAC)

MindSet is a unique program designed to encourage positive thinking—a major creativity attribute. It functions as a desk accessory that allows you to read positive affirmations as they appear on the menu bar (the affirmations disappear instantly whenever the mouse pointer approaches the menu bar). You also can add your own sayings, determine how long each saying appears, and select appearance intervals.

Comments. The ability to add your own sayings also makes MindSet a special value for designing your own idea-generation technique. You easily can add words from an idea-generation tool such as the Product Improvement CheckList (PICL) and watch the stimulus words appear across your computer screen. This could be particularly useful for group idea-generation sessions.

Synchronicity (Visionary Software, Inc., P.O. Box 69191, Portland, OR 97201. 503-246-6200. $59.95. MAC/PC)

Synchronicity was designed to improve intuitive decision making by providing a computer screen for incubation. It is based on psychologist Carl Jung's theory of synchronicity, that all things are connected and that most events that seem coincidental actually have some meaning. It uses the ancient Chinese Book of Changes (*I Ching*) to suggest general answers to your problems. You type in your problem and Synchronicity then responds by randomly selecting from 64 main readings and over

266,000 permutations. Although most of the responses are not directly relevant to your problem, they usually are close enough to prompt some ideas.

Comments. Well-conceived and -implemented graphics and sounds enhance the Synchronicity experience. A Japanese garden with an animated screen and croaking frog sounds, for instance, helps you relax. It is the perfect complement to programs that force you to focus intensely on a problem, providing the balance in creative thinking that we all need. Whether or not you believe in the concept of synchronicity, you will find this relaxing program useful.

11

Computer Software
for Groups

Both the business and the academic worlds recognize the importance of using work teams to increase organizational competitiveness. Environmental pressures and organizational time constraints have forced companies to look for tools to enhance their problem-solving abilities. As a result, research on computer-enhanced group creativity has intensified tremendously since the early 1980s. Computers and related technology now have been developed to facilitate and enhance group outcomes. These systems enhance efficiency, since technology reduces the time and travel requirements for collaborative work. They also enhance effectiveness, since technology helps structure the decision-making process.

Researchers in the literature refer to computer-enhanced group creativity as group decision support systems (GDSS), electronic meeting support (EMS), computer supported cooperative work (CSCW), group process support systems (GPSS), groupware, or a variety of other names. Despite the variety of nomenclature, some researchers suggest there really are two categories of these systems: GPSS and groupware.

GPSS uses special software and hardware to link together individuals. The technology may include telephones, electronic mail, manual aids, computer conferencing, and other computerized tools. These technologies offer alternative communication channels for group interaction. Groupware, in contrast, may use the same technology but structures the communication process in other ways; that is, a groupware environment influences how individuals communicate and what they discuss, helps perform calculations, and otherwise focuses a

This chapter was coauthored by Joseph B. Walther, Ph.D., Assistant Professor of Communication, Northwestern University.

group's activities as it works through different problem-solving procedures. GPSS provides the technology to bridge barriers of time and place and allows larger groups to work together more smoothly. On the other hand, GPSS participants are left on their own to structure their interactions and procedures.

This chapter describes major GPSS and groupware systems. Because of the rapid rate of technological development and related research, this review is limited in its scope. Not all systems are included; however, there is an extensive bibliography at the end of this chapter.

Group Process Support Systems (GPSS)

GPSS use hardware, software, and various machine display variations to enhance group-member interaction. A typical example of GPSS uses computers and cables in a network connected via phone or data lines. This enables multiple users to communicate with each other without resorting to face-to-face meetings. Electronic mail (e-mail) systems function this way, speeding communication between collaborators who can read and reply at their convenience. E-mail systems also may incorporate group distribution lists (a list of electronic addresses for all members of a group), which can send a message to all group members at once. While simple e-mail systems may do little more than combine functions of answering machines and photocopying machines, this power has made e-mail the third most popular office technology application. Only word processing and spreadsheet programs are used more frequently than e-mail.

Another variation of advanced e-mail technology is asynchronous computer conferencing. Participants using this system access a common conference file hosted in a mini- or mainframe computer. A conferencing program alerts users to new messages from other members, allows for easy review of previous group messages, and permits participants to attach their comments to others' ideas left in the system. A common characteristic of e-mail and conferencing systems is that group members access the communication program at their own discretion. Other members may not be on-line at the same time; hence the communication is asynchronous since members can read or write at their convenience. This feature can be an advantage for busy executives or partners separated by time zones.

In addition to asynchronous GPSS, there also are synchronous GPSS that involve simultaneous (real-time) interaction among group members. Participants can type their comments at the same time and then distribute them to the group. This provides a handy record of communications. In some systems, participants' computer screens are divided into several sections with one for typing and editing one's own comments, another for scrolling through the group's growing record of comments, and a third for nonpublic side conversations among two or more group members.

There are several advantages to synchronous systems. First, travel costs are avoided and attention is focused on the task at hand. Second, a larger number of people can participate in a group, since taking turns is not required and interruptions are not possible. Third, they can accommodate both geographically dispersed groups and groups in the same location. A disadvantage of synchronous systems is that they do not structure interactions among group members. Members must add structure or rely on a facilitator.

GPSS provide an alternative communication channel for group problem solving. Other tools are available that permit a variety of conferencing configurations. Some of the tools described in the following sections are generic computer hardware and software systems (e.g., e-mail systems), while others are designed specifically for group interaction.

Aspects (Group Technologies, Inc., 800 North Taylor Street, Suite 204, Arlington, VA 22203. 703-528-1555. $299)

Aspects is a simultaneous conference software program for the Apple Macintosh. Users on up to sixteen modem-linked or networked computers can view the same graphic and text documents in a real-time environment. They can do this whether they are in the same room or, more likely, in different offices dispersed throughout an organization. Participants can react to documents by making changes at any time. When the group reaches consensus, each member can save his or her own file. Or members can unlink their screen views and work on different parts of the same document simultaneously. They also can chat with each other without interrupting ongoing work. Telephones can be added to provide an integrated audio and visual teleconference.

Aspects offers three levels of meeting structure with a special mediation function. Small groups can use a free-for-all mode in which all participants can input ideas or make changes simultaneously. For larger groups, Aspects can require participants to take turns, thus ensuring equal input. Finally, a conference initiator can exert full control over who may work on a document at a specific time.

Aspects does not require a file server, but each workstation must have its own program copy and at least 1 megabyte of memory just for the program. Although the lack of need for a file server is a distinct advantage, the need for multiple program copies is a distinct cost disadvantage.

Carbon Copy Mac (Microcom Software Division, 500 River Ridge Drive, Norwood, MA 02062. 617-551-1999. $199; 2 for $299)

This program allows Macintosh users to view and control documents on other Macintosh computers, working as a desk accessory on a network or with a modem for remote interaction. The degree of interaction depends upon specification of a host Macintosh and guest privileges. (A "host" is the computer available to other computers; "guests" can visit hosts and control them as much as the host allows.) All guests can have equal control over your computer and can view, send, and receive files. You can't specify which guests can interact with you, however. The host Mac's screen appears as a separate window that can be resized and moved on the guest Mac screen.

Carbon Copy is easy to install and use. It helps facilitate collaborative group effort. And its ability to run either on an AppleTalk network or over a modem gives it added flexibility. A disadvantage is that your computer must be either a host or a guest—it can't be both. However, its competitive pricing may outweigh this weakness. A sister product, Carbon Copy Plus, is available for IBM PCs and compatibles.

Caucus (Megasystems Design Group, Inc., 2000 North 15th Street, Suite 103, Arlington, VA 22201. 703-892-9433. IBM)

Caucus was developed to help work groups conduct conferences, coordinate calendars, monitor projects, and schedule meetings. It allows up to sixteen PC users at a time to communicate in the same or geographically dispersed locations. Commands can be customized using built-in dictionaries. It also can be linked to data bases to provide users with technical information needed to discuss issues and solve problems.

The Coordinator (Da Vinci Systems, P.O. Box 17449, Raleigh, NC 27619. 919-881-4320. $295, single-user DOS; $395, 10-user DOS)

Da Vinci Systems developed the Coordinator to facilitate communication among work group members. It helps users clarify messages they plan to send, and aids receivers in responding to requests by either accepting, rejecting, or suggesting alternatives. A special feature is its ability to change the way people normally interact by providing a history of each conversation. This provides a context for discussions as well as establishing an explicit group history. It also provides a tool for listing commitments to actions and a calendar to monitor them. A Windows version is available.

Flash (Beagle Bros., 6215 Ferris Square, Suite 100, San Diego, CA 92121. 619-452-5500. $199.95)

Flash is a Macintosh file transfer desk accessory (INIT). In contrast to programs that permit collaboration only, Flash provides a "chat" feature for real-time group discussions. A special feature is the ability to create a group folder with folders for several people inside. When you drop a file in the group folder, the program automatically sends a copy to all group members. It works in the background or under MultiFinder (a Macintosh system feature that permits switching between applications without quitting the current one), so you can continue working with other applications while using Flash. A dedicated file server is not required.

Instant UpDate (On Technology, Inc., 155 Second Street, Cambridge, MA 02141. 617-876-0900. MAC, $495, 2-user pack; $995, 4-user pack)

Incorporates word processing in a network environment. It allows group members to collaborate by creating and editing live documents. (A "live" document is one that members can access at any time and find the latest version.) Whenever a change is made in a document, all members are notified. It works on a client-server–data base model over an AppleTalk network. Separate files are maintained for each document.

Users interact within a Document Management window where documents are organized by folder. Each user has a personal folder, a public folder, and a folder that allows moving any document anywhere on their disk. Clicking on a document opens a word processor with all the features of a modest, conventional word processor, including support for graphics and tables.

Users can create documents with this word processor or import them from other word processors. After a document is saved, the user calls up a list of others who are to work on it and then sends the list to the server. All the participants are notified and the document is sent to their machines. From that point on, only changes to the document are sent between local machines and the server.

Strengths of Instant UpDate include its ability to allow users to work locally on a live document, a well-implemented system for tracking current versions of a document, good coordination of group input, a user-friendly interface, and a useful word processor. Instant UpDate also is superior to some of its competitors. For instance, MarkUp creates copies of original documents and allows users to work on overlays of the originals. Aspects permits users to work on a live document, but only if all group members are present. Instant UpDate has a better approach in that it lets users work locally on live copies of a master document that is continuously updated to and from a server. Although it may be a little pricey for some small offices, volume discounts and site licenses are available.

Lotus Notes (Lotus Development Corp., 55 Cambridge Parkway, Cambridge, MA 02138. 617-577-8500)

This program was designed as a complete e-mail work group environment for PC users. It tracks and records messages and responses while allowing group members to use word processing, communication, and graphics programs. A unique feature is its ability to allow anyone to create applications. That person then becomes an application manager who controls access privileges. Lotus Notes includes a macro language so that data can be categorized, sorted, and manipulated in a number of ways within views ("views" enable an application's users to access forms in progress with other group members).

MarkUp (Mainstay, 5311-B Derry Avenue, Agoura Hills, CA 91301. 818-991-6540. $295, 1 user; $495, 2 users; $995, 5 users)

MarkUp is a Macintosh work-group productivity tool that enables group members to review and annotate text or graphics documents simultaneously. Notations and comments do not affect the original and can be merged together automatically. Each reviewer can track changes, eliminating duplicate effort and increasing understanding of the document. If desired, annotations can be confidential and modified only by the person making them. Once a group is satisfied with its changes, it can transfer them automatically to the original document. Another nice feature is that users don't need the application used to create the original document (e.g., a word processing or graphics program). A disadvantage is that the overlays used can be confusing, especially in regard to the most recent changes.

PacerForum (Pacer Software, Inc., 7911 Hershel Avenue, Suite 402, La Jolla, CA 92037. 619-454-0565. MAC, $549 for 5 users and 1 server)

This unique program uses a bulletin board metaphor to facilitate interaction among group users, in contrast to other network applications.

Although it is similar to other e-mail systems in that it can distribute messages, files, and pictures, PacerForum is much more efficient. This is because it is organized into multiple bulletin boards. Each board can contain multiple topics that, in turn, consist of messages posted by users. The messages may include attached files, pictures, and sounds.

Icons with titles are presented in the main PacerForum window, one title per bulletin board. Buttons are provided for creating new bulletin boards, modifying a current board, or searching for a board by name. Clicking on a button opens a second window for an icon for each topic in that bulletin board. Double-clicking on a topic opens a topic window that shows the name, date, and time of each response.

PacerForum provides a structured, real-time conferencing environment that is easy to navigate. Its use of icons and windows for managing the electronic bulletin board is well conceived; as a result, it will require relatively little training. Another advantage is that its ease of use and efficiency will help ensure that users actually use the program. Pacer-Forum should prove useful for a variety of tasks such as brainstorming, group planning, design and specification discussions, news broadcasting, schedule and budget monitoring, and software distribution and updating.

QuickMail (CE Software, P.O. Box 65580, West Des Moines, IA 50265. 800-523-7638. $189.95, 1 user; $339.95, 5 users; $499.95, 10 users)

QuickMail is an easy-to-use Macintosh or PC mail system with real-time conferencing capabilities. It contains many powerful features that have made it a popular choice among e-mail users. You can send and receive messages using a customized form and choose recipients from a list. It has a voice-mail feature that lets you record sounds and attach them to any message. You can share files containing spreadsheets, drawings, or charts and send them with a message (up to sixteen files per message). A message log tracks your mail and sorts it in a variety of ways (urgency, date, read versus unread). You also can add a mail menu to any application so you can send documents automatically. QuickMail connects to information services such as GEnie and CompuServe, and you can link it with UNIX mail and fax. It also has a remote access feature so you can use any computer, regardless of its communications software.

Perhaps the most useful feature of QuickMail for GPSS is its conference capability. With it you can send and receive messages to multiple users at the same time. You select the conferees, type in your message in an entry field, and click a send button to send your message. Any responses are signaled with a bell and are displayed on your screen. If you wish to send a message to only one or two conferees, you can use a whisper function to control who receives your message. QuickMail also eliminates interruptions from unwanted messages with a privacy command. (You can control the number of minutes you wish to stay away from conferencing messages.)

QuickMail is an example of how to implement an e-mail system. It makes collaborative work easy and, like similar programs, should increase work-group productivity.

Timbuktu (Farallon Computing, 2000 Powell Street, Emeryville, CA 94608. 415-596-9100. $195 per node)

Timbuktu is a Macintosh desk-accessory, file-sharing program. Once you are established as a guest, you can run any application, open and close folders, and operate just as if you were sitting in front of the host computer. Thus, you can view your desktop screen while controlling the screens of several other computers networked together. You also can send files to other computers and receive them as well. It is easy to set up and use.

Unlike Carbon Copy Mac, another file transfer program, Timbuktu allows you to send more than one file or folder at a time. However, Carbon Copy Mac also lets you transfer files over a modem. With Timbuktu, you need a separate program—Timbuktu Remote—to transfer remote files. On the other hand, Timbuktu is the better choice for viewing several screens simultaneously. Its major disadvantage is cost. Timbuktu is overpriced when compared to Carbon Copy Mac. Carbon Copy Mac's cost is $299 per AppleTalk zone, or $99 per user. Timbuktu is $195 per node. On a 250-node zone, Carbon Copy Mac costs $299; Timbuktu, in contrast, costs $12,500 on the same zone—even with a quantity discount!

Groupware

Most groupware systems are located at research universities and a few large corporations. In contrast to GPSS, many of these systems are expensive and involve software written specifically for each environment. As a result, users may need to go on-site, although there are exceptions.

Like GPSS, groupware systems may rely on electronic mail and provide synchronous and asynchronous communication. However, groupware systems provide an additional, important advantage over GPSS functions: They help structure interactions among group members—that is, they specify how individuals communicate as they work through different problem-solving activities. Such programs generally are known as group decision support systems (GDSS).

Professors Seibold and Contractor developed a fivefold taxonomy that describes the range of functions GDSS provide. The systems in the taxonomy range from the simple to the complex, with the more sophisticated systems adding more complex features. The functions of GDSS are described as levels of effects, as follows:

The first level, displaying, describes the most basic GDSS function: the projection of each participant's comments to all the others. This may be done by hooking one or more computers to a single, large-display screen, or through redistribution of comments of all participants using a chain of computers.

The second level, linking, adds communication alternatives. According to Seibold and Contractor, systems that link participants offer members the opportunity for both one-on-one and public message exchanges. Systems that alter communication practices by offering anonymity also are considered to contain a linking function.

Pooling is the third level. It refers to a system's capability to tabulate votes, rankings, ratings, and other measures of group agreement on an issue. Automated pooling is an important contributor to electronic group support. Its computational speed is far quicker than humans', especially when tabulating votes for different alternatives. Another characteristic of pooling is the ability to describe the degree of "discon-sensus" about an issue and its priority—that is, pooling also can describe the amount of deviation or range of scores. Such data can be vital to group decision making. By pooling, the computer gives group members feedback on how they feel as a group and the overall direction of group opinion.

Structuring adds a fourth level of support by incorporating rules and protocols that affect participant interactions directly. These rules may be set to alternate the order in which participants may contribute or to limit the amount or length of messages. Structuring with agreed-upon rules ensures uniformity, consistency, and equal participation. By implication, users who want to influence others must learn to be concise in their communications. These systems also may guide participants automatically through a prescribed agenda; thus, they may move members through a meeting from one stage to another as they complete each activity.

The fifth level, leading, is the most sophisticated. In this configuration, the system incorporates data bases, dictionaries, expert systems, or other such intelligent technology. These systems may become active automatically during group interaction or be activated as desired by participants. Some systems provide decision trees and group-defined vocabularies. This technology also has the ability to monitor discussions and notify participants about knowledge bases with relevant information. At this level, more than the others, the computer becomes an active participant in sharing information and decision making.

A variety of groupware systems are used throughout the United States. Although many are installed in major universities, increasing numbers are being offered commercially or in collaborative research agreements. Some representative groupware systems are described next.

Colabs

Among the newest groupware installations are two colabs at the University of Illinois. The "colab" concept was developed at Xerox's Palo Alto Research Center. The first of the Illinois installations was a twenty-four-computer laboratory employing Apple Macintosh SE/30s. This colab has been used primarily for collaborative education classes. The second colab is a fully furnished conferencing room with ten Macintosh IIci's placed inside recessed tables. In both facilities, the Macintoshes are connected via AppleTalk networks with gateway access to the university's supercomputer mainframe system. This allows high-speed access to communication and information networks around the world. The conferencing site also has a scanner, a CD-ROM player, and an interactive videodisc player connected to the network that provides access to a variety of data bases during a meeting.

The collaborative software currently used in the labs are Aspects (discussed previously) and SAGE (Software Aided Group Environment), both made by Group Technologies, Inc. Aspects is used for collaborative document preparation and conferencing. SAGE adds HyperCard-based group decision support system software.

Both of these tools have been used in communication courses at the University of Illinois. In the spring of 1991, over 200 students in eight courses used the systems as part of their educational experience. Students put their comments and questions about their reading on disks and brought them to class meetings. Their readings were linked and cross-referenced in the HyperCard stack, and participants then added to common research documents during class. Illinois researchers (with support from Apple Computer's Advanced Technologies Group, the National Center for Supercomputing Applications, and the National Science Foundation) now are exploring how these technologies affect the ways groups conduct their tasks.

gIBIS/GROVE/rIBIS

The Microelectronic Computer Corporation (MCC) of Austin, Texas, developed gIBIS (group Issue Based Information Systems) as part of its Software Technology Program (STP). The basic premise of an IBIS network is to track the decision process by problem issues, developing courses of action and generating pros and cons of the alternatives. gIBIS is used to represent decision data as a pictorial network of nodes and arcs. Users view the network in either close-up or wide angle and modify the network as desired. For instance, they could delete some nodes to indicate a change in viewpoint regarding the arguments for and against some position. According to Seibold and Contractor's typology, this type of system illustrates the value of level-two effects of GDSS: the recording and monitoring of discussion and decision progress.

GROVE (Group Outline Viewing Editor) allows group members to add, delete, or edit items in outlines. It includes special features to facilitate group interaction:

- Still photos of participants that appear and disappear as members join or leave the group
- Public screens that permit all members to add or delete data
- Private screens for individuals to research data (e.g., using a data base or spreadsheet)
- Shared screens in which one member is given control and the screen contents are temporarily locked for that individual

The third component of the MCC system is rIBIS (real-time IBIS). With rIBIS, members create an IBIS network on a shared screen so that only one member can work on the screen. If group members are dispersed geographically, they are linked with a speakerphone conference call. The person controlling the screen then records and facilitates the discussion.

GroupSystems

GroupSystems, developed at the University of Arizona in cooperation with IBM and other manufacturers, is one of the oldest groupware systems in the country. It was established in 1985 and involves an extensive set of tools known as PLEXSYS. It has been installed in six other universities as well as several corporate sites. GroupSystems is built around five decision-making stages:

1. *Session planning* uses a session manager to plan the agenda and select tools to use during the session.
2. *Idea generation* is an electronic brainstorming tool used to record anonymous comments from group members. GroupSystems uses traditional brainstorming, Delphi, and nominal group methods to generate ideas.
3. *Idea organization* uses three decision aids: policy formulation to develop a consensus on policy statements, issue analyzer to identify and consolidate key ideas from the idea-generation stage, and idea organizer to promote independent idea generation for later consideration.
4. *Idea evaluation* relies on two tools for support. There's the voting tool, which provides methods to assign priorities (e.g., Likert scales, rank-ordering, multiple choice); it permits casting of private ballots and displays cumulative results. There also is an alternative evaluator, which is a multicriteria tool for evaluating many alternatives.
5. *Issue exploration* contains three tools. The first is topic commentor, which visually resembles a series of file folders on the computer screen. It can be used to solicit ideas and enter, exchange, or review comments about any of several proposals. The other tools, stakeholder identification and assumption surfacing, help identify and evaluate assumptions behind policies and plans.

GroupSystems also contains other tools including an on-line questionnaire tool, a file reader for obtaining organizational data, a group dictionary for defining common terms, a tool for depicting organizational characteristics, and a graphic semantic browser for viewing data. The output of all these tools is a knowledge base that can be used as a collective memory for an organization.

The Innovator

The Innovator is a portable GPSS developed by the Wilson Learning Corporation in Minnesota. It uses individual keypads to provide instant polling on group issues. Because its major hardware requirements are small keypads and a portable computer, it can be used at Wilson Learning Corporation or transported on-site.

The Innovator contains three modules to help with problem diagnosis, analysis, and action planning. Most sessions using The Innovator produce an "opportunity map," which categorizes responses to an issue according to their relative value and the company's performance. This map classifies responses as: opportunities (low performance, high value), emergents (potential future opportunities), gripes (low performance and value), strengths (high performance and value), maintainers (satisfactory performance and value), and overkills (high performance, low value).

The Innovator follows a basic problem-solving process in which a facilitator uses a series of questions to solicit issues or opinions from group members. Next, the members use a variety of techniques to generate ideas. The facilitator records all ideas on the computer. Finally, the members use their individual keypads to vote anonymously on the central issues of best ideas. The facilitator then evaluates the results using a paired-comparison procedure* and displays the results on a public screen.

Because it requires a facilitator to structure activities, The Innovator is intermediate between groupware and GPSS. The computer software adds structure, but a facilitator is needed to move a group through the different phases. Although this may be a disadvantage, The Innovator also is considerably less expensive than more full-feature systems. Its portability also is a major advantage.

MeetingWare

MeetingWare is a groupware environment that originated as a Facilitator GPSS package at the University of Louisville and then was adapted for research at Western Washington University. It can be set up with a maximum of ten workstations with one of the stations serving as a controller and dedicated file server.

MeetingWare uses expandable software tools for each of its four modules: idea generation, idea organization, idea discussion, and idea evaluation.

During idea organization, members use a "list" tool to enter up to three ideas on their private screens and a "brainstorm" tool to send selected ideas to a public screen. Next, the group moves to idea discussion, where members can view and discuss all the ideas they submitted using a "discuss" tool. They then modify the ideas during idea discussion using "list edit" and "organizer" tools. List edit works best with short lists and enables users to delete, add, or edit ideas. Organizer is designed for longer lists and can structure ideas based on similarity, different levels of analysis, or sequence. During the last module of the MeetingWare system process—idea evaluation—members select the best

---

*A paired-comparison procedure involves comparing the votes for each item with every other item.

ideas using "vote, rank, rate, weight factors analysis, and cross-impact analysis" tools.

SAMM (Software-Aided Meeting Management)

The SAMM system at the University of Minnesota is a menu-driven, user-controlled system for idea generation and evaluation. Although it can be run in a chauffeured environment (controlled by others), users can select from a variety of tools to structure the problem-solving process. It also attempts to meet group members' social needs by allowing them to express feelings during their meetings.

Hardware for SAMM consists of nine workstations and one public screen attached to an NCR Tower 32 computer. System software involves a public program to control information to and from the public screen and a private program to manage interactions of the individual participants. The public program sends messages to the private program and collects, stores, and displays on the public screen communications from individuals. The private program collects individual communications and sends them to the public program.

The system configuration uses a setup module and an operations module. The setup module allows users to select features to use before beginning a meeting. The operations module contains three divisions: agenda, options, and utilities. The agenda holds a list of topics to discuss during the meeting but can be altered during the meeting.

The options feature is the core component of SAMM. It includes tools for brainstorming, idea evaluation, decision making, and attitude measurement and "meeting thoughts." The brainstorming or idea-gathering tool allows group members to send their ideas anonymously. The ideas are then combined with others; any group member can display them publicly whenever desired. During idea evaluation, the group can weight, rank, rate, and vote on ideas. Members also can display the results of this analysis. Decision aids in SAMM include stakeholder analysis, paired comparisons, snowcard technique, and problem formulation. Finally, meeting thoughts allows individual group members to express their feelings on the public screen or send private messages to the system administrator. Members also can assess the group's attitude toward the meeting with a "mood meter."

The third division of the operations module is utilities. It contains tools for storing, retrieving, and printing meeting minutes, notes, or user log files.

SAMM has been used by the Internal Revenue Service as well as several universities and corporations to improve group decision making.

Its latest version, affectionately called "Son of SAMM," currently is on-line at the University of Minnesota.

VISIONQUEST

VISIONQUEST is a groupware system developed by Collaborative Group Technologies Corporation in Austin, Texas. It is designed to improve access to information and the quality of communication among members. VISIONQUEST contains tools similar to those found in GroupSystems and SAMM; however, it provides a more flexible approach than these systems. VISIONQUEST allows multiple users to control their progress through several "agendas." It uses a structured problem-solving format but allows members to deviate whenever they wish. Most other groupware requires participants to follow a predetermined agenda as coordinated by a single session facilitator.

VISIONQUEST is built around meeting procedures and processes. Collaborative Group Technologies Corporation recommends its usefulness for meeting procedures including sending out announcements, preparing rosters, establishing purposes and goals, developing agendas, accessing other application software programs (word processing, spreadsheets, data bases, graphics), and documenting meeting proceedings. Other useful meeting processes include opinion gathering, ensuring anonymity, documenting conclusions and commitments, recording how decisions were developed, and creating a knowledge base. The opinion-gathering process is similar to idea-generation and -evaluation features in other systems. For opinion gathering, VISIONQUEST uses electronic brainstorming, the nominal group technique, a topic commentor-annotator, group rating, ranking, voting, pairwise comparisons, subgroup selection, multiple choice, and meeting critique and evaluation.

VISIONQUEST can be set up in five different modes. First, it can be used as a private workstation to develop announcements, agenda items, or visuals, and to rehearse presentations. In the second mode, it can be configured for face-to-face interaction. While members generate ideas, a "technographer" records them into VISIONQUEST. The ideas are then displayed on a public screen for evaluation. In this mode, however, individuals do not have access to computers. The third mode is similar to the second, except that all members have access to PCs and may type in their own ideas, rankings, and ratings. The fourth mode is arranged so that real-time meetings can be conducted with remote members or separated groups. In this situation, videoconferencing technology is used to link together two groups in different places. Finally, the fifth mode allows members to interact in an asynchronous meeting. This allows participants to join the conference at their convenience, to read and add their own contributions, or to use an analysis tool before moving to the next agenda item. Members may participate in a central location or via a LAN or dial-in system. This flexibility is what VISION-QUEST developers refer to as the "any time—any place" potential of VISIONQUEST meetings.

The Effects of Computer Support

Although users often heap praise on GPSS and groupware technology, there is little definitive research to validate just how well it works. Researchers who have summarized results of research studies usually conclude that most findings are inconsistent. One problem is that system developers use different approaches, thus making it difficult to compare one system to another. Researchers also vary in their interests and backgrounds. For instance, systems engineers look at data-handling capacities of systems; social scientists analyze participation data, decision quality, and social interactions; and business school professionals study cases for impressions and emergent patterns. It is no wonder that generalizing across settings and group sessions is a perplexing task.

Given these limitations, the review of the effects of computer support that follows must be viewed with some caution. In this review, the variables of participation, efficiency, effectiveness, and satisfaction are examined.

Participation

GPSS and groupware systems, in general, tend to equalize participation among group members. The findings have been relatively consistent in regard to this variable. The reasons for this range from the complex to the simple. One complex explanation is that users focus less on the presence of others in computer-mediated interaction. This reduces their communication apprehension, lowers their anxiety, and causes them to be less inhibited by higher-status members. As a result, they are more likely to speak their minds. In groupware meetings in which anonymity is structured, this effect may be even more apparent.

A simpler explanation is that people express themselves more in synchronous GPSS systems, since there is little else to do on-line except read and write. The pace of keyboards clicking can be frenetic as participants read each other's comments and are spurred to additional thoughts. There is little need to interrupt and interject one's ideas out of turn. This also holds true for asynchronous conferencing, where users read and write at their convenience (there also are no interruptions). It is not known if the computer equalizes participation more than similar paper-based groups (such as brainwriting groups). It does appear, nevertheless, that computer support encourages shy and hesitant people to participate more.

Efficiency

Are GPSS more efficient for group decision making than face-to-face meetings? The evidence is inconsistent. GPSS originally were thought to make users more task oriented by reducing the social cues that usually distract or inhibit people. These same computer-mediated groups also have been found to exhibit more hostile comments and to agree less than face-to-face groups. This lack of agreement has been attributed to the greater task orientation of computer-supported groups.

Recent research, however, suggests that these effects may not be inherent features of GPSS. Characteristics of research settings may have affected the results in misleading ways. For instance, as users get to know each other over time, the interpersonal differences between the conditions disappear. In most business settings, many groups exist over time and are composed of people who know each other. Newer research suggests that the impersonality found in lab experiments may not exist in business settings. Thus, it may not be fair or accurate to conclude that computer-supported groups are more task oriented.

There are some clear advantages of computer-supported groups in terms of efficiency, however. It is evident, for example, that computer-mediated groups reduce travel costs to meetings and time lost to dialing unanswered phones. There also is an added advantage of the written word that has not received much attention: the ability to think out and edit one's comments before making them public. This factor alone can help individuals become more efficient in their interactions with others. If you have time to think before responding, you can focus on precisely what you need to say.

On the other hand, GPSS groups also have a characteristic that can make them inefficient. Although they tend to use just as many comments to reach decisions as face-to-face groups, it often takes three to four times longer to express these ideas in GPSS groups. The reason is that GPSS responses are typed rather than spoken; because it takes longer to type than to speak, computer-supported groups can be inefficient.

Effectiveness

Are the decisions reached in computer-mediated groups superior to those in face-to-face groups? Again, the results are somewhat mixed.

Several studies show that more unique ideas are proposed in GPSS groups. When other attributes of groupware are introduced, the effects are more dramatic. For instance, using anonymity and a bogus group member (confederate) who was either critical or supportive of others, research has found that:

- Anonymous group members generated more comments when a confederate was critical than when supportive.
- The most original solutions were produced when members were both anonymous and used an evaluative, critical tone. When group members were not anonymous and used a supportive tone, they were more satisfied with their experience but produced fewer creative ideas.

Recent research at the University of Oklahoma examined idea generation, degree of consensus, and satisfaction across four conditions for both idea generation and evaluation: (1) groups using computers for brainstorming and meeting face-to-face for evaluation, (2) groups meeting face-to-face for brainstorming, but going on-line for idea evaluation, (3) groups communicating via computer for both stages, and (4) face-to-face discussion in both stages. This study found that computer-mediated groups generated more ideas during brainstorming; however, no differences with regard to satisfaction or consensus were found.

Satisfaction

Most research on satisfaction suggests that people initially do not perceive GPSS to be very useful for complex, interpersonal tasks; however, once they use GPSS for some time, they develop more favorable impressions. Numerous studies report high levels of satisfaction with groupware meetings. It is difficult to compare these meetings with face-to-face groups, since satisfaction is related to the task, the way conflict is handled, the amount of participation, and the attributes of the computer terminal and other related equipment. Overall, however, most groups are satisfied with the systems once they have experienced them and become comfortable using them.

Suggested Reading List for
Group Process Support Systems

Adelman, L. (1984). "Real-Time Computer Support for Decision Analysis in a Group Setting: Another Class of Decision Support Systems." *Interfaces*, 14, pp. 75–83.

Adrianson, L., and E. Helmquist. (1987). "Group Processes in Face-to-Face Computer-Mediated Communication." University of Goteborg, Sweden. *Goteborg Psychological Reports, 17*, pp. 1–24.

————. (1985). "Small Group Communication in Two Media: Face-to-Face Communication and Computer-Mediated Communication." University of Goteborg, Sweden. *Goteborg Psychological Reports, 15*, pp. 1–16.

Aldag, R. J., and D. J. Power. (1986). "Computer-Assisted Decision Analysis: An Empirical Assessment." *Decision Sciences, 17*, pp. 572–588.

Bawden, D. (1986). "Information Systems and the Stimulation of Creativity." *Journal of Information Science, 12*, pp. 203–216.

Bugg, P. W. (1986). *Microcomputers in the Corporate Environment*. Englewood Cliffs, N.J.: Prentice Hall.

Burns, A., M. A. Rathwell, and R. C. Thomas. (1987). "A Distributed Decision-Making System." *Decision Support Systems, 3*, pp. 121–131.

Carlson, E. D., B. F. Grace, and J. A. Sutton. (1977). "Case Studies of End User Requirements for Interactive Problem-Solving Systems." *MIS Quarterly, 1*, pp. 51–63.

Casey, J. T., C. F. Gettys, R. M. Pliske, and T. Mehle. (1984). "A Partition of Small Group Predecision Performance Into Informational and Social Components." *Organizational Behavior and Human Performance, 34*, pp. 112–139.

Cats-Baril, W. L., and G. P. Huber. (1987). "Decision Support Systems for Ill-Structured Problems: An Empirical Study." *Decision Sciences, 18*, pp. 350–372.

Connolly, T., L. M. Jessup, and J. S. Valacich. (1990). "Idea Generation in a GDSS: Effects of Anonymity and Evaluative Tone." *Management Science, 36*, pp. 689–703.

Crawford, A. B., Jr. (1982). "Corporate Electronic Mail—A Communication Intensive Application of Information Technology." *MIS Quarterly, 6*, pp. 1–14.

Culnam, M. J., and M. L. Markus. (1987). "Information Technologies." In F. M. Jablin, L. L. Putnam, K. H. Roberts, and L. W. Porter (eds.). *Handbook of Organizational Communication: An Interdisciplinary Perspective*. Newbury Park, Calif.: Sage, pp. 420–443.

Dennis, A. R., J. F. George, L. M. Jussup, J. F. Nunamaker, and D. R. Vogel. (1988). "Information Technology to Support Electronic Meetings." *MIS Quarterly, 12(4)*, pp. 591–624.

DeSanctis, G., and B. Gallupe. (1987). "A Foundation for the Study of

Group Decision Support Systems." *Management Science, 33,* pp. 589–609.

———. (1985). "Group Decision Support Systems: A New Frontier." *Data Base, 16,* pp. 3–10.

Dreyfuss, J. (1988, September). "Catching the Computer Wave." *Fortune,* pp. 78–80.

Dubrovsky, V. J., S. Kiesler, and B. N. Sethna. (1991). "The Equalization Phenomenon: Status Effects in Computer-Mediated and Face-to-Face Decision-Making Groups." *Human-Computer Interaction, 6,* pp. 119–146.

Easton, G. K., J. F. George, M. O. Pendergast, and J. F. Nunamaker. (1989). *An Experimental Comparison of Two Group Decision Support Systems for Solving the Same Problem.* Working paper, Dept. of MIS, University of Arizona.

Finholt, T., and L. Sproull. (1990). "Electronic Groups at Work." *Organization Science, 1,* pp. 41–64.

Foulger, D. A. (1990). *Medium as Process: The Structure, Use and Practice of Computer Conferencing on IBM's IBMPC Computer Conferencing Facility.* Unpublished dissertation, Temple University.

Gallupe, B., G. DeSanctis, and G. W. Dickson. (1988). "Computer-Based Support for Group Problem-Finding: An Experimental Investigation." *MIS Quarterly, 12,* pp. 277–296.

———. (1986a). *The Impact of Computer-Based Support on the Process and Outcomes of Group Decision Making.* Minneapolis: Management Information Systems Research Center, Working Paper 86–08.

———. (1986b). *The Impact of Computer-Based Support on the Process and Outcomes of Group Decision Making.* Minneapolis: Management Information Systems Research Center, Working Paper MISRC-WP-86–08.

Geisler, E. (1986, July–August). "Artificial Management and the Artificial Manager." *Business Horizons,* pp. 17–21.

George, J. F., A. R. Dennis, J. F. Nunamaker, and G. K. Easton. (1989). *Experiments in Group Decision Making: Performance in an EMS Decision Room.* Working paper, University of Arizona.

Gerrity, T. P. (1971, Winter). "Design of Man-Machine Decision Systems: An Application to Portfolio Management." *Sloan Management Review,* p. 59.

Goslar, M. D., G. I. Green, and T. H. Hughes. (1986). "Decision Support Systems: An Empirical Assessment for Decision Making." *Decision Sciences, 17,* pp. 79–91.

Hiemstra, G. (1982). "Teleconferencing, Concern for Face, and Organizational Culture." In M. Burgoon (ed.). *Communication Yearbook 6.* Beverly Hills, Calif.: Sage.

Hiltz, S. R., K. Johnson, and G. Agle. (1978). *Replicating Bales' Problem Solving Experiments on a Computerized Conference: A Pilot Study.* Newark: New Jersey Institute of Technology, Research Report No. 8.

Hiltz, S. R., K. Johnson, C. Aronovitch, and M. Turoff. (1980). *Face-to-Face vs. Computerized Conferences: A Controlled Experiment. Vol. 1. Findings.* Newark: New Jersey Institute of Technology, Research Report No. 12.

Hiltz, S. R., K. Johnson, and M. Turoff. (1986). "Experiments in Group Decision Making: Communication Process and Outcome in Face-to-Face Versus Computerized Conferences." *Human Communication Research, 13,* pp. 225–252.

Hiltz, S. R., and M. Turoff. (1985). "Structuring Computer-Mediated Communication Systems to Avoid Information Overload." *Communications of the ACM, 28,* pp. 680–689.

———. (1978). *The Network Nation: Human Communication via Computer.* Reading, Mass.: Addison-Wesley.

Horwitt, E. (1984). "DSS: Effective Relief for Frustrated Management." *Business Computer Systems, 3*(7), pp. 44–47, 52–54, 56.

Huber, G. P. (1982). "Group Decision Support Systems as Aids in the Use of Structured Group Management Techniques." Honolulu, Hawaii: *Transactions of the Second International Conference on Decision Support Systems* (June), pp. 96–108.

———. (1984a). "Issues in the Design of Group Decision Support Systems." *MIS Quarterly, 8,* pp. 195–204.

———. (1984b). "The Nature and Design of Post-Industrial Organizations." *Management Science, 30,* pp. 928–951.

———. (1981). "The Nature of Organizational Decision Making and the Design of Decision Support Systems." *MIS Quarterly, 5,* pp. 1–10.

Humphreys, P., and W. McFadden. (1980). "Experiences With MAUD: Aiding Decision Structuring Versus Bootstrapping the Decision Maker." *Acta Psychologica, 45,* pp. 51–69.

Jarvenpaa, S. L., V. S. Rao, and G. P. Huber. (1988). "Computer Support for Meetings of Medium-Sized Groups Working on Unstructured Problems: A Field Experiment." *MIS Quarterly, 12.*

Jessup, L. M. (1987). "Group Decision Support Systems: A Need for Behavioral Research." *International Journal of Small Group Research, 3,* pp. 139–158.

Jessup, L. M., T. Connolly, and J. Galegher. (1987). *The Effects of Anonymity on GDSS Group Process With an Idea Generating Task.* Working paper, University of Arizona.

Johansen, R. (1988). *Groupware: Computer Support for Business Teams.* New York: Free Press.

Johansen, R., J. Vallee, and K. Spangler. (1979). *Electronic Meetings: Technical Alternatives and Social Choices.* Reading, Mass.: Addison-Wesley.

Joyner, R., and K. Tunstall. (1970). "Computer Augmented Organizational Problem Solving." *Management Science, 17,* pp. B212–B225.

Keen, P. G. W., and M. S. Scott Morton. (1978). *Decision Support Systems: An Organizational Perspective.* Reading, Mass.: Addison-Wesley.

Keim, R. T., and S. Jacobs. (1986). "Expert Systems: The DSS of the Future?" *Journal of Systems Management, 37,* pp. 6–14.

Kerr, E. B., and S. R. Hiltz. (1982). *Computer-Mediated Communication Systems: Status and Evaluation.* New York: Academic Press.

Kiesler, S., J. Siegel, and T. W. McGuire. (1984). "Social Psychological Aspects of Computer-Mediated Communication." *American Psychologist, 39,* pp. 1123–1134.

Kiesler, S., and L. Sproull. (1987). "The Social Process of Technological Change in Organizations." In S. Kiesler and L. Sproull (eds.). *Computer and Change on Campus.* New York: Cambridge University Press.

Kiesler, S., D. Zubrow, A. M. Moses, and V. Geller. (1985). "Affect in Computer-Mediated Communication." *Human Computer Interaction, 1,* pp. 77–104.

Kull, D. (1982). "Group Decisions: Can Computers Help?" *Computer Decisions, 14,* pp. 70–84, 160.

Leduc, N. F. (1979). "Communicating Through Computers: Impact on a Small Business Group." *Telecommunications Policy,* pp. 235–244.

Lewis, F. L. (1987). "A Decision Support System for Face-to-Face Groups." *Journal of Information Science, 13,* pp. 211–219.

———. (1982). *Facilitator: A Micro-Computer Decision Support System for Small Groups.* Unpublished dissertation, University of Louisville.

Loy, S. L., W. E. Pracht, and M. Kersnick. (1987). "Effects of a Graphical Problem-Structuring Aid on Small Group Decision Making." *Journal of Management Information Systems, 129.*

McCartney, L. (1987, January). "Brainstorming Problems With the Computer." *Dun's Business Month,* pp. 71–72.

McGuire, T. W., S. Kiesler, and J. Siegel. (1987). "Group and Computer-

Mediated Discussion Effects in Risk Decision Making." *Journal of Personality and Social Psychology, 52,* pp. 917–930.

Malhotra, N. K., A. Tashchian, and E. Mahmoud. (1987). "The Integration of Microcomputers in Marketing Research and Decision Making." *Journal of the Academy of Marketing Science, 15,* pp. 69–82.

Meyer, N. D., and J. C. Bulyk. (1985, Summer). "Increasing Meeting Effectiveness Through Augmented Support." *Journal of Information Systems Management,* pp. 63–67.

Nunamaker, J. F., Junior. (1988, November–December). "Computer-Aided Deliberation: Model Management and Group Decision Support." *Journal of Operations Research.*

———. (1987). "Facilitating Group Creativity: Experience With a Group Decision Support System." *Journal of Management Information Systems, 3.*

Olaniran, B. A. (1991). *Computer-Mediated Communication in Small Group Decisional Stages.* Unpublished dissertation, University of Oklahoma.

Pinsonneault, A., and K. L. Kraemer. (1990). "The Effects of Electronic Meetings on Group Processes and Outcomes: An Assessment of the Empirical Research." *European Journal of Operational Research, 46,* pp. 143–161.

Poole, M. S., and G. DeSanctis. (1990). "Understanding the Use of Group Decision Support Systems: The Theory of Adaptive Structuration." In J. Fulk and C. Steinfield (eds.). *Organizations and Communication Technology.* Newbury Park, Calif.: Sage.

Quinn, R. E., J. Rohrbaugh, and M. R. McGrath. (1985). "Automated Decision Conferencing: How It Works." *Personnel, 62,* pp. 49–55.

Rathwell, M. A., and A. Burns. (1985). "Information System Support for Group Planning and Decision Making Activities." *MIS Quarterly, 9,* pp. 255–271.

Rice, R. E. (1980). "Computer Conferencing." In B. Dervin and M. J. Voigt (eds.). *Progress in Communication Sciences. Vol. 7.* Norwood, N.J.: Ablex.

———. (1984). "Mediated Group Communication." In R. E. Rice and Associates (eds.). *The New Media: Communication, Research, and Technology.* Newbury Park, Calif.: Sage.

Rice, R. E., and Associates (eds.). (1984). *The New Media: Communication, Research, and Technology.* Newbury Park, Calif.: Sage.

Rice, R. E., and D. Case. (1983). "Electronic Message Systems in the University: A Description of Use and Utility." *Journal of Communication, 33,* pp. 131–152.

Rockart, J. F., and D. W. DeLong. (1988). *Executive Support Systems: The Emergence of Top Management Computer Use.* Homewood, Ill.: Dow Jones-Irwin.

Seibold, D. R., and N. S. Contractor. (1991). *Evaluating Group Decision Support Systems: Taxonomy, Research Review, and Effects.* Paper presented at the annual meeting of the International Communication Association, Chicago.

Siegel, J., V. Dubrovsky, S. Kiesler, and T. W. McGuire. (1986). "Group Processes in Computer-Mediated Communication." *Organizational Behavior and Human Decision Processes, 37,* pp. 157–187.

Sprague, R. H. (1980). "A Framework for the Development of Decision Support Systems." *MIS Quarterly, 4,* pp. 1–26.

Sprague, R. H., and E. D. Carlson. (1982). *Building Effective Decision Support Systems.* Englewood Cliffs, N.J.: Prentice Hall.

Sproull, L., and S. Kiesler. (1986). "Reducing Social Context Cues: Electronic Mail in Organizational Communication." *Management Science, 32,* pp. 1492–1512.

Steeb, R., and S. Johnston. (1981). "A Computer-Based Interactive System for Group Decision Making." *IEEE Transactions on Systems, Man, and Cybernetics, SMC-11,* pp. 544–552.

Steinfield, C. W. (1986). "Computer-Mediated Communication in an Organizational Setting: Explaining Task-Related and Socioemotional Uses." In M. L. McLaughlin (ed.). *Communication Yearbook 9.* Newbury Park, Calif.: Sage, pp. 777–804.

Stodolsky, D. (1981). "Automatic Mediation in Group Problem Solving." *Behavior Research Methods & Instrumentation, 13,* pp. 235–242.

Turoff, M., and S. R. Hiltz. (1982). "Computer Support for Group Versus Individual Decisions." *IEEE Transactions on Communications, Com-30(1).*

Tydeman, J., H. Lipinski, and S. Spang. (1990). "An Interactive Computer-Based Approach to Aid Group Problem Formulation." *Technological Forecasting and Social Change, 16,* pp. 311–320.

Valee, J., R. Johansen, H. Lipinski, K. Spangler, T. Wilson, and A. Hardy. (1975). *Group Communication Through Computers. Vol. 3: Pragmatics and Dynamics.* Menlo Park, Calif.: Institute for the Future.

Walther, J. B. (In press). "A Longitudinal Experiment on Relational Tone in Computer-Mediated and Face-to-Face Interaction." *Proceedings of the Twenty-Fifth Hawaii International Conference on System Sciences.* Los Alamitos, Calif.: IEEE Computer Society Press.

———. (In press). "Interpersonal Effects in Computer-Mediated Communication: A Relational Perspective." *Communication Research.*

Walther, J. B., and J. K. Burgoon. (1991, May). *Relational Communication in Computer-Mediated Interaction.* Paper presented at the annual meeting of the International Communication Association, Chicago.

Watson, R. T., G. DeSanctis, and M. S. Poole. (1988). "Using a GDSS to Facilitate Group Consensus: Some Intended and Unintended Consequences." *MIS Quarterly, 12,* pp. 462–477.

Weidlein, J. R., and T. B. Cross. (1986). *Networking Personal Computers in Organizations.* Homewood, Ill.: Dow Jones-Irwin.

Weisband, S. P. (In press). "Discussion, Advocacy, and Computer-Mediated Communication Effects in Group Decision Making." *Organizational Behavior and Human Decision Processes.*

Zigurs, I., M. S. Poole, and G. DeSanctis. (1988). "A Study of Influence in Computer-Mediated Communication." *MIS Quarterly, 12,* pp. 625–644.

Bibliography

Ackoff, R. L. (1978). *The Art of Problem Solving*. New York: Wiley.

Andersen, H. R. (1991). *The Idea of the Diamond Idea Group*. Chicago: Mitsubishi Heavy Industries of America.

Basadur, M., G. B. Graen, and S. G. Green. (1982). "Training in Creative Problem Solving: Effects on Ideation and Problem Finding and Solving in an Industrial Research Organization." *Organizational Behavior and Human Performance*, 30, pp. 41–70.

Bharadwaj, A., D. Cheslow, J. K. Ellisor, R. Mahapatra, J. C. Potts, and S. S. Syam. (1990). *A Platform for Research on Group Process Support Systems at Texas A&M University*. College Station, Tex.: College of Business.

Brilhart, J. K. (1966). "An Experimental Comparison of Three Techniques for Communicating a Problem-Solving Pattern to Members of a Discussion Group." *Speech Monographs*, 33, pp. 168–177.

Brilhart, J. K., and L. M. Jochem. (1964). "Effects of Different Patterns on Outcomes of Problem Solving Discussions." *Journal of Applied Psychology*, 48, pp. 175–179.

Buzan, T. (1976). *Use Both Sides of Your Brain*. New York: Dutton.

Connolly, T., L. M. Jessup, and J. S. Valacich. (1990). "Idea Generation in a GDSS: Effects of Anonymity and Evaluative Tone." *Management Science*, 36(6), pp. 689–703.

Crovitz, H. F. (1970). *Galton's Walk*. New York: Harper & Row.

Delbecq, A. L., A. H. Van de Ven, and D. H. Gustafson. (1975). *Group Techniques for Program Planning: A Guide to Nominal Group and Delphi Processes*. Glenview, Ill.: Scott-Foresman.

DeSanctis, G. L., and B. Gallupe. (1987). "A Foundation for the Study of Group Decision Support Systems." *Management Science*, 33(5), pp. 589–609.

Doyle, M., and D. Straus. (1976). *How to Make Meetings Work*. New York: Berkley.

Ellis, S. K. (1988). *How to Survive a Training Assignment*. Reading, Mass.: Addison-Wesley.

George, J. F., A. R. Dennis, J. F. Nunamaker, and G. K. Easton. (1989). *Experiments in Group Decision Making: Performance in an EMS Decision Room*. Working paper, University of Arizona.

Gordon, W. J. J. (1961). *Synectics*. New York: Harper & Row.

Gouran, D. S., C. Brown, and D. R. Henry. (1978). "Behavioral Correlates of Perceptions of Quality in Decision-Making Discussions." *Communication Monographs*, 45, p. 62.

Grossman, S. R. (1984). "Releasing Problem Solving Energies." *Training & Development Journal*, 38, pp. 94–98.

Haefele, J. W. (1962). *Creativity and Innovation*. New York: Van Nostrand Reinhold.

Huber, G. P. (1984). "Issues in the Design of Group Decision Support Systems." *MIS Quarterly*, 8, pp. 96–108.

Isaksen, S. G., and D. J. Treffinger. (1985). *Creative Problem Solving: The Basic Course*. Buffalo, N.Y.: Bearly.

Jessup, L. M., T. Connolly, and J. Galegher. (1987). *The Effects of Anonymity on GDSS Group Process With an Idea Generating Task*. Working paper, University of Arizona.

Jurma, W. E. (1979). "Effects of Leader Structuring Style and Task-Orientation Characteristics of Group Members." *Communication Monographs*, 46, pp. 282–295.

Kepner, C. H., and B. B. Tregoe. (1976). *The Rational Manager*. Princeton, N.J.: Kepner-Tregoe.

Koberg, D., and J. Bagnall. (1976). *The Universal Traveller*. Los Altos, Calif.: William Kaufmann.

Lawrence, P., and J. Lorsch. (1967). *Organization and Environment: Managing Differentiation and Integration*. Cambridge, Mass.: Harvard Graduate School of Business Administration, Division of Research.

Maier, N. R. F., and A. R. Solem. (1952). "The Contributions of a Discussion Leader to the Quality of Group Thinking: The Effective Use of Minority Opinions." *Human Relations*, 5, pp. 277–288.

Mansfield, R. S., T. V. Busse, and E. J. Krepelka. (1978). "The Effectiveness of Creativity Training." *Review of Educational Research*, 48, pp. 517–536.

Morrison, D. (1991). *Facilitation Skills*. Frisco, Tex.: Involvement Systems.

Noller, R. B., S. J. Parnes, and A. M. Biondi. (1976). *Creative Actionbook*. New York: Scribner's.

Olsen, R. W. (1980). *The Art of Creative Thinking*. New York: Barnes & Noble.

Osborn, A. F. (1963). *Applied Imagination*, 3rd ed. New York: Scribner's.

Parnes, S. J. (1992). *Sourcebook for Creative Problem Solving*. Buffalo, N.Y.: Creative Education Foundation Press.

———. (1987). "The Creative Studies Project." In S. Isaksen (ed.). *Frontiers of Creativity Research: Beyond the Basics*. Buffalo, N.Y.: Bearly.

———. (1985). *A Facilitating Style of Leadership*. Buffalo, N.Y.: Bearly.

———. (1967). *Creative Behavior Guidebook*. New York: Scribner's.

Parnes, S. J., and R. B. Noller. (1972). "Applied Creativity: The Creative Studies Project" (Part II). *Journal of Creative Behavior*, 6, pp. 164–186.

Pearson, A. F. (1979). "Communication, Creativity, and Commitment: A Look at the Collective Notebook Approach." In S. S. Gryskiewicz (ed.). *Proceedings of Creativity Week, I, 1978*. Greensboro, N.C.: Center for Creative Leadership.

Poole, M. S. (1983). "Decision Development in Small Groups II: A Study of Multiple Sequences in Decision Making." *Communication Monographs*, 50, pp. 224–225.

Prince, G. M. (1970). *The Practice of Creativity*. New York: Harper & Row.

Rebibo, K., J. Reel, C. Woodford, and J. Reiser. (1987). *Word Finder*. East Rochester, N.Y.: Microlytics.

Ribler, R. L. (1983). *Training Development Guide*. Reston, Va.: Reston Publishing.

Rose, L. H., and H-T. Lin. (1984). "A Meta-Analysis of Long-Term Creativity Training Programs." *Journal of Creative Behavior*, 18, pp. 11–22.

Rosenfield, L. B., and T. B. Plax. (1975). "Personality Determinants of Autocratic and Democratic Leadership." *Speech Monographs*, 42, pp. 203–208.

Simon, H. A. (1977). *The New Science of Management Decisions*, rev. ed. Englewood Cliffs, N.J.: Prentice Hall.

Tatsuno, S. M. (1990). *Created in Japan: From Imitators to Innovators*. New York: Harper Business.

Taylor, J. W. (1961). *How to Create Ideas*. Englewood Cliffs, N.J.: Prentice Hall.

Torrance, E. P. (1974). *Torrance Tests of Creative Thinking*. Lexington, Mass.: Ginn/Xerox.

VanGundy, A. B. (1991). *Training Your Creative Mind*. Buffalo, N.Y.: Bearly.

———. (1988). *Techniques of Structured Problem Solving*, 2nd ed. New York: Van Nostrand Reinhold.

———. (1987). *Creative Problem Solving: A Guide for Trainers and Management*. Westport, Conn.: Quorum.

———. (1985). *The New Product Creative Process*. Presentation at the National New Products Conference, Chicago.

———. (1984a). *Managing Group Creativity: A Modular Approach to Problem Solving*. New York: AMACOM.

———. (1984b). *How to Get the Idea That Leads to the Product*. Presentation at the National New Products Conference, Chicago.

———. (1983). *108 Ways to Get a Bright Idea*. Englewood Cliffs, N.J.: Prentice Hall.

Wagner, G. R. (1990). *Personal Communication*. Austin, Tex.: Group Technologies.

Watson, D. L. (1989). "Enhancing Creative Productivity With the Fisher Association Lists." *Journal of Creative Behavior*, 23(1), pp. 51–58.

Index

[The letter *n* after a number indicates a footnote.]